QSE
QUICK SMART ENGLISH

Pre-Intermediate

TEACHER'S GUIDE
with
Photocopiable Resources

Rebecca Robb Benne

with

Joanne Collie

BROOKEMEAD ENGLISH LANGUAGE TEACHING

QSE

QUICK SMART ENGLISH

Pre-Intermediate

TEACHER'S GUIDE

Series editor: Duncan Prowse
Contributors and consultants: Joanne Collie, Rosemary Harris, Anna Whitcher Kutz
Editor: Anna Whitcher Kutz
Illustrator: Belinda Evans
Designers: John Anastasio, Wendi Watson, Lapiz Digital Services

QSE Pre-Intermediate Common European Framework Level A2-B1

QSE Series *Title*	*Common European Framework*	*Cambridge ESOL*	*Michigan*	*TOEFL (New TOEFL)*	*Trinity College, London, ESOL*	*Edexcel London Test of English*
Quick Start English	A1-A2	KET			ISE 0 GESE Grade 1, 2, 3	Level (A1) 1
Quick Smart English Pre-Intermediate	A2-B1	PET	BCCE		ISE I, GESE Grade 4, 5, 6	Level 1- 2
Quick Smart English Intermediate	B1-B2	FCE	ECCE	450-525 Target 485 (NT 163)	ISE II, GESE Grade 7, 8, 9	Level 2-3
Quick Smart English Advanced	B2-C1	CAE	ALCE	Target 525 (NT 197)	ISE III, GESE Grade 10, 11	Level 3-4

ISBN: 978-1-905248-15-5

Also available:
QSE Pre-Intermediate Student's Book, ISBN 1-905248-08-3
QSE Pre-Intermediate Workbook, ISBN 1-905248-09-1
QSE Pre-Intermediate CD 1 Listening and Pronunciation, ISBN 1-905248-10-5
QSE Pre-Intermediate CD 2 Reading, ISBN 1-905248-11-3

Other books in the QSE Series:
QSE Intermediate (CEF B1-B2)
Student's Book, Workbook, Audio CDs, Teacher's Guide (with photocopiable resources)
QSE Advanced (CEF B2-C1)
Student's Book and Workbook, Audio and Video DVD, Teacher's Guide (with photocopiable resources)

Published by:
Brookemead English Language Teaching
P.O. Box 58230, London N1 1RP
www.brookemead-elt.co.uk

QSE
QUICK SMART ENGLISH

Pre-Intermediate

TEACHER'S GUIDE

CONTENTS

Unit	Title	Subject *The BIG question*	Functions, Language Banks (See SB cover flaps)	Grammar	Reading (CD 2, track)	Listening (CD 1, track)
1	**Adrenalin rush**	Hobbies and sports, holidays *Do we need danger?* SB8	1 Talking about permanent situations and repeated actions 2 Talking about the past and sequencing events SB10, WB40	The past simple / present simple, sequencing words SB9, WB4	1 Interviews with people who do extreme sports SB9	1 The experience of free-fall and skydiving SB1 WB4
2	**Carnival atmosphere**	Festivals and music *Why are we celebrating?* SB12	3 Giving advice (*should*) SB14, WB40 4 Describing frequency and manner SB14, WB41	Adverbs of frequency and manner SB13 WB6	2 Censorship and protest at the Rio de Janeiro Carnival SB13	2 Radio report from London's Notting Hill Carnival SB1 WB4
3	**Lifestyle choices**	Work, job satisfaction *What kind of job is best for you?* SB16	5 Comparing two things, more than two things SB18, WB41	Comparatives, superlatives of adjectives SB17 WB8	3 Three people talk about their ideal jobs; career changes and job satisfaction SB17	3 Office job, or outdoor job? SB18, WB4 4 Pronunciation: vowels WB
4	**Stranger than fiction**	Entertainment *Are reality shows good TV?* SB20	6 Expressing likes and dislikes SB20, WB41 7 Talking about future plans and intentions SB22, WB42	*Going to* future SB21 WB10	4 Reviews of reality TV shows SB21	5 Reality TV shows SB22, WB5 6 Pronunciation: consonants WB1
5	**Shopaholics**	Shops and shopping *Do shops rip you off?* SB24	8 Complaining 9 Quantifying SB26, WB42	Adverbials of quantity Quantifiers SB25 WB12	5 *Image* magazine letters about shopping and sales staff SB25	7 Telephoning customer services about a wrong order SB2 WB5
6	**Eat your greens!**	Food *Must we kill to eat?* SB28	10 Asking for and giving reasons 11 Making and replying to requests SB30, WB43	Connecting words: *and, but, because* SB29 WB14	6 Article about vegetarianism SB29	8 Buying a meal vegetarianism SB30, WB5 9 Pronunciation: word stress WB1
7	**For your eyes only**	Diaries, blogs *What do you keep private?* SB32	12 Talking about events in the indefinite or recent past SB34, WB43	Present perfect with *ever, never, just* SB33 WB16	7 Blogs – more than a modern diary SB33	10 Trouble with a blog SB34, WB5 11 Pronunciation: strong and weak forms WB1
8	**Fashionistas**	Fashion *Are you a fashion leader?* SB36	13 Talking on the phone 14 Expressing preferences SB38, WB44	Articles SB37 WB18	8 The styles of eight different fashionistas SB37	12 Fashion and mobile phones SB3 WB5
	Extended reading 1	Fame and success SB40			9 *Around the world in 71 days* SB41	

Key:
SB = Student's Book TG = Teacher's Guide
WB = Workbook PR = Photocopiable Resources in TG

QSE Pre-Intermediate MATERIALS MAP

Speaking	Writing	CLIL (Content and Language Integrated Learning)	Teacher's Guide Photocopiable Resources	Pages
ROLE PLAY: Persuading people that extreme sports are good idea CONVERSATION: Describing a dangerous situation YOUR TOPIC: Presenting the dangers and attractions of a sport SB10	Email to a friend about a sporting experience SB11 Email to a friend; an article for a magazine; a letter to a newspaper WB5	FIRST AID: Sports injuries and advice for emergency treatment SB11	Teacher's notes and answer key TG29 PET Exam 1 PR146 Quick Smart Test 1 PR162	Unit 1 SB8-11 WB4-5 TG29-35 PR146, 162
ROLE PLAY: Giving advice about going to a big event like a carnival CONVERSATION: What do you do to celebrate with family and friends? YOUR TOPIC: Presenting a local celebration SB14	A profile of a favourite band or singer; an article about a festival SB15 Article for college magazine Email to a penfriend Description of a concert WB7	MUSIC TECHNOLOGY: DJ mixing SB15	Teacher's notes and answer key TG36 PET Exam 2 PR147 Quick Smart Test 2 PR164	Unit 2 SB12-15 WB6-7 TG36-41 PR147, 164
ROLE PLAY: Discussing a job with a career adviser CONVERSATION: Listing the most important things for you in finding the right job YOUR TOPIC: Presenting your ideal job SB18	A letter asking for information about a job SB19 Email to a friend Article for a newspaper Description of a job WB9	BUSINESS STUDIES: Meetings, different kinds and how they work SB19	Teacher's notes and answer key TG42 PET Exam 3 PR148 Quick Smart Test 3 PR166	Unit 3 SB16-19 WB8-9 TG42-48 PR148, 166
ROLE PLAY: Persuading a friend to go on a reality TV show CONVERSATION: Discussing which reality shows to watch YOUR TOPIC: Presenting a popular TV show SB22	A review of a movie SB23 Email about plans Essay about likes and dislikes Article for a magazine WB11	MEDIA STUDIES: How film continuity works and continuity mistakes SB23	Teacher's notes and answer key TG49 PET Exam 4 PR149 Quick Smart Test 4 PR168	Unit 4 SB20-23 WB10-11 TG49-54 PR149, 168
ROLE PLAY: Complaining in a shop about something you bought CONVERSATION: Comparing shopping habits with a partner YOUR TOPIC: Presenting your best and worst buys SB26	Email of complaint to an online shopping site SB27 Email about shopping Tips for shoppers Description of a dream shop WB13	CONSUMER RIGHTS: Tips for online shoppers; safety and security online SB27	Teacher's notes and answer key TG55 PET Exam 5 PR150 Quick Smart Test 5 PR170	Unit 5 SB24-27 WB12-13 TG55-60 PR150, 170
ROLE PLAY: Customer and sales assistant in a hamburger restaurant CONVERSATION: Is it cruel to eat meat, or even plants? YOUR TOPIC: Presenting vegetarianism SB30	A report for a health magazine about healthy diets SB31 Email to a friend Report on food Story about food WB15	NUTRITION: Food pyramid guide to daily amounts of different foods for a healthy diet SB31	Teacher's notes and answer key TG61 PET Exam 6 PR151 Quick Smart Test 6 PR172	Unit 6 SB28-31 WB14-15 TG61-66 PR151, 172
ROLE PLAY: Class website: cause of trouble between teachers and students? CONVERSATION: What you use the internet for YOUR TOPIC: Presenting your own happy or sad experiences SB34	A blog about a recent event SB35 Email to a friend Essay about privacy Description of internet use WB17	CREATIVE WRITING: Tips for improving your writing skills SB35	Teacher's notes and answer key TG67 PET Exam 7 PR152 Quick Smart Test 7 PR174	Unit 7 SB32-35 WB16-17 TG67-73 PR152, 174
ROLE PLAY: Phoning a friend and leaving a message CONVERSATION: Discussing your own fashion image YOUR TOPIC: Presenting a favourite fashion item SB38	Email to a friend about fair trade clothes; email about the latest fashion SB39 Letter to a friend Description of clothes Story of life of a designer WB19	GLOBALISATION: Sustainable clothing and fair trade goods SB39	Teacher's notes and answer key TG74 PET Exam 8 PR153 Quick Smart Test 8 PR176	Unit 8 SB36-39 WB18-19 TG74-79 PR153, 176
Discussing what it is like to sail alone around the world SB40	Progress check 1 WB20-21			SB40-41 WB20-21 TG80-83

Unit	Title	Subject *The BIG question*	Functions, Language Banks (See SB cover flaps)	Grammar	Reading CD 2, track	Listening CD 1, track
9	**Rule of law**	Rules and regulations *Who needs rules?* SB42	15 Expressing obligation and necessity SB44, WB44	Modals of obligation and necessity: *must, have to, need to* SB43, WB22	10 Article about childhood in a commune SB43	13 Radio programme about silly laws SB44, WB5 14 Pronunciation: stress on verbs WB2
10	**What's next?**	Future developments *What will change the world next?* SB46	16 Giving and following instructions 17 Informing about and predicting the future SB48, WB45	*will* future for predictions SB47 WB24	11 *Eager*, extract from a science fiction novel about a thinking robot SB47	15 Father and son discuss attitudes to technology SB4 WB5
11	**Travel costs**	Travel and transport *Will air travel cost the Earth?* SB50	18 Asking about and stating the duration of events SB52, WB45	Present perfect with *for* and *since* SB51 WB26	12 Air travel and its effect on the environment SB51	16 Planting trees to reduce carbon dioxide levels SB52, WB5 17 Pronunciation: consonant clusters 1 WB2
12	**Money, money, money**	Money *How honest are you?* SB54	19 Using telephone banking SB54, WB46 20 Expressing certainty and uncertainty SB56, WB46	Modals of certainty and uncertainty: *will* and *might* SB55 WB28	13 Cash machines that gave out free money SB55	18 Quiz about honesty and your ow reactions SB5 WB5
13	**Destination disaster**	Cars and bicycles *Do cars rule our lives?* SB58	21 Expressing intention and purpose SB60, WB46	Infinitive of purpose SB59 WB30	14 Road rage, stress on drivers, SUVs SB59	19 Radio debate: Do we really need cars? SB60, WB5 20 Pronunciation: consonant clusters 2 WB3
14	**All in the family**	Special occasions, family *Families – hell or happiness?* SB62	22 Asking about and describing past activities 23 Asking about and describing events in the past SB64, WB47	Past continuous SB63 WB32	15 Two weddings – one formal, other on a beach SB63	21 Work in the house – does dad do his share? SB64, WB5 22 Pronunciation: intonation in statements WB3
15	**The new epidemics**	Health *Can we stop disease?* SB66	24 Talking about facts SB68, WB47 25 Requesting and expressing opinions and impressions SB68, WB48	Zero and first conditionals SB67 WB34	16 Bird flu – the dangers of pandemics, FAQs about epidemics SB67	23 A hypochondriac thinks he has many diseases SB6 WB5
16	**Adventures in language**	Seasonal activities, English-speaking world *Why are you learning English?* SB70	26 Making arrangements 27 Talking about future arrangements and intentions SB72, WB48	Present continuous for future arrangements SB71 WB36	17 Two students talk about their English language courses SB71	24 Teacher and studen discuss best ways to learn SB72, WB5 25 Pronunciation: intonation in question WB3
	Extended reading 2	Racism and prejudice SB74			18 *Face* by Benjamin Zephaniah SB75	
		Language Banks, exercises and answer key WB40–48, TG203				**Audio text** WB 49–5

Key:
SB = Student's Book TG = Teacher's Guide
WB = Workbook PR = Photocopiable Resources in TG

QSE Pre-Intermediate MATERIALS MAP

Speaking	Writing	CLIL (Content and Language Integrated Learning)	Teacher's Guide Photocopiable Resources	Pages
ROLE PLAY: What would you ban if you could make laws? CONVERSATION: Rules at home and what you usually do at home YOUR TOPIC: Presenting important rules of your college, home or country SB44	A magazine article about the EU; article about rules at home or college SB45 Article about communes Letter of comment Essay on rules WB23	EUROPEAN CITIZENSHIP: What is the European Union and how does it work? SB45	Teacher's notes and answer key TG84 PET Exam 9 PR154 Quick Smart Test 9 PR178	Unit 9 SB42-45 WB22-23 TG84-90 PR154, 178
ROLE PLAY: Explaining how something works so partner can guess what it is CONVERSATION: Making predictions about the future as you see it YOUR TOPIC: Presenting a technology that you think will change the world SB48	Email to a friend about robots SB49 Email about a gadget Essay about the future Description of invention WB25	INFORMATION TECHNOLOGY (IT): Robots that can dance and climb stairs SB49	Teacher's notes and answer key TG91 PET Exam 10 PR155 Quick Smart Test 10 PR180	Unit 10 SB46-49 WB24-25 TG91-96 PR155, 180
ROLE PLAY: Persuading your boss that he should travel by plane less often CONVERSATION: Discussing how long you have been doing certain things YOUR TOPIC: Presenting a recent trip you have made SB52	Cheap air travel – advantages and disadvantages SB53 Letter about a holiday Article about the environment Description of transport types WB27	BIOLOGY: Photosynthesis and how trees produce oxygen SB53	Teacher's notes and answer key TG97 PET Exam 11 PR156 Quick Smart Test 11 PR182	Unit 11 SB50-53 WB26-27 TG97-102 PR156, 182
ROLE PLAY: Attitudes to cheating at homework CONVERSATION: Using internet banking; your future in business YOUR TOPIC: Presenting your own examples of behaviour SB56	An essay about spending and saving money SB57 Email to a friend Article about money Story about you and money WB29	MATHS: Foreign exchange calculations between different currencies SB57	Teacher's notes and answer key TG103 PET Exam 12 PR157 Quick Smart Test 12 PR184	Unit 12 SB54-57 WB28-29 TG103-110 PR157, 184
ROLE PLAY: After passing your driving test, persuading someone to buy you a car CONVERSATION: Are you for or against a world without cars? YOUR TOPIC: Presenting a cycling campaign SB60	Describe a city without cars SB61 Letter about cycling Article about cars Story about an accident WB31	PHYSICS: The speed of sound; breaking the world land speed record SB61	Teacher's notes and answer key TG111 PET Exam 13 PR158 Quick Smart Test 13 PR186	Unit 13 SB58-61 WB28-29 TG111-117 PR158, 186
ROLE PLAY: Mum does all the work in the house – say what you think about this CONVERSATION: Describing what you were doing at various times throughout the day YOUR TOPIC: Presenting a special family occasion SB64	Email to a friend about a family argument SB65 Email about your family Essay about family life Description of special occasion WB33	THE FAMILY: Different types of family and its changing function SB65	Teacher's notes and answer key TG118 PET Exam 14 PR159 Quick Smart Test 14 PR188	Unit 14 SB62-65 WB32-33 TG118-125 PR159, 188
ROLE PLAY: Explaining to a friend the dangers of bird flu CONVERSATION: Giving your opinions about medical issues YOUR TOPIC: Presenting information about the healthcare system SB68	An essay on health and health improvement SB69 Email to a hypochondriac Article about disease Essay on smoking WB35	HEALTH AND FITNESS: What smoking does to the lungs; a healthy lifestyle SB69	Teacher's notes and answer key TG126 PET Exam 15 PR160 Quick Smart Test 15 PR190	Unit 15 SB66-69 WB34-35 TG126-132 PR160, 190
ROLE PLAY: Making an arrangement in the summer holidays CONVERSATION: Talking about your arrangements for the evening and weekend YOUR TOPIC: Presenting your ideas about learning English SB72	Email to a friend about an English course you are going to take SB73 Email about plans for the weekend Tips for students of English WB37	ENGLISH-SPEAKING WORLD: Where English is spoken and by whom SB73	Teacher's notes and answer key TG133 PET Exam 16 PR161 Quick Smart Test 16 PR192	Unit 16 SB70-73 WB36-37 TG133-139 PR161, 192
Discussion about the importance of beauty and appearance SB74	Progress check 2 WB38-39			SB74-75 WB38-39 TG140-143

Unit-by-unit glossary (with monolingual definitions) SB 76–86 **Unit-by-unit wordlist** WB 58–65

Introduction – Welcome to *QSE Pre-Intermediate*

- ***Quick Smart English*** is a topic-based English language course at various levels in line with the **CEF** (Common European Framework of Reference).
- ***QSE*** uses affective, topical and sometimes controversial reading and listening material to present and revise structures and vocabulary and to develop communication skills.
- The language structures are those found in widely-accepted international curricula.
- The topic-based vocabulary is wide-ranging and based on real-life ideas and issues.
- The learning tasks include integrated 4-skills activities, with a particular focus on speaking.
- Integrated **CLIL** (Content and Language Integrated Learning) activities in each Unit.
- Although ***QSE Pre-Intermediate*** is not a dedicated exam preparation course, the structure and vocabulary practice, skills work, question types and supplementary test materials are all designed to help students prepare for international ESOL examinations.
- ***QSE Pre-Intermediate*** is designed to cover a 70–80 hour course, with additional materials for further study and homework. It can also be used in modules for skills development, in particular speaking practice.

QSE and the CEF

The structure and approach of the course are based on the Council of Europe's Common European Framework of Reference (**CEF**). Like the CEF, ***QSE*** takes a very broad view of what language students need to learn in order to use a foreign language and what knowledge and skills they need to develop so as to be able to communicate effectively. ***QSE*** aims to provide the widest possible cultural context, using examples from the great cultural diversity of global English (British, American, Australian, South African and others).

The objectives, content and methods of ***QSE*** follow the guidelines of the CEF, aiming to equip students to deal with everyday communication, not only in English-speaking countries, but also in other countries and contexts where English is used as a *lingua franca*. Today one of the most common uses of English is as a medium of communication between non-native speakers.

QSE helps students to exchange information and ideas and to communicate their thoughts and feelings. Its wide range of topics, many of which are unusual for EFL courses, help students achieve a wider and deeper understanding of the way other people live and think of their cultural heritage. ***QSE***'s methods of language teaching and learning are based on the needs, motivations, characteristics and resources of the learners themselves. The course is therefore designed to be **student-centred**.

The topics (including the CLIL materials) help students face the modern challenges of global mobility and closer international understanding, not only in education, culture and science but also in work, trade and industry. ***QSE*** aims to promote mutual understanding and tolerance, respect for different identities and cultural diversity through more effective international communication.

The course visits all four **Domains** identified by the CEF: Personal, Public, Educational and Occupational. In ***QSE Pre-Intermediate***, the Personal Domain is represented, for example, in the topic of Family in Unit 14 and Fashion in Unit 8; the Public Domain in Shopping in Unit 5, in Law in Unit 9, in Travel and Transport in Units 11 and 13 and in Public Health in Unit 15; the Occupational Domain is to the fore in the topic of Jobs in Unit 3, the Educational Domain in Blogs and Creative Writing in Unit 7 and Learning English in Unit 16.

The CEF is a framework not only for language learning, but also for **assessment**, which is central to the methodology of ***QSE***. Trinity College London recognises that ***QSE*** makes a valuable contribution to preparation for the Graded Examinations in Spoken English for speakers of other languages (GESE) and Integrated Skills Examination (ISE). ***QSE*** is also compatible with preparation for the UCLES Cambridge suite of examinations, featuring a special set of exam preparation materials at **PET** (Preliminary English Test) level in ***QSE Pre-Intermediate***, at **FCE** (First Certificate) level in ***QSE Intermediate*** and at IELTS and CAE levels in ***QSE Advanced***. The chart below shows how the various levels of the ***QSE*** Series have been planned to match the levels of the CEF and the requirements of international examinations.

QSE, the CEF and international examination levels

QSE	*Common European Framework (CEF)*	*UCLES (University of Cambridge ESOL)*	*Trinity College, London ESOL*	*Michigan / HAU*	*TOEFL (New TOEFL)*	*IELTS*	*Edexcel London Test of English*
Quick START English	A1-A2	KET (Key English Test)	GESE Grade 1, 2, 3				Level (A1) 1
QSE Pre-Intermediate	A2-B1	PET (Preliminary English Test)	ISE 0, ISE I, GESE Grade 4, 5, 6	BCCE		3.0 to 4.0	Level 1-2
QSE Intermediate	B1-B2	FCE (First Certificate in English)	ISE II, GESE Grade 7, 8, 9	ECCE	450-525 Target 485 *(NT 163)*	4.0 to 5.5	Level 2-3
QSE Advanced	B2-C1	CAE (Certificate in Advanced English)	ISE III, GESE Grade 10, 11	ALCE	Target 525 *(NT 197)*	5.5 to 6.5 / 7.0	Level 3-4

QSE Pre-Intermediate takes students from Level **A2** to **B1**. These are the **CEF Reference Levels Global Descriptors** for the two levels. There are more detailed examples of the **CEF Can-do Statements** in the four skill areas in the **Self-assessment** charts on pages 200–202 of this book.

	A2 ▶	B1
Listening	• I can understand phrases and the highest frequency vocabulary related to areas of most immediate personal relevance (eg very basic personal and family information, shopping, local area, employment). I can catch the main point in short, clear, simple messages and announcements.	• I can understand the main points of clear standard speech on familiar matters regularly encountered in work, school, leisure etc. I can understand the main point of many radio or TV programmes on current affairs or topics of personal or professional interest when the delivery is relatively slow and clear.
Reading	• I can read very short, simple texts. I can find specific, predictable information in simple everyday material such as advertisements, prospectuses, menus, timetables and I can understand short simple personal letters.	• I can understand texts that consist mainly of high frequency everyday or job-related language. I can understand the description of events, feelings and wishes in personal letters.
Spoken interaction	• I can communicate in simple and routine tasks requiring a simple and direct exchange of information on familiar topics and activities. I can handle very short social exchanges, even though I can't usually understand enough to keep the conversation going myself.	• I can deal with most situations likely to arise whilst travelling in an area where the language is spoken. I can enter unprepared into conversation on topics that are familiar, of personal interest or pertinent to everyday life (eg family, hobbies, work, travel and current events).
Spoken production	• I can use a series of phrases and sentences to describe in simple terms my family and other people, living conditions, my educational background and my present or most recent job.	• I can connect phrases in a simple way in order to describe experiences and events, my dreams, hopes and ambitions. I can briefly give reasons and explanations for opinions and plans. I can narrate a story or relate the plot of a book or film and describe my reactions.
Writing	• I can write short, simple notes and messages relating to matters in areas of immediate need. I can write a very simple personal letter, for example, thanking someone for something.	• I can write a short, simple connected text on topics which are familiar or of personal interest. I can write personal letters describing experiences and impressions.

QSE and exams

QSE is not designed to be a specific exam-preparation course. But no teacher or class these days can ignore the fact that exams are a very important and almost unavoidable presence in the language classroom. All international exams today have been written or have been calibrated to fit into the levels and requirements of the CEF. Styles of examination differ, however. As ***QSE*** is a course with a very strong emphasis on **spoken English** and developing **oral skills**, the authors decided to use the syllabus of the **Trinity College, London, GESE** (Graded Examinations in Spoken English) and **ISE** (Integrated Skills in English) examinations. However, we are aware that many students will take other exams, so there are many question types, tasks and exercises in the Student's Book and Workbook that provide exam practice in all four skills for several exam types. In addition, there are photocopiable pages in this Teacher's Guide (see pages 144–194) that practice the **University of Cambridge ESOL PET** (Preliminary English Test), plus Quick Smart Tests for each Unit. This makes ***QSE*** an ideal course for general study where students may go on to take a variety of exams.

QSE and the Cambridge PET Exam

QSE provides practice of all the papers in the Cambridge ESOL PET exam.

PET Paper 1 Reading and Writing

Reading: All five parts of the reading component of Paper 1 (formats and task types) are practised in the photocopiable **Exam practice pages** in this Teacher's Guide (pages 146–161). Part 1: short texts with multiple choice (for example, Reading Activity 1, PET exam practice pages). Part 2: matching descriptions of people to short adapted-authentic texts (Reading Activity 3 and 11, PET exam practice pages). Part 3: an adapted-authentic text with True / False questions (Reading activity 5 and 13, PET exam practice pages). Part 4: an adapted-authentic long text with multiple choice (Reading activity 7, PET exam practice pages). Part 5: factual or narrative text with multiple-choice cloze (Reading activity 9 and 15, PET exam practice pages).

Writing: Part 1: theme-related sentence transformations. This part is practised in the Use of English section in every unit of the Workbook (For example, U1 Ex 4, U2 Ex 4, U3 Ex 3). Part 2: a short communicative message such as an email. This part is covered by the Portfolio Writing section (Activity 9) in the Student's Book (For example, SB U1 Ex 9, U5 Ex 9; WB U1 question 1, U3 question 1) and the extra Portfolio Writing tasks in the Workbook. These tasks are slightly longer than the PET tasks but practise similar text types.
Part 3: a longer piece of continuous writing such as a letter or story. This is practised in the Portfolio Writing tasks as above (For example SB U2 Ex 9, U7 Ex 9; WB U1 question 3, U6 question 3).

PET Paper 2 Listening

The listening formats and task types of Parts 1–4 are practised in the **LISTEN IN** section (Activity 5) of each Unit. Part 1: short monologues or dialogues with multiple-choice (U4 Ex 5). Part 2: longer monologue or interview with multiple-choice (U9 Ex 5). Part 3: longer monologue with gap fill (U8, Ex 5). Part 4: longer dialogue with True / False items (U7, Ex 5)

PET Paper 3 Speaking

Parts 2–4 of Paper 3 (formats and task types) are practised in the photocopiable exam practice material in the Teacher's Guide. Part 1: candidate / interlocutor interaction about factual personal information (no practice material necessary).
Part 2: candidate / candidate simulated situation using visual material (Speaking activity 4, 8, 12, 16, PET exam practice pages)
Part 3: extended turn, photograph description (Speaking activity 2, 6, 10, 14, PET exam practice pages). Part 4: candidate / candidate conversation developing the theme in Part 3 (Speaking activity 6, 14, PET exam practice pages).

QSE and the Trinity College, London GESE and ISE exams

Because they are based on the structures, functions and subject areas of Trinity's GESE (Grades 4, 5 and 6) and ISE (0 and I) examinations (covering CEF levels A2+ to B1+), the Units in ***QSE Pre-Intermediate*** provide a thorough preparation for students taking examinations at these levels.

The **Reading** (Activity 3 of each Unit) and **Listen In** (Activity 5 of each Unit) sections in the book offer the opportunity to become familiar with the vocabulary specific to the subject areas in the Trinity examinations. Students then learn how to present and discuss their knowledge and ideas with the examiner in **Your Turn to Speak** (Activity 6) and **Your Topic** (Activity 7) in each Unit, using the structures and functions of the appropriate grade. This preparation applies to the Interview component of both GESE and ISE examinations.

In the GESE and ISE **Interviews**, Trinity examiners will be looking for candidates to show their ability to use a good range of the communicative skills, grammar, lexis and functions in the syllabus for the appropriate grade, while having a sufficient grasp of English pronunciation to be intelligible to the examiner.

Students will need guidance in selecting a **Topic**, which may be any theme that they are interested in, knowledgeable about and able to talk readily about. In preparing the Topic, candidates should be actively discouraged from producing and memorising a written text, as this will result in the candidate not being prepared to use spontaneous spoken English. Candidates are also advised to think carefully about the amount of material necessary for their topic, bearing in mind the time available. They should prepare enough material to sustain a discussion of the topic for up to five minutes, but not more. The points on the Topic form, which must be handed to the examiner at the beginning of the examination, should provide opportunities for the candidate to use the language of the specific grade, eg at Grade 4 or ISE 0, not just general statements about the present but also references to future plans, intentions and past events.

In the Trinity GESE exams the candidate needs to be prepared to:

- give information about the prepared topic in a series of limited long turns under the given headings;
- answer questions and participate in informal discussion, during which the examiner might request more information, facts or details;
- ask the examiner at least one question about the topic area.

Also, it is a good idea to mention that students may like to take with them into the exam one or more pictures, photos, models or other suitable objects to illustrate their prepared topics.

QSE Pre-Intermediate also provides ongoing guidance in the writing skills needed to tackle the Portfolio tasks and Controlled Written Examination of the ISE. On page 25 of this Introduction, under the heading **Portfolio Writing** (Activity 9), you will find details of what this element of the ISE consists of. There is also a requirement for candidates to talk to the examiner about one or more of their pieces of Portfolio Writing, giving more details about what they have written. In the ISE Controlled Written examination, which takes place at the candidates' place of learning, students are expected to complete a Reading into Writing task which requires them to read a text of about 100 (ISE 0) or 200 (ISE I) words and then use their understanding to complete the accompanying Writing task. This part of the exam takes place before the examiner comes to mark the Portfolio and interview the candidates.

QSE Pre-Intermediate covers the necessary skills, knowledge and range of language for students who want to take the three Elementary grades (4, 5 and 6) of Trinity's 12 Graded Examinations in spoken English. At this point, when students have successfully made the **transition from the Initial stage**, Trinity examiners are looking for increasing fluency and the ability to play a limited part in initiating and maintaining the conversation. The candidate is expected both to ask and answer questions on the prepared topic and the subject areas for conversation as well as demonstrate that she or he can produce exponents of the functions and grammatical items of the relevant grade.

A further transition is that at two points candidates have the option of taking Trinity's Integrated Skills in English examinations instead of the spoken GESE grades: ISE 0 (equivalent to Grade 4 GESE) and ISE I (equivalent to Grade 6). These test both reading and writing skills as well as speaking and listening. ***QSE Pre-Intermediate*** provides a thorough grounding in the skills needed to tackle the ISE Portfolio and written examination, as well as the Interview, in which the examiner discusses the Portfolio with its author.

Rosemary Harris, Trinity Examiner

QSE and CLIL

One of the most significant aims of recent educational thinking in many countries has been to make learning a relevant preparation for the students' real lives in the widest sense. This can mean relevance not just to vocational training but also to personal development, citizenship, further education and the use of information technology. In addition, education reforms in many countries now encourage a greater emphasis on political, economic, historical and cultural world awareness, as **globalisation** affects everyone's lives.

QSE features a cross-curricular **CLIL** (Content and Language Integrated Learning) topic as part of every Unit. Some of these are traditional school subjects like Maths, Physics and Biology. Others reflect the changing nature of the modern syllabus with subjects like Business Studies, Media Studies, European Citizenship and Information and Communications Technology (ICT). The course approach to CLIL also reaches out more widely to embrace a range of topics that interest and are useful to students even if they are not being formally studied. These include ideas such as First Aid, Music Technology, Health and Fitness and the English-speaking World. In ***QSE,*** CLIL is truly integrated so that it becomes a natural part of what we use language for – talking about the things that interest us.

The objective of the cross-curricular sections in this book is not to add to the students' own knowledge of maths, science, history or geography. Instead it is to equip students with an English language strategy (and the relevant conceptual and linguistic tools) so that they can extend their understanding of the world through the use of a foreign language. It is not aiming to teach mathematics to the students – they are already learning that separately. It is intending to give them the equipment to combine their language studies with their other subject areas.

'CLIL is an approach to bilingual education in which both curriculum content – such as science or geography – and English are taught together….. Hence it is a means of teaching curriculum subjects through the medium of the language still being learned….. CLIL can also be regarded the other way round – as a means of teaching English through study of a specialist content. … CLIL is compatible with the idea of JIT education (Just In Time learning) and is regarded by some of its practitioners as the ultimate communicative methodology.' (David Graddol, *English next*, British Council, 2006)

QSE and Multiple Intelligences

The theory of Multiple Intelligences, first posited by Dr Howard Gardner in 1983 and modified many times since then, has divided teachers and educators as much as it has brought them together. But this is really a matter of the details. Most educational theorists now agree that the long-established methods of teaching and testing, which only appealed to a learner's linguistic or logical-mathematical intelligences, work well for some students but exclude others whose intelligences are of a different type.

What we have tried to do in this book is address certain other aspects of the theory, particularly the distinction between interpersonal and intrapersonal intelligences. Students do not always want to interact with each other and provision needs to be made for 'lone' activities as well as pair and group work. However, we also feel that the notion of bodily-kinaesthetic intelligence is a key factor in language learning and enjoyment of the process. But as these are choices and decisions which are best made by the teacher, activities that involve sharing, moving around to find the answers with other students, participating and mingling have been included here in the Teacher's Guide rather than on the pages of the Student's Book. Auditory learners will find plenty of stimulation in the 116 minutes of varied audio material on the two CDs. Visual learners will find that ***QSE*** is lavishly illustrated with photos that make the texts come alive. Most of the photographs are authentic news pictures and there are Picture notes that describe the back story to many illustrations in the Unit-by-Unit part of the guide.

English as a meme

Content and Language Integrated Learning (CLIL) represents an evolution in second language acquisition. It is an idea that is changing the way people learn English. One of the key concepts of CLIL is that, by changing the context in which a foreign language is learned, teachers can make it more relevant to the students' needs and thus more readily acquired.

In 1976, Professor Richard Dawkins of Oxford University suggested that there are units of cultural inheritance and transfer which he called 'memes'. He suggested that they work in a way that is similar to the way that genes pass on biological information. Memes are ideas (such as the Earth is flat) or fashions (like short skirts) or skills (such as skiing), which can be rapidly transmitted from one person to another.

The skill of speaking English as a foreign or second language is now a globally successful idea, or a meme. Over a billion people worldwide are learning English as a Foreign Language. Dawkins and others think that memes reproduce by both mutation and recombination, rather like genes in process of biological evolution itself. A mutation in thought may take centuries to take root. For example, Leonardo da Vinci's ideas on mechanical flight never caught on in the fifteenth century because the technical environment of the time could not support them. Five hundred years later, the meme of flight is so commonplace we hardly question it.

Memes are also propagated by recombination, such as when existing ideas and skills come up against a new environment and adapt rapidly to suit it. Thus, mobile phones and the internet have dramatically changed the ways in which people communicate. We still talk and write, but now we do this instantly with people anywhere in the world. The result is an explosion of global communication – an extremely successful meme, evolved to fit the 21st century environment.

CLIL may be another example of memetic recombination. The learning environment is filled with subjects like geography, history and physics. If language learning moves into these new environments, it becomes an improved meme – one that combines old ways of teaching with new situations and thus provokes students to acquire improved skills and new ideas.

Students not only learn *about* the subject of geography or maths with CLIL, they also turn the process upside down and learn the language *from* the subject. If they are already learning geography, discussing it in English enables them to recombine the subject with the second language, producing a form of learning that is better adapted to their environment. It's more fun, more relevant and more motivating, and like a gene or a meme, more successful.

QSE Pre-Intermediate – at-a-glance

QSE Pre-Intermediate consists of 16 separate Units of six-pages each, plus various additional materials, such as Extended Reading, Exam Practice, Tests and Language Banks. Every Unit of the course works in the same way. The same ingredients appear in the same order in each Unit. The activities are explained with an intentionally limited repertoire of rubrics, which are repeated throughout. The activities are varied, but the instructions are kept as simple as possible. This means that students only have to learn how to use the course once in the first Unit, and can then expect the same structure in the rest of the Units. This makes it exceptionally clear and user-friendly, further defining the student-centred approach of the whole course.

Scope and sequence of the course:

Contents pages of Student's Book (see also Materials Map pages 4–7 of this Teacher's Guide) *and the* ***Workbook***

Every Unit consists of:

4 Student's Book pages

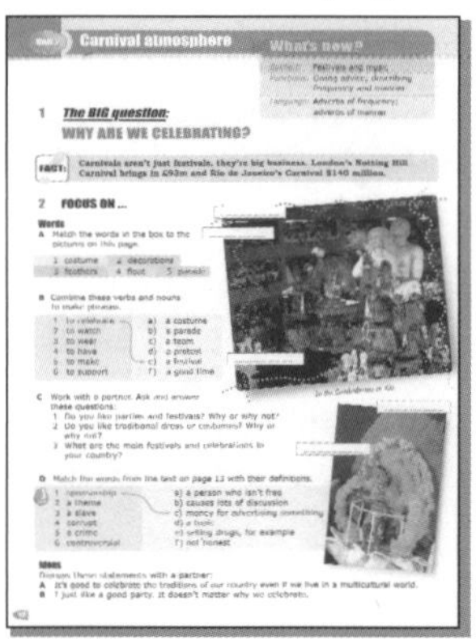

Page 1:
Focus on Words and Ideas

Page 2:
Reading, Grammar

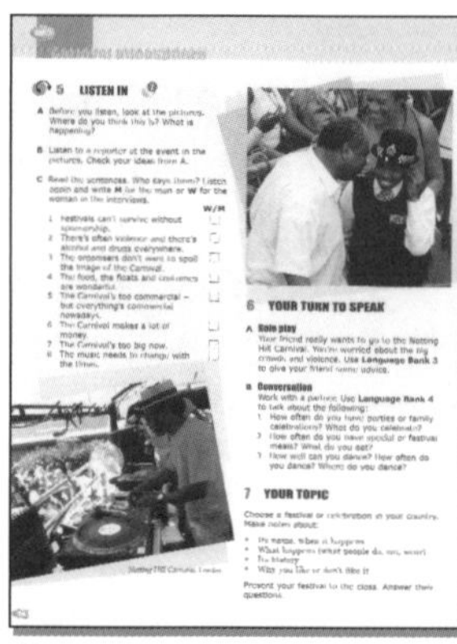

Page 3:
Listening, Speaking

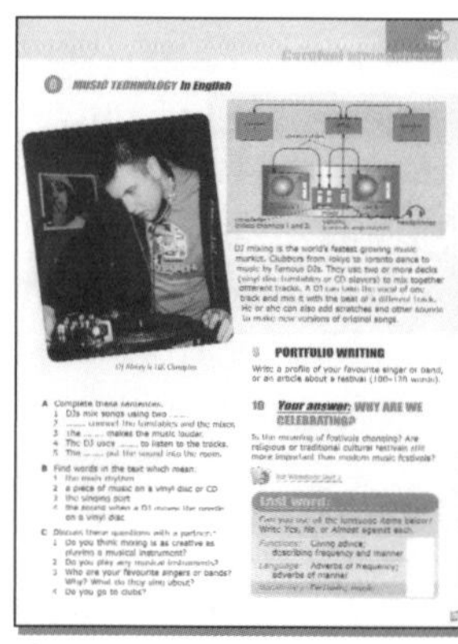

Page 4:
CLIL, Writing, Speaking

2 Workbook pages

Grammar explanations and exercises

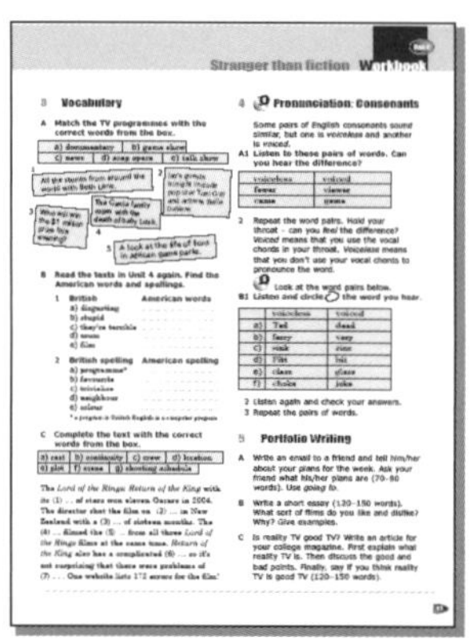

Use of English, Vocabulary Pronunciation, Writing

Listening on CD1 (Blue)
Reading on CD2 (Red)

Cambridge PET Exam practice and Quick Smart Tests for each Unit

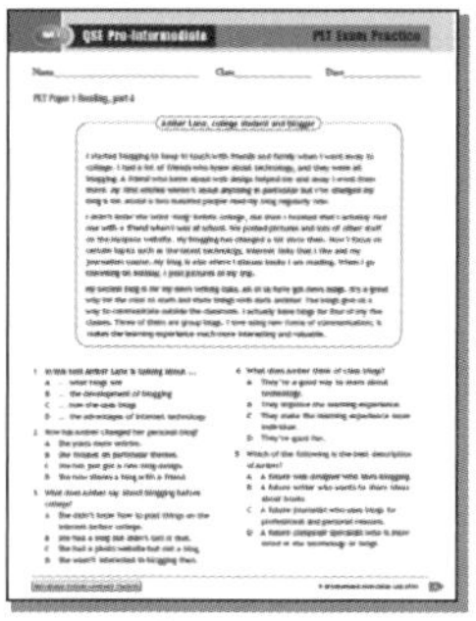
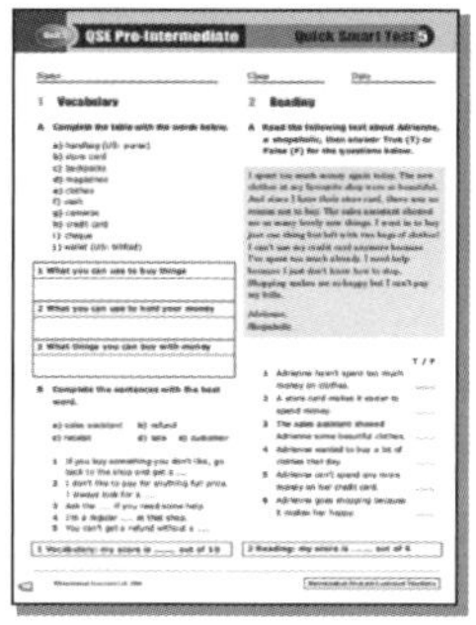
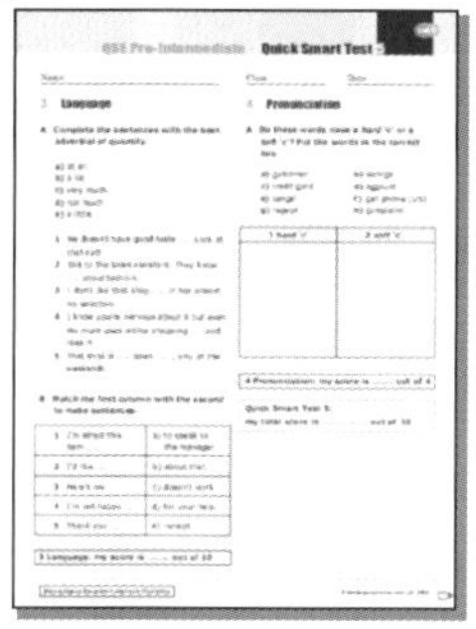

Photocopiable pages in this Teacher's Guide

Plus various other resources:

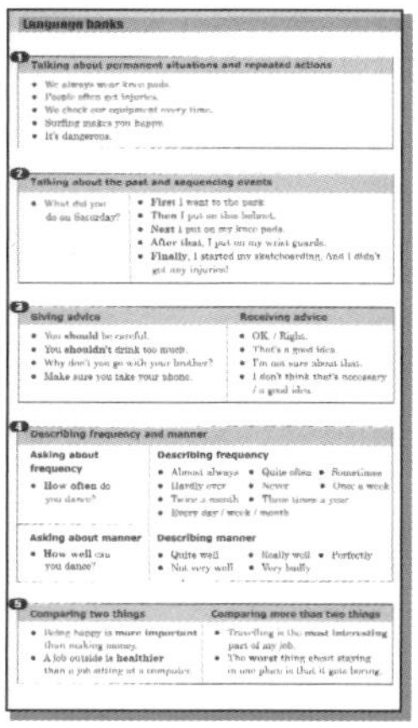
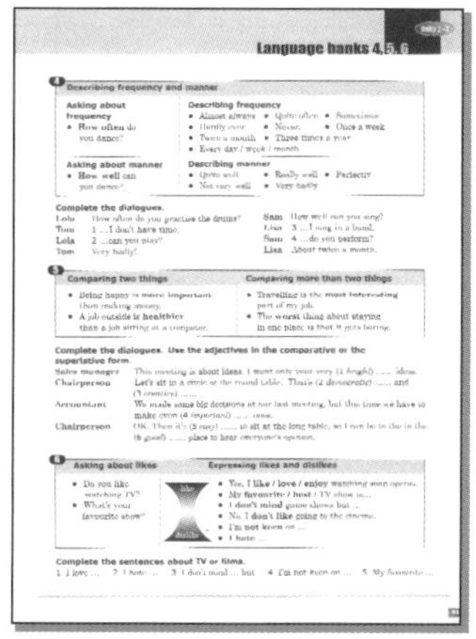

***27 Language Banks**, on the Student's Book cover flaps*

The Language Banks are also in the Workbook with exercises

2 Extended Reading sections in the Student's Book

2 Progress Checks in the Workbook

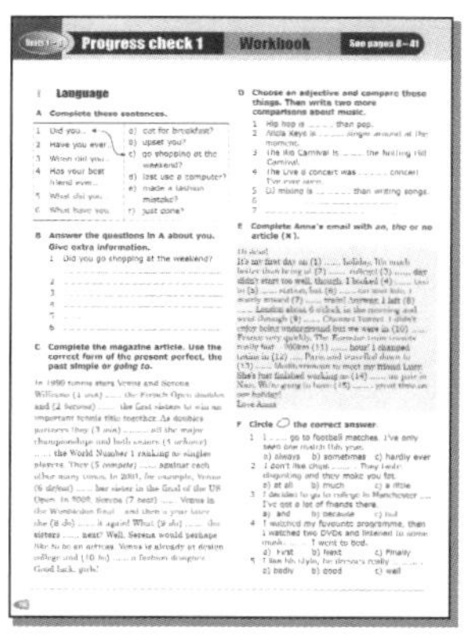
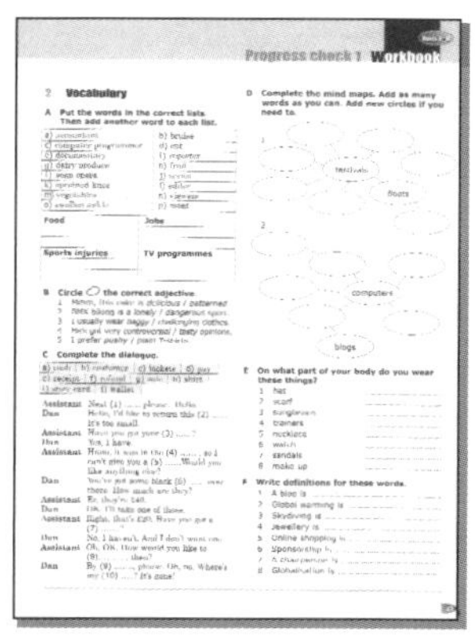

***Audio texts** (Listening & Pronunciation)*

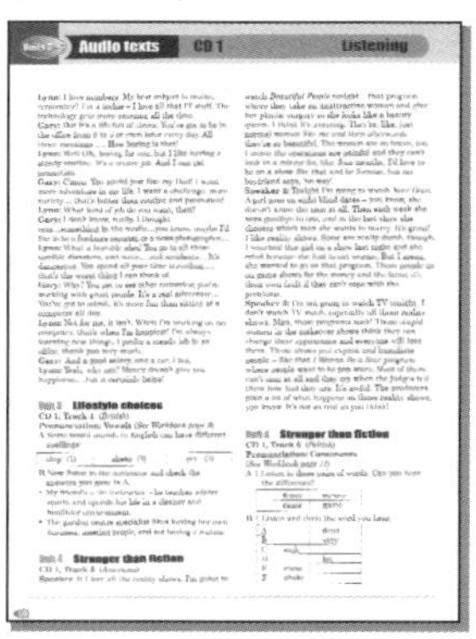

*Unit-by-Unit **Glossary** in the Student's Book*

***Wordlist** in the Workbook*

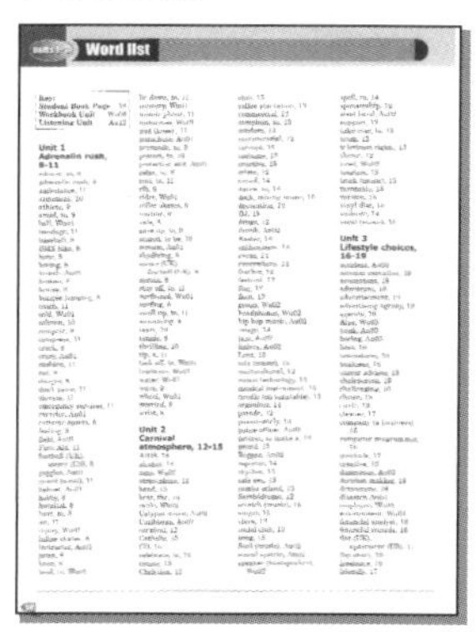

QSE Pre-intermediate – guide to the Unit structure

The 4 pages of each Unit in the Student's Book consist of:

Student's Book Page 1

What's new?
Subjects, functions and language introduced in the Unit

1 *The BIG question*
Grabs the attention of the students.

FACT box
An amazing or amusing fact to engage immediate attention on the topic.

2 FOCUS ON ...
Words
Pre-teaching of new vocabulary using word fields and collocations. Developing new and wider lexis for the students is an important element of the course.

Ideas
Personalised and intercultural speaking activities based on the new vocabulary. Introduction to thinking about the reading text on the next page.

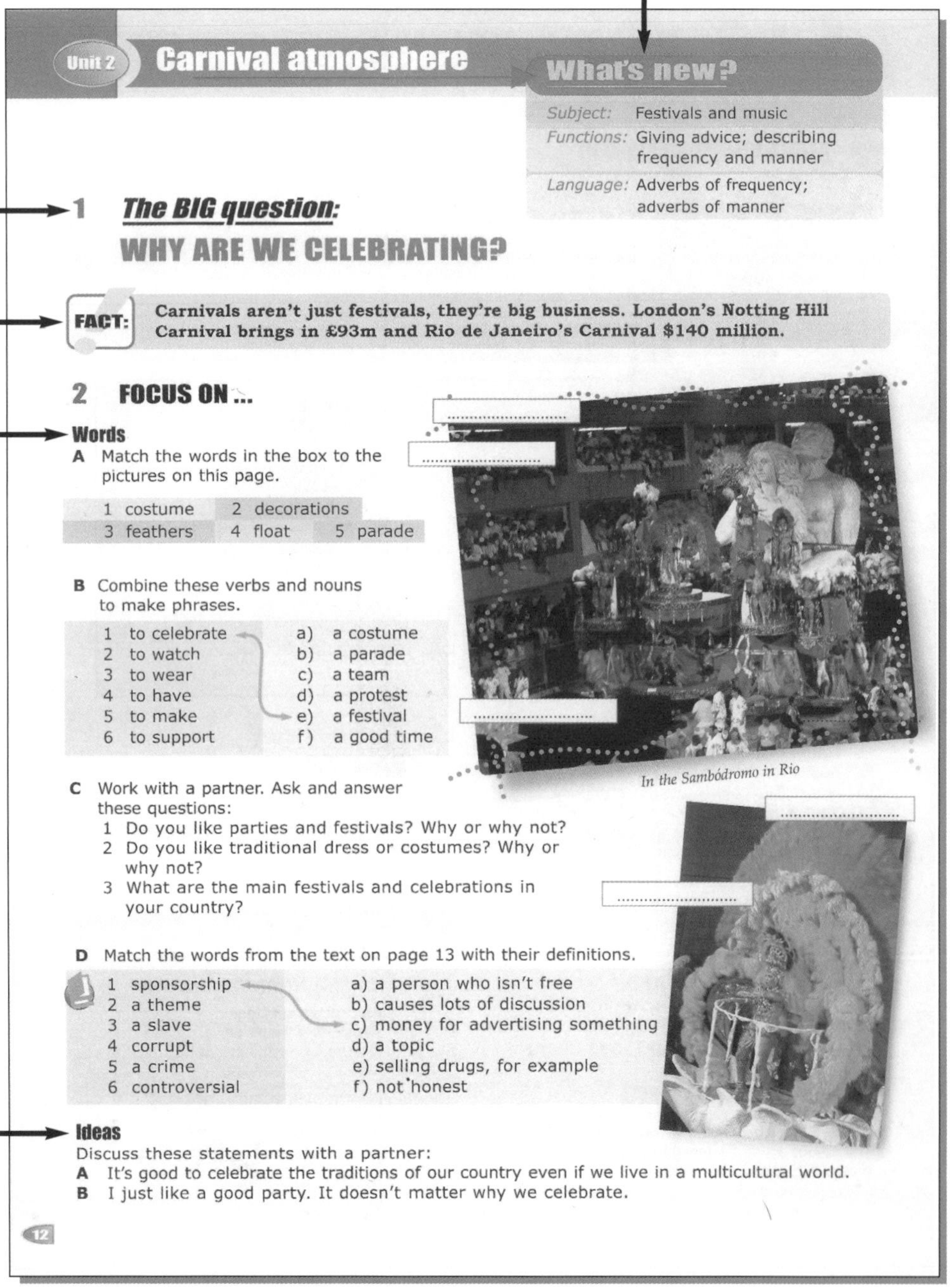

Unit 2 **Carnival atmosphere**

What's new?

Subject:	Festivals and music
Functions:	Giving advice; describing frequency and manner
Language:	Adverbs of frequency; adverbs of manner

1 ***The BIG question:***
WHY ARE WE CELEBRATING?

FACT: Carnivals aren't just festivals, they're big business. London's Notting Hill Carnival brings in £93m and Rio de Janeiro's Carnival $140 million.

2 FOCUS ON ...

Words

A Match the words in the box to the pictures on this page.

1 costume	2 decorations	
3 feathers	4 float	5 parade

B Combine these verbs and nouns to make phrases.

1 to celebrate	a) a costume
2 to watch	b) a parade
3 to wear	c) a team
4 to have	d) a protest
5 to make	e) a festival
6 to support	f) a good time

In the Sambódromo in Rio

C Work with a partner. Ask and answer these questions:
1 Do you like parties and festivals? Why or why not?
2 Do you like traditional dress or costumes? Why or why not?
3 What are the main festivals and celebrations in your country?

D Match the words from the text on page 13 with their definitions.

1 sponsorship	a) a person who isn't free
2 a theme	b) causes lots of discussion
3 a slave	c) money for advertising something
4 corrupt	d) a topic
5 a crime	e) selling drugs, for example
6 controversial	f) not honest

Ideas

Discuss these statements with a partner:
A It's good to celebrate the traditions of our country even if we live in a multicultural world.
B I just like a good party. It doesn't matter why we celebrate.

12

Student's Book Page 2

All texts are based on research from authentic sources. They have in many cases been carefully adapted to reflect the structural and lexical aims of the unit.

The photographs and illustrations are an important aid to learning. They provide talking points, aid understanding and motivate students to read the text.

3 READING
Text(s) with track number (❷) for audio CD2 Reading

Pre-reading questions (reading for gist; prediction, personal reaction)

Comprehension questions on the Reading text(s)

Reading for gist and reading for detail

4 LANGUAGE
Inductive grammar activities cross-referenced to grammar explanations and exercises in the Workbook.

Cross-reference to Workbook page grammar explanation and exercises

Unit 2

Carnival atmosphere

3 READING

A Read the article quickly. What happens at Carnival time in Rio?

❷

CELEBRATION OR PROTEST?

The Rio de Janeiro Carnival is a time to drink, dance and celebrate before Lent. As in Catholic Europe, Lent is the forty days before Easter when many Christians stop doing things they enjoy. But the Rio Carnival also includes African dance and music traditions from the time when slaves worked on Brazil's coffee plantations.

Millions of people usually watch the street parades all over the city and about 70,000 see the top samba schools in the Sambódromo, Rio's parade street. Rio's samba schools are local social clubs. The schools choose different themes for every Carnival and members work hard all year to build the floats and make the costumes. Their supporters are proud of them and support them passionately – like their favourite football team. At the samba parade the schools get points for music, costumes, dancing and enthusiasm.

Slavery, corrupt politicians and crime were Carnival themes in past years and the themes are becoming more controversial each year. Brazil's Roman Catholic Church often complains. In 2004, for example, the church complained about the Acadêmicos da Grande Rio School and its theme of safe sex and AIDS. However, anti-AIDS groups supported the school and protesters gave out free condoms at the Carnival. "Festivals like the Rio Carnival are a good way to teach young people about AIDS," one supporter said. "We're using the Carnival to make a protest," said another.

But a lot of people ask whether protest and education are what the Carnival is really about. Others say that commercial interests such as television rights, tourism and sponsorship are taking over the traditional meaning of Rio's Carnival. Some think it just doesn't matter – what's important is the party.

A float with the word CENSORED on it. The church often complains about Carnival themes

B Read the text again. Who or what do these sentences refer to?
1 They worked in coffee plantations.
2 They dance in the parade at the Sambódromo.
3 They choose different themes every year.
4 They work hard all year.
5 They are becoming more controversial.
6 It complained.

C Are these sentences about the Rio Carnival true (**T**)? or false (**F**)?

		T/F
1	There is one parade.	
2	The Carnival takes place before Lent.	
3	The Carnival combines European and African traditions.	
4	It isn't a commercial event.	

D Discuss these questions with a partner.
1 Do you have a carnival in your country? Do you think it's a good tradition?
2 What do you think about commercial sponsorship of festivals?
3 Is it right that particular groups use festivals to promote their ideas?

4 LANGUAGE

Look at the adverbs of frequency and manner in **bold** in these sentences:
- They **usually** watch the parade.
- Members work **hard** all year.
- They support their schools **passionately**.
- They **often** complain.

A Which adverbs answer the question 'How often'? Where do these adverbs go in the sentence?

B Which adverbs answer the question 'How'? Where do they go in the sentence?

C Can you think of other examples of adverbs of frequency and manner?

Workbook Unit 2: Adverbs of Frequency and Manner

13

Student's Book Page 3

5 LISTEN IN

Listening material with track (❷) number for audio CD 1 Listening & Pronunciation

All audio recordings made in broadcast standard London studio, using authentic native-speaking British and American actors. Listening texts are adapted to suit the structural and lexical aims of the Unit.

Photos and illustrations aid understanding and improve motivation to listen.

Pre-listening activities (pre-discussion of the general topic, prediction, pre-teaching of vocabulary)

Listening comprehension questions (listening for gist and listening for detail; personal reactions and opinions)

6 YOUR TURN TO SPEAK

A Role play

B Conversation

Role play and discussion using the language and functions introduced in the Unit.

7 YOUR TOPIC

Presentation and discussion of a topic using a pre-prepared list of points.

Unit 2

Carnival atmosphere

5 LISTEN IN ❷

A Before you listen, look at the pictures. Where do you think this is? What is happening?

B Listen to a reporter at the event in the pictures. Check your ideas from A.

C Read the sentences. Who says them? Listen again and write **M** for the man or **W** for the woman in the interviews.

		W/M
1	Festivals can't survive without sponsorship.	☐
2	There's often violence and there's alcohol and drugs everywhere.	☐
3	The organisers don't want to spoil the image of the Carnival.	☐
4	The food, the floats and costumes are wonderful.	☐
5	The Carnival's too commercial – but everything's commercial nowadays.	☐
6	The Carnival makes a lot of money.	☐
7	The Carnival's too big now.	☐
8	The music needs to change with the times.	☐

Notting Hill Carnival, London

6 YOUR TURN TO SPEAK

A Role play

Your friend really wants to go to the Notting Hill Carnival. You're worried about the big crowds and violence. Use **Language Bank 3** to give your friend some advice.

B Conversation

Work with a partner. Use **Language Bank 4** to talk about the following:

1. How often do you have parties or family celebrations? What do you celebrate?
2. How often do you have special or festival meals? What do you eat?
3. How well can you dance? How often do you dance? Where do you dance?

7 YOUR TOPIC

Choose a festival or celebration in your country. Make notes about:

- Its name, when it happens
- What happens (what people do, eat, wear)
- Its history
- Why you like or don't like it

Present your festival to the class. Answer their questions.

14

Student's Book Page 4

8 *CLIL TOPIC in English*

A cross-curricular topic connected with Unit. Comprehension, specialist vocabulary questions and other CLIL activities using the cross-curricular material presented charts, diagrams, maps and illustrations in the style used in the cross-curricular subject area.

9 PORTFOLIO WRITING

Guided writing tasks designed to be collected into a varied Portfolio of work.

10 *Your answer*

Sub-questions to help answer The BIG question that opened the Unit.

Last word

Self-assessment progress check, helping students to judge their own achievement in the areas of functions, grammar and lexis.

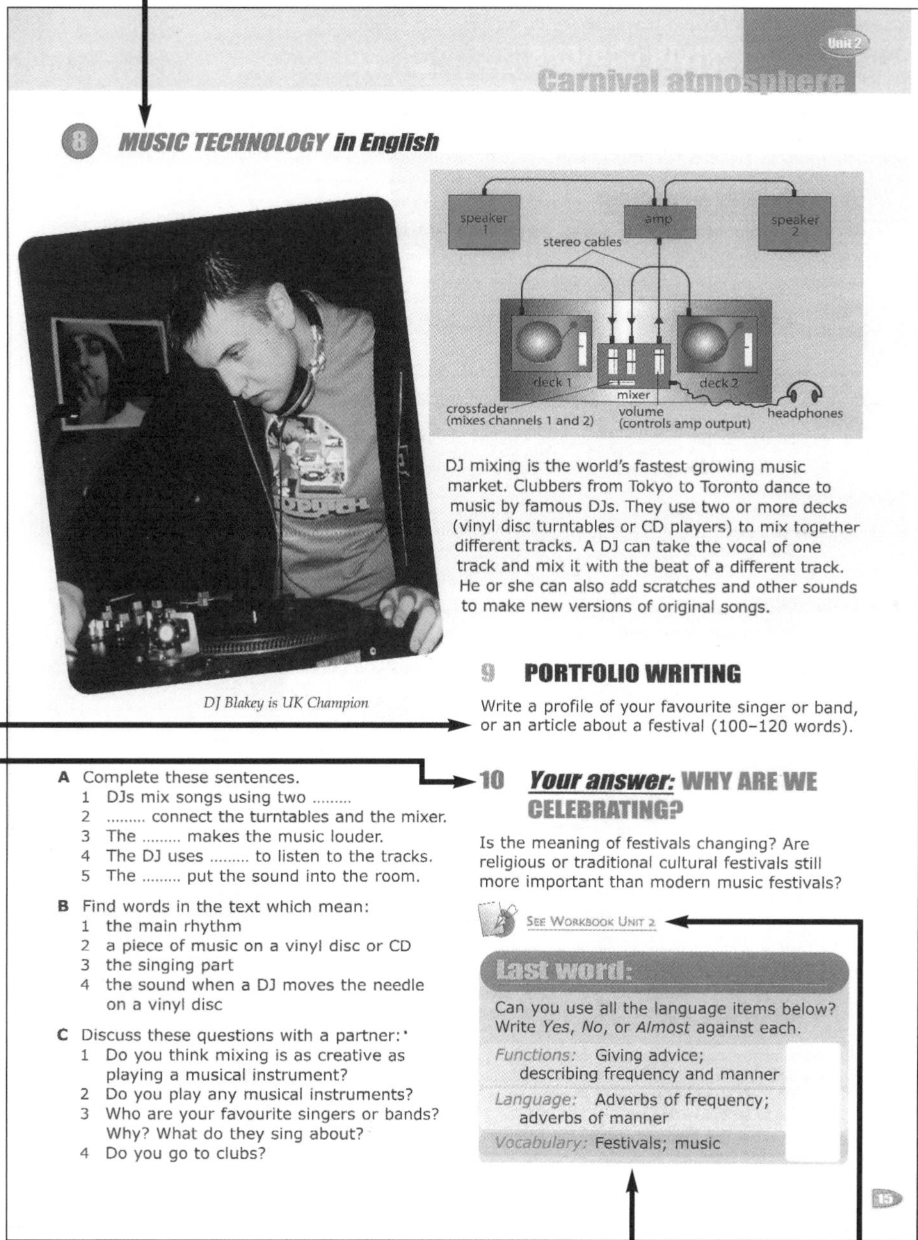

Unit 2

Carnival atmosphere

8 *MUSIC TECHNOLOGY in English*

DJ Blakey is UK Champion

DJ mixing is the world's fastest growing music market. Clubbers from Tokyo to Toronto dance to music by famous DJs. They use two or more decks (vinyl disc turntables or CD players) to mix together different tracks. A DJ can take the vocal of one track and mix it with the beat of a different track. He or she can also add scratches and other sounds to make new versions of original songs.

A Complete these sentences.
1 DJs mix songs using two ....
2 .... connect the turntables and the mixer.
3 The .... makes the music louder.
4 The DJ uses .... to listen to the tracks.
5 The .... put the sound into the room.

B Find words in the text which mean:
1 the main rhythm
2 a piece of music on a vinyl disc or CD
3 the singing part
4 the sound when a DJ moves the needle on a vinyl disc

C Discuss these questions with a partner:
1 Do you think mixing is as creative as playing a musical instrument?
2 Do you play any musical instruments?
3 Who are your favourite singers or bands? Why? What do they sing about?
4 Do you go to clubs?

9 **PORTFOLIO WRITING**

Write a profile of your favourite singer or band, or an article about a festival (100–120 words).

10 ***Your answer:*** **WHY ARE WE CELEBRATING?**

Is the meaning of festivals changing? Are religious or traditional cultural festivals still more important than modern music festivals?

See Workbook Unit 2

Last word:

Can you use all the language items below? Write *Yes*, *No*, or *Almost* against each.

Functions: Giving advice; describing frequency and manner
Language: Adverbs of frequency; adverbs of manner
Vocabulary: Festivals; music

15

Cross-reference to Workbook page exercises

Workbook Page 1

Unit number
Page cross-reference to Student's Book

1 Language

Grammar explanations and examples with exercises based on language presented in the Unit. Presentation in the Unit is inductive, so students can refer to these pages for quick explanations.

2 Use of English

Simple rewriting exercises in Cambridge PET exam style.

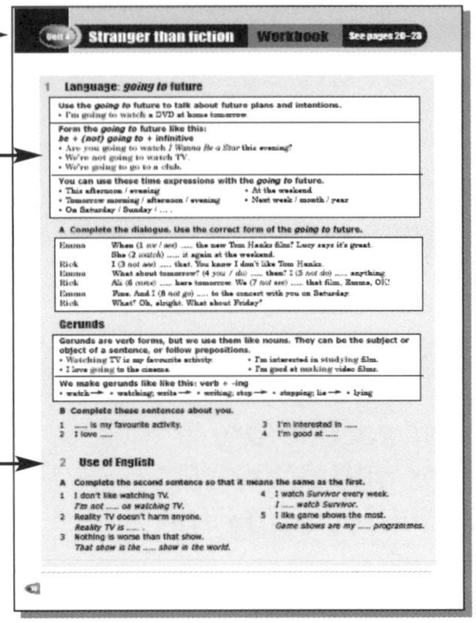

Workbook Page 2

3 Vocabulary / Word Building

Cloze sentences, dialogues and mini-texts, puzzles, mind maps and matching exercises, word families and word building strategies (one of the above sections per Unit).

Connections

Prepositions and opposites, language awareness, idioms.

4 Pronunciation

Self-study pronunciation exercises (individual sounds, word stress and sentence stress) with CD track number (❻).

5 Portfolio Writing

Exam-style writing activities.

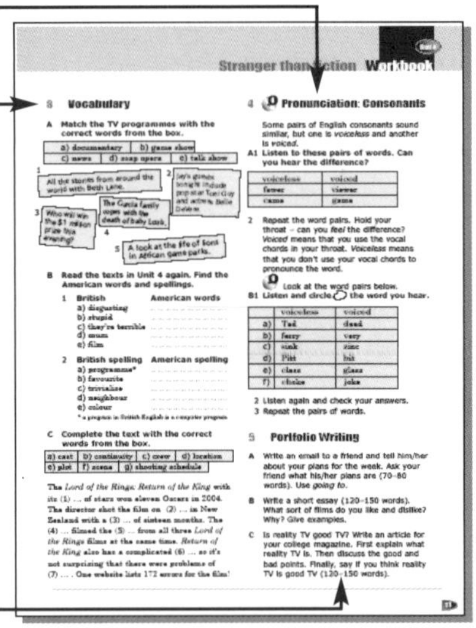

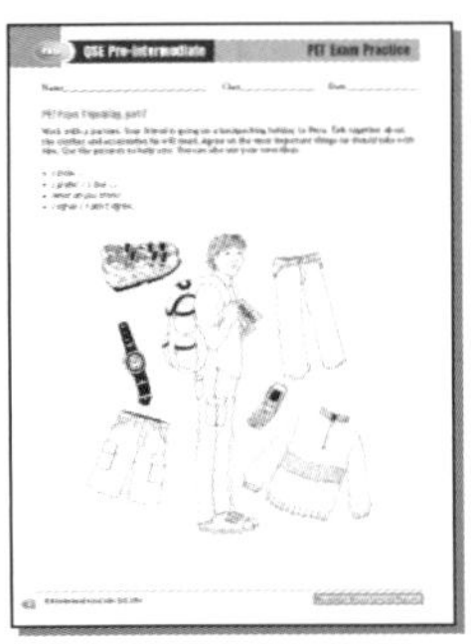

Photocopiable Resources

PET Exam Practice

For each Unit there is a photocopiable Exam Practice page. These prepare students for various parts of the Cambridge ESOL PET Examination (CEF Level B1).
See pages 144-145 and 146-161.

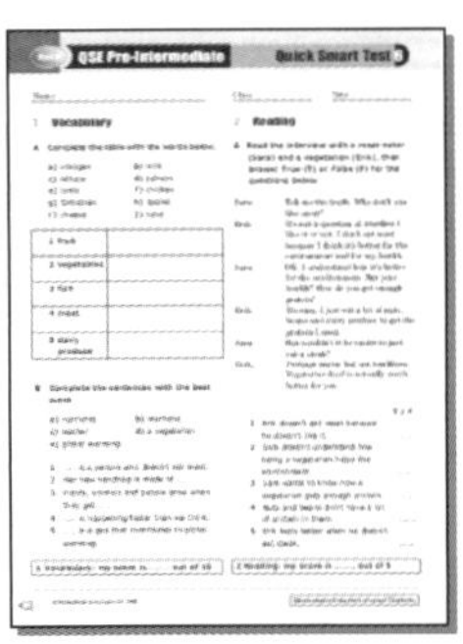

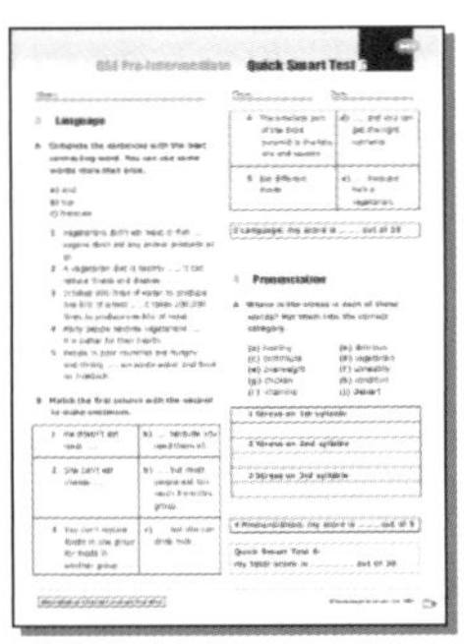

Quick Smart Tests

For each Unit there is a photocopiable Quick Smart Test that reviews and reinforces vocabulary, reading, language and pronunciation studied in the Unit.
See pages 144-145 and 162-193.

QSE Pre-Intermediate – how the sections of each Unit work

Map of the course

Student's Book Contents pages 4–7, Workbook page 3, Teacher's Guide pages 4–7.

The syllabus of ***QSE Pre-Intermediate*** is based on an extensive survey of current international standards in EFL teaching. Increasingly these are based on the CEF, or, if non-European, they are now aligned with it (for example the University of Michigan examinations). The functional, structural and topical basis of the course is the syllabus of Trinity College, London, but it also takes into account the requirements of the University of Cambridge ESOL syllabus.

Given that **communicative competence** is one of the main aims of the ***QSE*** course, care has been taken not to overload the students with grammar. However, extra language work is available in this Teacher's Guide. The Student's Book takes care to concentrate on skills work, particularly speaking. The Contents pages show the scope and sequence of each Unit, with headings for **Topic** (or Subject), ***The BIG question*,** **Functions (Language Banks), Grammar, Reading, Listening, Speaking, Writing** and **CLIL**. These pages can be used as a quick reference for both students and teachers, including a list of **CD tracks** for both CDs.

Student's Book Units

The colour pages of the Student's Book contain all the main language input material of the course. The authors have chosen to have many short Units, rather than a few long ones, so there is lots of variety and interest for students of widely different tastes. There are **16 Units**, plus two **Extended Reading** sections.

Unit title and What's new?

Student's Book Unit, page 1

The title gives a clue to the Unit topic. It is often an idiom or catch phrase that native speakers use frequently, for example *Stranger than fiction*. This may be worth an explanation to set the scene for the Unit. It also provides a chance to ask: Is there a similar expression in your language? There is an arrow leading from the Unit title to the **What's new?** box, which tells you the subject, language functions and grammar that will be covered in the Unit. The subjects have been chosen to cover the areas specified in the various examination syllabi, which are in turn also compatible with the domains, themes and sub-themes outlined in the CEF. These topics are, according to the CEF, the subjects of discourse, conversation, reflection or composition, as the focus of attention in particular communicative acts.

1 *The BIG question*

Every Unit begins and ends with a key question related to the topic. The question is intended to grab the attention of the students, but when it first appears, they are not required to give their opinion or respond to the question unless they wish to give a brief initial reaction. At the end of the Unit, after consideration of the evidence presented in the Unit and consultation with other students about their opinions, the class will be much more prepared and confident to answer ***The BIG question***. One way of working with ***The BIG question*** is to ask students to write a 1–2 sentence answer in their notebooks at the beginning of the class. Tell them that at the end of the Unit you will ask them to reread their answers and see if they have changed their minds.

FACT box

There is also a boxed Fact at the beginning of the Unit. The Fact is informative and / or surprising and is often based on statistics. You may not want to exploit the Fact, but simply tell students it is something for them to think about. Alternatively, you can use the question to stimulate interest in the topic by asking questions (for example, *What's your reaction to this? Does this surprise you? Why / why not?*) If you do this, spend only one or two minutes eliciting answers and don't worry about correcting mistakes.

2 FOCUS ON …

This section prepares students for the reading task on the next page. It consists of two parts: **Words** and **Ideas**.

Words

This section presents and highlights words that appear in the page 2 **READING** text on the opposite page and also adds other related vocabulary. In other words, the vocabulary that the students need to help them deal with the Reading text appears with words from the same context, providing students with a wider lexical set. Students are often encouraged to provide words they already know at this stage, as well. The words section is accompanied by photos, which provide illustrations of new words and stimulus for their activation.

Because all the topics are real life ones and the materials taken from authentic published or internet sources, the vocabulary range is challenging. The benefit for students is that they have to deal with language they would actually meet in genuine written or spoken exchanges with native English speakers. It is important then to always encourage students to use their dictionaries for help. Vocabulary enrichment is one of the benefits of using authentic and topical materials. The Workbook recycles and practises vocabulary items with various activities. This helps learners to consolidate their knowledge and to become more confident in using the structures and expressions they have learnt. There is a **monolingual Glossary** in the Student's Book and a Wordlist for each Unit in the Workbook.

Ideas

In this section, students focus on the global ideas behind the Reading text. This enables students to approach the Reading text with a framework of expectations about the text, thus facilitating the student's reading experience. Put students in pairs to discuss their answers. Then encourage brief discussion and correct only major errors.

3 READING ⑩

Student's Book Unit, page 2

The Reading text is the main feature of this page. The text is designed to give students practice in the skill of reading. It also aims to present the target structure and vocabulary in context, and to provide students with material to help them deal with later activities in the Unit, including answering ***The BIG question*** at the end.

The Reading text may be in the form of one long text or two or more short ones on the same topic. The Reading texts at the beginning of the book are approximately 300 words long, increasing successively with each Unit to about 400 words in later Units. Longer reading passages are available in the two **Extended Reading** sections. Further reading texts are featured in the CLIL sections. All the Reading texts (except the CLIL texts) are available as audio recordings on **CD2**, which is red. The circles (⑩) on the page next to the heading indicate the CD track number of the relevant recording. Some teachers may wish to use the reading section as reading only and not use the audio, at least in the first instance. Others may like to make this into a read-and-follow activity using the audio.

The reading materials offer a wide variety of text types and topics. In some Units the reading texts have been slightly adapted from authentic or literary texts (for example, Unit 6 and Unit 10). Other texts have been more heavily adapted or specially written while still retaining the flavour and feel of the authentic text types, such as newspaper and magazine articles, brochures, websites and interviews on which they are based. It is worth noting that the enormous range and variety of both texts and illustrations for all the Units in ***QSE*** would not have been possible before the internet age. The sources are truly global.

We have chosen Reading texts which will always draw the attention of the reader and are designed to make students want to express their own views. The general topics in ***QSE Pre-Intermediate*** are those required for international examinations, but always with a stimulating twist. Unit 1, for example, is about sport but the focus in the reading is on danger. Unit 5 is about shopping but the reading focuses on the pushy sales methods of shop assistants. Unit 11 is about travel, but deals with the environmental threat of cheap air flights, while Unit 15 takes the topic of health and discusses the threat of avian or bird flu. Students will want to find out more after seeing the illustrations and reading the photo captions, the headline and the first few lines of text. The notion of grabbing the attention of the reader through the triple attractions of arresting images, catchy headlines and affective first paragraph is a fundamental principle behind all kinds of print and online journalism. It also provides a strong motivation to read ELT materials.

Thanks to the preparatory work on page 1, students should be in a position to deal with the Reading text confidently, so the first reading can be done quite quickly. Students should try to grasp the overall gist of the text and not worry at this stage if they don't understand everything. There is a reading-for-gist exercise to help students with the overall meaning. The exercises which follow are designed to get students to re-read the text for more detailed understanding.

The Reading text is accompanied by standard examination-style activities and exercises, comprehension questions and activities designed to help the students read for detail. They also promote the sharing of ideas and opinions, the aim being to present both sides, or sometimes the many sides, of a debatable issue. Students can do the activities individually, in groups or in pairs.

4 LANGUAGE

This section deals with the main language structure(s) of each Unit. In ***QSE Pre-Intermediate*** the choice of structures reflects those required for the Trinity GESE examinations, Grades 4, 5 and 6, but which are also common to most syllabi in language texts at this stage. The structural material may be new to the students, or it may be revision. Only you, the teacher, know the realities for your class, which may contain a wide range of abilities. We will therefore make suggestions for the aspects of the structure item that you need to revise or present so that students can deal with the material they encounter later in the Unit.

In the Student's Book we have chosen to use the **inductive** method for initial presentation. Students are presented with example sentences from the Reading text which are highlighted because of their grammatical structure content. Students then reflect on the example sentences using questions to help them. There is no attempt at this stage in the Student's Book to provide an explanation of the grammar point. However, a detailed **grammar explanation** is available in the **Workbook** with a cross-reference provided. If you wish, you can at this point spend some time working on the structure practice material you will find on the left-hand page of the **Workbook** for each Unit, under the heading **1 Language**. In this section there is sometimes a **secondary grammar item** featured, with explanations and exercises.

5 LISTEN IN ⑩

Student's Book Unit, page 3

The main features of this page are the activities which relate to the listening text. Each of the audio tracks is shown on the page by a CD symbol (⑩), with the relevant track number on audio **CD 1 Listening & Pronunciation** (blue). The **Audio Text** is available in the **Workbook**.

Listening is a vitally important language skill and it is important that listening material sounds authentic as well as interesting. However, we appreciate that listening can be quite arduous for the students. To begin with, listening to a CD player on the teacher's desk is not the same as listening to a real native speaker. The ***QSE*** recordings have been made using professional English native speaker actors in a broadcast standard studio in London, but the quality of the sound may be affected by the machine it is played on and the room it is played in. Often the speed of the delivery is daunting for students, and sometimes they lose the thread of the meaning and find it hard to pick it up again.

Slowing down the texts to an artificial degree is not the answer – this does not prepare students for real listening experiences. What we try to do in ***QSE*** is present focused pre-listening activities, which make the listening experience a successful one. Often there is more than one pre-listening task. These tasks focus on predicting the topic through pictures, pre-discussion of the general topic of the listening text and pre-teaching of key lexical items. The first of the comprehension activities focuses on the gist of the listening passage, while the second deals with more detailed comprehension. The final activity or activities are speaking activities based on topics arising from the passage.

In our view, it is pointless to make the listening tasks so challenging that students lose both confidence and motivation. As with the presentation of the reading material, the listening tasks are designed to motivate students to listen with a purpose.

Whilst the listening texts are all specially recorded, the text types are authentic and varied – from street *vox pop*, where people give their opinions, to private conversations, radio interviews and discussions and telephone calls. Whilst all factual information in the listening is to the best of our knowledge accurate, the texts may contain some non-standard opinions. For example in Unit 12 *Money, money, money,* a teenager says that she would keep money found on the street or quietly pocket extra change at the supermarket. The aim of the authors has been throughout to present the widest possible range of views, opinions, ideas and facts in order to challenge and stimulate the student's ideas and imaginations and lead them into meaningful discussion. That means giving space to all shades of opinion – none of which are endorsed or recommended by the authors or the publishers, who remain neutral in what they hope will be active classroom discussions!

There are usually 4–5 activities in the **LISTEN IN** section. The first activity prepares students for the listening passage, often by focussing on key vocabulary items that will appear in the passage.

6 YOUR TURN TO SPEAK

This section combines the chance to discuss the topic and also activate some key functional language. **YOUR TURN TO SPEAK** offers a role play and a topic for conversation, one or both of which are cross-referenced to the numbered **Language Banks**. As stated earlier, the choice of functional material follows an established syllabus (which is shown in the Contents list, or map of the course on pages 4–7 of the Student's Book and on page 3 of the Workbook). However, the functional practice is, of course, relevant and useful whether or not the students are doing exams.

Before you ask students to try to carry out the **YOUR TURN TO SPEAK** tasks, ask them to check the relevant Language Bank (on the cover flaps of the Student's Book and in the Workbook with exercises) to see the kind of language that they should try to use. However, and this will be a recurrent theme in these notes, with any productive task, speaking or writing, successful completion of the task is more important than actually using the target functional language. In other words, if students carry out the task successfully, but don't use any of the target expressions, this is not a reason to criticise them! It can prove to be very helpful, in a follow-up session, to briefly go through the activity again as a way of revising the language.

Students can use the **Language Banks** on the **fold-out cover flaps** of the Student's Book for handy reference to functional language exponents presented in meaningful and useful written or spoken examples. The **Language Banks** also appear in the **Workbook**, where they are accompanied by exercises with answers on page 203 of this Teacher's Guide.

7 YOUR TOPIC

This task gives students the opportunity to talk about various aspects of a prepared topic, with the help of the structures and functional language introduced in this Unit. Before speaking, students make notes on a list of given points, which they then use as the basis of their presentation. Presentations should be about two minutes long.

The presentations can be individual or group presentations and can be made to a group or to the whole class. Listeners should be encouraged to listen attentively, ask questions, add information or give their own point of view.

In the Trinity GESE examinations, students are required to talk about a prepared list of topic points but in random order, selected by the examiner. The lists of points in ***QSE Pre-Intermediate*** often represent a logical sequence but can also be asked and answered in random order. You can therefore use this activity to practise for the Trinity examinations by formulating the points as questions in a different sequence and asking students to answer.

8 *CLIL in English*

Student's Book Unit, page 4

In this section, the **cross-curricular** aspects of the central theme of the Unit are explored. The title of each CLIL section makes this connection clear. Titles include ***MATHS in English, CREATIVE WRITING in English*** and ***BIOLOGY in English***.

Cross-curricular work is more and more in demand not only because teachers like the idea but also because certain national education policies and educational reforms now require it. However, we haven't only included a CLIL section for these reasons. We think there is great value in cross-curricular study, with students using English to accomplish tasks which refer directly to other aspects of their studies or work.

The CLIL sections are not designed to teach biology or maths from the beginning. In many cases, students may have already covered topics such as IT (Information Technology, Unit 10) in their other classes. A well-established tenet of good practice is to bring existing knowledge into a novel environment. This enables students to learn *from* as well as *about* the topics they are studying. They can take what they know already and apply it to the new circumstances of using that knowledge in English. However, all the CLIL topics can also be classified as general knowledge, being angled for use by non-specialists as well as those who already know the topics. The point is not to teach the content, but to practise the language in the context of the content. The language teacher does not need to be an expert in the relevant CLIL subject area. He or she can use the simple information presented on the page, plus the students' own knowledge, to promote language learning in a new context. The students may or may not have already studied Photosynthesis, for example (Unit 11), but discussing it in English should be a collaborative, stimulating, and useful part of language learning. If the students are using English to tell the teacher and other class members about their specialist subject, then a language learning aim has been successfully achieved.

The input material is presented in a variety of forms – conventional reading texts, pictures, facts and figures, diagrams and charts. Often the reading is more dense and challenging, and we recommend that the class should deal with it in a different way from the Reading texts on page 2. Group work, with students supporting each other and adding their own prior knowledge, is important here.

As with the more conventional reading texts on the second page of each Unit, the texts are accompanied by vocabulary and comprehension activities.

9 PORTFOLIO WRITING

This section requires students to carry out writing tasks based on various international forms of assessment, including the European Portfolio. Tasks include emails, letters, reports and essays, blogs or diaries, creative writing and reviews. Most tasks give some guidance as to how the writing activity should be approached, either in the form of content ideas and / or a paragraph plan. The Unit-by-Unit notes in the Teacher's Guide give detailed guidance for content, organisation and language which you can use to help your students prepare for the task.

Portfolio writing is a student-centred activity that many teachers and learners will find motivating and creative. It is intended that students collect the best examples of the different types of writing they have created during the course and make up a Portfolio which demonstrates the level of their achievement.

When you go through student's written work, make notes of sentences containing major errors. In a follow-up session, write these sentences on the board or hand them out as a photocopy. Ask students to correct the sentences in pairs or groups. When correcting written work, devise symbols for different types of errors, (eg 'G' for grammar, and 'Sp' for spelling). Give students a photocopied handout of these symbols. Make sure that students write out incorrect sentences correctly.

This section is particularly useful for students preparing specifically for the Portfolio component of Trinity's ISE examinations. The Portfolio forms part of the ISE examinations at all four levels. It provides an important opportunity for candidates to present to Trinity examiners the best work they can produce, rather than the best they can produce on a single occasion in the examination room. ISE portfolios are learner-led; they are able to draw on a wide range of resources and they can use different media. From a published list of fifteen tasks for each ISE level, candidates choose one task to present from each of the three sections, which are:

1 Correspondence (eg memos, notes, forms, postcards, letters and emails)
2 Factual writing (eg reports, articles, reviews, giving instructions or directions)
3 Creative and descriptive writing

It is strongly recommended that candidates prepare more than three tasks and then select their best three pieces of work for inclusion in the Portfolio. Teachers are not allowed to correct their learners' portfolio writing, but a feedback form is provided to help teachers to provide focussed and appropriate feedback. It is recommended that candidates should work on the Portfolio over a period of 6–12 weeks.

Because candidates have every opportunity to draft and correct their work, using spell-checkers and dictionaries, a very high level of accuracy is expected at all levels.

10 *Your answer*

And finally, we come back to ***The BIG question*** which opened the Unit. Students will now be in a much better position to answer it. To prove this, we recommended earlier that, before you start the Unit with your class, you all read ***The BIG question*** together and students make notes of what their answers would be on first reading. Then when you have completed the Unit, read the question again. Ask students if there is anything they would change or add from their original notes.

Depending on the amount of discussion you have had in your class throughout your work on the Unit, you can deal with answers to ***The BIG question*** in one of the following ways:

- Have a full-class discussion using the sub-questions for guidance. Write useful language on the board to help students express themselves (they can use the **Language Banks**).
- Ask two or three students to answer the sub-questions or sum up their opinion. Ask students if their opinions have changed since they first answered ***The BIG question***, and if so, why?
- You can also ask students to write a paragraph to answer the question for homework.

Last word

This section sends students back to the **What's new?** section at the very start of the Unit. As a form of self-assessment they can answer *Yes, No* or *Almost* to the questions. These reflect the objectives of the Unit, laid out in the map of the book and at the opening of the Unit. If there are too many *Almosts,* students will need to go back over their work and revise grammar, functions or vocabulary that they have not mastered.

Extended reading

The two **Extended Reading** Units are situated after Units 8 and 16. The reading texts here are longer and more substantial than the texts on page 2 of the other Units. In ***QSE Pre-Intermediate***, the texts are an authentic online interview with the round-the-world sailor Ellen MacArthur and an extract from a teenage novel, *Face* by British writer Benjamin Zephaniah. The interview has been adapted in places, whereas the novel extract has been abridged but not changed in any other way. Apart from the text itself, these two-page Units provide practice in working out the meaning of words from context and interpreting information, as well as questions for further discussion. This Teacher's Guide also offers optional Portfolio Writing tasks on these texts.

Glossary

At the back of the Student's Book there is a monolingual **Glossary** section. This contains approximately 800 head words, with English-language explanations in the style of popular learner's dictionaries. This does not replace a dictionary, which students will need and should use frequently, but it does provide a quick reference to the most difficult vocabulary in a lexically rich book. There is a fuller Unit-by-Unit Wordlist without explanations at the back of the Workbook.

Language Banks

There are **27 Language Banks** (**LBs**) on the cover flaps of the Student's Book. In this way they can be kept open in front of the students for constant reference. These Language Banks (LBs) also appear in the Workbook, with accompanying exercises. There is one LB for each of the **Functions** listed in the scope and sequence of the course (see Contents pages 4–7 of the Student's Book). The functions chosen for the ***QSE Pre-Intermediate*** Language Banks are taken from the Trinity College examination list of requirements, levels 4, 5 and 6, which equate to CEF levels A2-B1.

Students should be encouraged to use the LBs for ready reference in speaking activities particularly. Each LB can be used in conjunction with many different Units of the book. However, each one is introduced and practised for the first time in the order of Units shown in the Contents list. Reference to the new LB for each unit is usually made in Activity **6 YOUR TURN TO SPEAK**. Thereafter students are expected to be able to use the LBs on their own initiative, and when prompted in the text.

Workbook Units

The Workbook is designed to be used either for self-study, for **homework**, or in class. The contents follow those of the Student Book Units, the aim being to reinforce knowledge of the main themes as well as to provide further practice of language structures, vocabulary, and writing skills. Nine of the Units have **Pronunciation** activities, using audio recordings on CD1 (blue). There are also two **Progress check** sections, located at the same position in the Workbook as the **Extended Reading** Units are in the Student Book, namely after Units 8 and 16. There are up to six sections to each Workbook Unit. Not all the sections appear in every Unit and the numbers (apart from **1 Language**) vary according to the choice of activities. The various activities are listed below.

Language

On the left hand page of every Unit, the main grammar item is presented in diagrammatical form, with **grammar explanations** and information about rules. This is in contrast to the **inductive grammar** presentation of the new language in the Student's Book. Following the Workbook left-hand page explanations, there are practice exercises. In addition, there is sometimes information and exercise material relating to a **secondary grammar item**, which was featured in the Student Book reading text but was not focused on in **4 LANGUAGE** in the Student's Book.

Vocabulary

At the top of the right-hand Workbook page, this section features tasks such as cloze sentences, dialogues and mini-texts, puzzles, mind maps and matching exercises. These tasks aim to provide more practice of the lexis of the main Unit theme and of the CLIL topic area. **Vocabulary development** is an important feature of the course.

Word Building

Some of the ***QSE Pre-Intermediate*** **Workbook** Units contain tasks to heighten students' **language awareness**, by looking at word families and providing them with strategies to extend their vocabulary.

Connections

The **Connections** tasks provide a further opportunity for students to widen their awareness of related words – how words connect. In ***QSE Pre-Intermediate*** the tasks focus on prepositions and opposites.

Pronunciation ⑩

Pronunciation exercises can be found in nine out of the sixteen Units. They offer basic practice and help with some of the phonetic problems experienced by most students at this level. Tasks focus on individual sounds, word stress and sentence stress. All the pronunciation exercises are recorded on audio **CD1** (blue) **Listening & Pronunciation**, with track numbers (⑩) shown on the page.

Use of English

This section has easy exercise material in the format of Part 1 of the PET Examination Writing paper, based on the topic area of the Student Book Unit. These tasks provide useful practice for all students, regardless of whether they are doing the Cambridge Exams or not.

Portfolio Writing

The writing section offers a choice of tasks and is of the length and type specified in various exams. The writing tasks are diverse and range from short informal emails to longer *for* and *against* opinion pieces. We encourage students to appreciate the differences in register and style that are needed when writing for different purposes. The tasks here are useful ideas for homework.

QSE Audio CDs

There are two Audio CDs for ***QSE Pre-Intermediate.***

CD1 (blue) is the **Listening & Pronunciation CD** with 25 tracks and a running time of 60 minutes. All of the **LISTEN IN** activities are on CD1, together with nine pronunciation activities for which the text is in the Workbook.

CD2 (red) Reading contains 18 tracks with a running time of 56 minutes. All 16 of the **READING** activities are on this, together with the two **Extended Reading** sections.

Transcripts of all the listening material are provided with track numbers. At the beginning of each Unit text there is a description of the type of **accents** used in the recording. These vary considerably, from standard American and British (with, in each case, a few light regional accents), to South African and Australian. All of the accents are light and do not interfere with comprehension. The **pronunciation**

activities are all recorded in British RP (received pronunciation).

Wordlist

Finally, there is a list of words and collocations. The words are listed Unit-by-Unit, alphabetically and with a page reference. The simple number page references (*56*) give the relevant page of the Student's Book, in which almost all new vocabulary is introduced. Where there is a new word in the Workbook or the Audio, the reference is to the Workbook Unit number (*Wu6*), or the Audio script with a Unit number (*Au10*). Students can use these **Wordlists** as the basis of their own **topic wordlists**, building up vocabulary on related areas of study and interest. Some students like to make up their own topic-based **vocabulary cards**, with their own translations and ideas for remembering the words (mnemonics or homophones for example). In the Student's Book there is a glossary with monolingual English language explanations.

Vocabulary enrichment

Because all the topics are real life issues, and the input materials for them are from authentic sources, the vocabulary range is challenging. *QSE* is intentionally a rich source of new vocabulary for students' use. The benefit for students is that they have to deal with language they would actually meet in genuine written or spoken exchanges with native English speakers.

In addition, we provide activities to help students understand and activate new terms or concepts, both before they read or listen and afterwards. Then, after they have worked through the Student Book activities, the Workbook recycles and practises vocabulary items. This too helps learners to consolidate their knowledge and to become more confident in using the structures and expressions they have learnt.

Internet sources

There are lists of **internet references** for further research in each of the Unit-by-Unit sections of this Teacher's Guide. We also recommend that teachers and students take advantage of the fantastic research and study opportunities offered by search engines such as *Google*. Online sources are correct at time of print. The publishers cannot guarantee that websites will not change. This is the reason why the internet links have not been printed in the Student's Book. Both teachers and students should be aware that all websites and online resources are constantly changing. They should be checked before they are used for educational purposes.

The contents of any online references cited in this book do not represent the opinions of, or any manner of endorsement from the publishers, who cannot be responsible for any online content beyond their control.

QSE illustrations

The illustrations in *QSE* have been selected with great care from worldwide authentic sources, the scope of which can be seen from a brief glance at the acknowledgements list at the beginning of the Student's Book. The illustrations which accompany all the texts and exercises serve not only to grab attention, but also to aid understanding. They are often used to predict information in pre-reading tasks. There are suggestions for making class-time use of the photos in the Unit-by-Unit Teacher's Guide. Where it is useful and appropriate, there are separate background **Picture notes** with some extra information about the photographic material. Many forms of testing today require students to discuss and comment on images, and the pages of *QSE* provide ample opportunities for students to develop this form of **visual awareness** which is such an important part of modern literacy and communication.

QSE Photocopiable Resources

On pages 144–145 is an Introduction to the use of the ***QSE* Photocopiable Resources**, which are on pages 146–206 of this Teacher's Guide, also available online at www.brookemead-elt.co.uk/downloads/. These include examination practice and Quick Smart Tests for every Unit.

We hope you enjoy using ***Quick Smart English Pre-Intermediate*** and find the ideas in this Teacher's Guide useful and productive for your classroom teaching.

Rebecca Robb Benne
Joanne Collie
Ken Wilson, Mary Tomalin

What's new?

Subject: Sports, extreme sports, injuries, first aid
Language: The past simple / present simple; sequencing words
Functions: **Language Bank 1** Talking about permanent situations and repeated actions
Language Bank 2 Talking about the past and sequencing events

1 *The BIG question:* DO WE NEED DANGER?

The theme of this first unit is sports, especially extreme or dangerous sports. ***The BIG Question*** is: Do we need danger? Do we prefer 'ordinary' sports – baseball, basketball and football – which reflect traditional values such as cooperation, character building and group competition, or extreme sports which promote different values such as risk-taking, the thrill of the 'adrenalin rush' and fierce individualism?

- Read ***The BIG Question*** with the class and use the visuals to elicit initial reactions.
- Ask students if they think traditional or extreme sports produce more injuries. Then read the **FACT** box and see whether they think the same is true of their country.

2 FOCUS ON...

Words

Picture / background information

For more information on extreme sports:
www.extreme.com
www.allextremesports.com
For more information on bungee jumping:
www.bungeezone.com

- Look at the unit title with the class. Pre-teach 'adrenalin rush' or get students to use their dictionaries and suggest meanings.
- If your class is just beginning a course and the students don't know each other very well yet, you may wish to use a warm-up activity. A well-known ice-breaker is the following mingling activity which can be used to teach the material in A1 and A2.

Extra activity: A mingling activity

- Ask students to write three facts about themselves on a slip of paper, as follows:
  1 *My favourite sport*: (elicit names of sports and write them on the board if students need help)
  2 *The extreme sport I'd like to do*: (again, elicit and list on board)
  3 *Injuries I've had*: (elicit and list; also teach 'none')
- Write the three questions on the board:
  1 What's your favourite sport?
  2 What's the extreme sport you'd like to do?
  3 What injuries have you had?
- Students mingle, asking the three questions of as many students as they can within a set amount of time.

One way of introducing a game element is to ask students to give themselves a point each time the other student has written the same answer to one of the questions. The activity can also be used to create pairs: as soon as students find one (or two) similar answers, they pair off.

2 A 1

- Alternatively, if you have not used the mingling activity, look at the three categories and the words in the box with the class. Ask students what the photo in each category shows. Point out that the American English word for football is soccer.
- In pairs, students put the other words and phrases from the box in the correct categories.
- Check the answers and write lists on the board.

2 FOCUS ON... Words A 1 **Answers**

Traditional sports: football, baseball, tennis, swimming, basketball
Extreme sports: bungee jumping, BMX biking, skydiving, inline skating, surfing
Sporting injuries: sprained knee / wrist, cuts and bruises, broken bone, cracked rib

2 A 2

- Elicit further words from students for the three categories in exercise A1 and add them to the lists on the board.

2 FOCUS ON… Words A 2	Suggested answers
Traditional sports: golf, hockey, rugby, cricket Extreme sports: skiing, kayaking, white-water rafting, skateboarding Sporting injuries: head/back injury, dislocated shoulder	

2 B

Here students work with short phrases that they can use in their own discussions later.

- The symbol indicates that students consult their dictionaries for help with the exercise. If classes are not familiar with dictionary work, use this exercise to show them how to locate and interpret entries.
- Students match the sentences with their opposite meaning. Check the answers.

2 FOCUS ON… Words B	Answers
1 d **2** c **3** e **4** b **5** a	

2 C

This exercise is a pre-reading exercise which focuses on key vocabulary in the interviews.

- Students work in pairs and match the sentences to one of the meanings. Check the answers.

2 FOCUS ON… Words C 1 / 2	Answers
1 I want to show that girls can do anything; I love the adrenalin rush. **2** I cracked a rib.	

2 D

These questions elicit personal reaction to some of the ideas in the unit.

- Students discuss the questions with a partner. In monolingual classes, they may go back into their L1, which usually indicates that they are actually finding the questions interesting. Circulate and help with concepts and vocabulary.
- Ask students to report back to the class.

2 FOCUS ON…

Ideas

This section takes the discussion to a more abstract level.

- Read out the two statements and then discuss them with the class. As there are no 'right' or 'wrong' answers, encourage students to give their own views, whatever these are.

Picture / background information

The four photos show the four extreme sports discussed in the interviews. For more information on the sports, see these websites:

BMX biking:
www.sportsinfocentral.com
www.BMXtreme.com
Surfing:
www.surfing-waves.com
www.britsurf.co.uk
Skydiving:
www.skydiving.com
Inline skating:
www.skatefaq.com
www.iisa.org

3 READING CD2 (Red) track 1, page 9 SB

3 A

This question aims to provide training in reading for gist.

- Students should read the four sections through by themselves, and then match each one with a picture. This is a deliberately easy task, the purpose being to encourage learners to have the confidence to continue with this first reading even if there are some words or structures they don't understand.
- Students can also listen to the interviews on CD as they read. Check the answers.

3 READING A	Answers
1 b (Gary Lansdowne)	**2** c (Francine O'Reilly)
3 d (Juan Julia)	**4** a (Paula Carrera)

3 B 1

- Read out the first task and check that students understand it.
- Students read the interviews again and work through the questions individually or in pairs. Check the answers.

3 READING B 1 **Answers**

1 a) Gary: at 5, then went back at 20; Francine, as a child, then started competing at 16; Juan: at 20; Paula: at 15.
b) Gary: parents hated it; Francine: parents were supportive; Juan: his mum can't watch (must be frightened for him); Paula: at first, parents didn't think surfing was OK for girls, then they accepted it and now find it exciting.
c) Gary: lots of injuries when he started; Francine: a sprained knee; Juan: never had any injuries; Paul: none mentioned.
d) Gary: loves the adrenalin rush; Francine: loves the sport, wants to show that girls can do it; Juan: the thrill of danger makes him feel alive; Paula: loves it and it makes her happy.

3 B 2

- Read out question **2**. Students answer orally.
- Look at the sequencing words in **3** with the class. Students write sentences with the words. Check by asking individual students to read them out.
- Students write sentences like those in **3** for Francine.

3 READING B 2 **Answers**

2 a) started racing BMX bikes **b)** played tennis and football **c)** got back to biking
3 a) First, he started racing when he was 5. **b)** Then, at 16, he played tennis and soccer. **c)** Finally, at 20, he went back to BMX biking.
4 *(Example answer)*
First Francine's parents gave her a pair of roller skates. Then they bought her some inline skates. Finally, she started competing.

3 C

Read out the questions.
- Students compare their ideas in pairs.
- Ask students to report back to the class and compare ideas.

4 LANGUAGE: The present simple and past simple

4 A

This section is the grammar focus of the unit. Many students will have learnt the forms without necessarily internalising the rules of use. This inductive exercise helps them to see when the two tenses are used.
- Look at the example sentences with the class.
- Read out the questions in turn and ask students to answer orally.

4 LANGUAGE A **Answers**

1 stays **2** started **3** comes, watches **4** got

4 B

- Ask students to read the interviews again and find the past forms. Check the answers.

4 LANGUAGE B **Answers**

was (interview 4) got (interview 4)
gave (interview 2) thought (interview 4)
learnt (interview 1)

- Refer students to the explanation of the present simple and the simple past in Workbook Unit 1. They can read the explanation and do the exercises in class or for homework.

5 LISTEN IN CD1 (Blue) track 1, page 10 SB

Picture / background information

The photos show a student and instructor parachuting together. It is usual on the first jump for the student to be strapped to the instructor, who controls the parachute completely. If they are free-falling, the plane will take them up to about 10,000 feet. After they jump, they free-fall for about 5,000 feet and then the instructor opens the parachute. The student does not have to do anything. Before parachuting alone, the student trains on the ground and then does several jumps in which the parachute opens automatically.

The listening conversation focuses on injuries in this sport and more ordinary sports.
More information on sports injuries:
www.sportsinjuryclinic.net
www.americansportsdata.com
www.unc.edu/depts/nccsi
The speakers in the listening text are both American.

5 A

The activities in these listening sections are designed to help learners overcome difficulties and gain the confidence they need to understand gist the first time they listen, then to pick up more specific details when they listen again.

- Explore the two questions in **A** with students, bringing out some of the vocabulary and even the expressions they are going to hear, for example, *people die, protective suit, helmet, goggles.*
- Write these on the board to help students recognise them when they hear them.

5 LISTEN IN A	**Suggested answers**
1 Twisted /sprained knees (ankles), broken legs (bones), cracked ribs, cuts and bruises	
2 Wear wrist guards, a helmet	

5 B

- Read out the task. Once again, the first question is quite a simple one, to help students focus on the overall gist.
- Play the CD. Students listen and answer the questions. Check the answers.

5 LISTEN IN B	**Answers**
1 Alicia likes skydiving.	
2 Tim likes soccer (US) / football (UK).	

5 C

This time students listen for detail.

- Read out the arguments and check that students understand them.
- Play the conversation again. Students listen and put the arguments in the correct column. Alternatively, students can do this exercise in pairs, with one of them noting what Alicia says, and the other what Tim says.

5 LISTEN IN C	**Answers**
What Alicia says: 1, 2, 4, 6	
What Tim says: 3, 5, 7, 8	

5 D

- Tell students that they have looked at the positive aspects of extreme and traditional sports; now they are going to listen for negative aspects. Pair students so that each partner takes one of the tasks.
- Play the CD again. Students listen and make notes.
- Students exchange information with their partner.
- Check the answers. Write the arguments on the board.

5 LISTEN IN D	**Answers**
AGAINST extreme sports: it's dangerous; it's wrong to do dangerous things; people die.	
AGAINST traditional sports: they're boring; most accidents happen in traditional sports; people don't wear protection.	

6 YOUR TURN TO SPEAK

A Role play

The **Role Play** section builds on the conversation that students have listened to. The two learners take turns as teacher and student so that they have the opportunity of taking the initiative in the conversation, and rehearsing the two opposing sides of the argument.

- Go through the phrases in **Language Bank (LB) 1** with the class.
- Divide the class into pairs. Students practise the role play. They can take turns playing both parts.
- Ask for volunteers to perform the role play in front of the class. Choose one pair or choose a 'teacher' from one pair and a 'student' from another.
- To consolidate the language used in this activity, students can do the exercise in **LB 1** orally in pairs in class. Alternatively, ask students to review the phrases in **LB 1** at home and do the exercise for homework.

B Conversation

- Go over the sequencing expressions in **LB 2** with the class. It may help to write the five sequencing experiences on the board.
- If students need an example, provide one from your own experience, and get them to ask questions: What did you do next? What did you do after that?
- Instead of a whole class feedback, you can put two pairs together when they are ready and ask them to compare the conversations they have just been having.
- As a final feedback, ask the groups what was the most interesting thing they heard.
- To consolidate the language used in this activity, ask students to do the exercise in **LB 2** AFTER they have worked through *FIRST AID in English* on page 11.

7 YOUR TOPIC

This is preparation for a more formal piece of oral presentation or for a student-led discussion as used in oral examinations. The topic has been well prepared by now and students should have a bank of available vocabulary, expressions and opinions to include.

- Read out the points learners have to prepare to speak about.
- Students prepare this first presentation in class. Use the preparation time to train learners to structure their talk in a logical way with a clear beginning, middle and end.
- Circulate while students are preparing, encourage them to write key words or ideas on cards rather than write the whole talk out.
- Ask them to think about the audience so that they prepare interesting things to say, and help with language difficulties.
- Before students give their short talk, go over the aspects that they have to consider when they are speaking: they should make sure they speak clearly, don't mumble or speak too quickly, make eye contact with members of the audience, breathe deeply before they start (as this helps to control nervousness), etc.
- Encourage students to be friendly and supportive of each other's efforts, give them a check list of things to listen for, always starting with positives: What did they find most interesting in the talk?

Extra activity: A balloon debate

A balloon debate is an activity often used in British schools to help students gain confidence in public speaking. A number of people are in a hot air balloon; all except one have to jump out to keep the balloon in the air.

- Students prepare in four groups. Two groups are in favour of ordinary sports and two groups are for extreme sports. Each group chooses a sport and three coaches or instructors to represent them.
- The groups write three presentations – two or three sentences each – to argue why their sport is important and safe, and should not be eliminated.
- One instructor/coach from each group gives the first prepared presentation. The rest of the class votes. Which instructor or coach was least persuasive? That one is out of the balloon.
- Repeat with the second presentation. A new instructor/coach of each group argues their case. After a vote, two are left in the balloon.
- Students give the final presentations, and the final vote takes place.

8 *FIRST AID in English* Page 11 SB

8 A

This first cross-curricular section focuses on first aid, which many young people will be learning about in their health or sports lessons.

- Set the scene by getting students to imagine that you've just had a fall and have sprained your knee or ankle. What can they do to help?
- Elicit suggestions. Accept suggestions in their own language in monolingual classes, and get the class to help you find English equivalents and to write them on the board. Elicit the key words that they will encounter in the text – *rest, ice, compress* and *elevate* by asking questions if necessary: Do I rest the ankle now? etc.
- Ask the class to read the two letters quickly. Ask a few gist questions: What kind of text is it? (A web page of advice for teen readers about sports-related matters.) What are the letters about? What injuries have the teenagers had?
- Read out the definitions in **A**. Ask students, individually or in pairs, to find words and phrases in the text that match the definitions. Check the answers.

8 *FIRST AID in English* A **Answers**

1 a wrist guard **2** stay off **3** ice **4** a cushion
5 an ambulance **6** Emergency Services

8 B

- Students read the two letters again.
- Students do the exercise either individually, or together, in class using a checklist on the board. Explain *avoid* if necessary.

8 *FIRST AID in English* B **Answers**

1 ✗ 2 ✓ 3 ✓ 4 ✓ 5 ✗ 6 ✓

Optional project: Finding out about first aid

Divide the class into two or more groups. They are going to find out more about the work of organisations that give first aid (or courses in first aid) in their town or region.

- Students do some preliminary research in the library, online or by using the phone book. Each group focuses on one organisation or one type of course.
- Students arrange to interview a member of their chosen organisation, and find more about courses available. They collect brochures or download information.
- Each group presents their findings to the class, with the materials collected.
- Encourage the class to ask questions and make comments.

9 PORTFOLIO WRITING

- Go over the questions with the students.
- Elicit some general ideas about the style of an email from the class. Is the language formal or informal? (Informal.) What ways of greeting and signing off are they familiar with? Elicit and write expressions on the board: *Dear / Hi* and your friend's name and then *See you soon / Take care / Love / Cheers / All the best* and your name.
- Use the questions as support to elicit some of the words and expressions students may need. Write them on the board.
- The email can be written in class or done for homework. A useful exercise is for students to work in pairs, once they have written their first drafts. They tell their partner what they find interesting in his or her draft, suggest improvements and ask for help if there are any language difficulties. The students can then be asked to prepare a second draft taking account of the suggestions made.
- When students have written their final drafts, ask them to swap with a different partner and read their partner's work.
- Collect the emails and check them.

10 *Your answer*

- Students now have the vocabulary and concepts to be able to express their opinions more fully than they did at the beginning. Finish the unit with a final whole class discussion of ***The BIG Question***: *Do we need danger?* Discuss the questions given and then ask two or three students to give their answer to the main question.
- Alternatively, students can have a mini-debate in which they take sides about ***The BIG Question.***
- Refer students to the Workbook Unit 1 activities.

Last word

- After doing the workbook exercises, students check their own performance and reflect on their ability to use the language items highlighted in the unit. Discuss with students what steps they can take if they feel they need further practice. For example, they could use a grammar practice book with exercises; in groups, they can design further role plays on related topics; in groups, they can write practice tests for other groups, and so on.

WORKBOOK answers — Pages 4–5 WB

1 Language: the present simple and past simple

1 A

1 Yes, she thought it was. No, she didn't think it was.
2 I started at five. I didn't start until I was 10.
3 I was scared at first. Later, I wasn't scared at all.
4 Yes, I always wore it. No I didn't wear it.
5 Yes, I had a lot of fun. No, I didn't have any fun at all.

1 B

1 bought	**2** started	**3** tried	**4** said	**5** was
6 feel	**7** cracked	**8** sprained	**9** love	**10** pays

1 C

(Individual answers)

2 Vocabulary

2 A

(Example answers)
1 car racing, cycling
2 football, tennis, baseball, rugby, squash
3 surfing, sailing, water polo, diving, canoeing
4 bruises, broken bones, sprained wrist / ankles

2 B

1 Then we got into the plane and took off.
2 Next, I stood at the open door, feeling scared.
3 The next minute, I was out in the air, flying.
4 Finally, I landed safely.

2 C

1 great	**2** dangerous	**3** elevated
4 bandage	**5** scared	

3 Word Building

Noun	**Adjective**
tradition	**traditional**
protection	protective
sport	**sporting**
sprain	**sprained**
thrill	thrilling
relaxation	**relaxed**
danger	dangerous
injury	**injured**

4 Use of English

1 Football is *boring*.
2 This sport is thrilling because it's *dangerous*.
3 *I didn't* like the sport.
4 *Stay off* your sprained ankle.
5 Keep your injured friend *warm*.

5 Portfolio Writing

(Individual answers)

What's new?

Subject: Festivals, music
Language: Adverbs of frequency, adverbs of manner
Functions: LB 3 Giving advice
LB 4 Talking about frequency and manner

1 *The BIG question:* WHY ARE WE CELEBRATING?

The theme of this unit is festivals and celebration, in particular carnivals, and ***The BIG Question*** is: Why are we celebrating? Do celebrations need to have a tradition or a deeper meaning than just fun?

- Start with a warmer: write the word CELEBRATION in the middle of the board and ask students what they associate with that word. Write all their ideas on the board in the form of a mind map.
- Read out ***The BIG Question***. Elicit a few initial ideas but don't discuss them in detail.
- Read through the **FACT** box with students. Ask them if the information surprised them.

Picture / background information

Carnivals in general:
www.wikipedia.org/wiki/Carnival
www.nationmaster.com/encyclopedia/Carnival

2 FOCUS ON...

Words

A

Picture / background information

The first photo shows a float in the parade through the Sambódromo, the parade stadium in Rio which can hold 70,000 people. In the background, the different levels of the spectator stadium can be seen. Other parades throughout the city are free, but spectators need tickets for the Samba Parade in the Sambódromo and they are quite expensive.

The second photo shows a dancer on a float in a typical costume. Naked dancers are not allowed, but many are topless or wear only body paint. Other costumes can be very complicated and heavy, so they use cranes to get the people in these costumes onto the floats. For more information on and photos of the Rio Carnival:
www.ipanema.com/carnival/home.htm
www.southamericaexperience.co.uk/brazil/brazil_carnival.html

- Look at the photos on page 12 and page 13. Ask: Have you ever seen the Rio Carnival on TV? Would you like to go to the Carnival? What sort of atmosphere do you think there is there?
- Read out the words in the box and make sure students can pronounce them. Then students match the words in the box to the correct parts of the pictures.

2 FOCUS ON...Words A — **Answers**
Picture 1: decorations, parade, float
Picture 2: feathers, costume

- You could extend the set of carnival words: bring in props to illustrate extra words such as *flag, mask, lantern* or the English words for anything particular to festivals in your country.

B

- Collocation work is a feature of this first page in the unit. Tell students it is important to learn words in combination. Here students combine verbs and nouns.

FOCUS ON...Words B — **Answers**
1 e 2 b 3 a 4 f 5 d 6 c

C

- Students discuss the questions with a partner. Then discuss the questions briefly with the whole class. Encourage them to talk about the general importance of traditional dress and festivals in their country.

D

- This exercise deals with words from the text in order to make the text less difficult for learners. Tell students to first try to match the words

with their definitions. Then they should use their dictionaries to check their answers.
- Check the answers. If there are any difficulties, provide or ask students to provide examples.

2 FOCUS ON...Words D	Answers
1 c 2 d 3 a 4 f 5 e 6 b	

2 FOCUS ON...

Ideas

- Read out the questions and make sure students understand them.
- Students discuss the questions with a partner. Alternatively, they can work in small groups. Give students help with learning the vocabulary and expressing their opinions.
- Ask students to report back to the class.

3 READING CD2 (Red) track 2, page 13 SB

Picture / background information

This photo shows a float of the Grande Rio School at the 2004 parade. The school had to cover up some parts of its float about safe sex. They protested with banners saying 'Censored' (*Censurado* in Portuguese). For further information, see:
www.news.bbc.co.uk/1/hi/world/americas/3505109.stm
www.news.bbc.co.uk/1/hi/programmes/panorama/3844985.stm
www.cnn.com/2004/WORLD/americas/02/23/rio.carnival.reut/

A

- This question aims to train reading for gist. Tell students to read the text quickly the first time and not to look up unknown words.

3 READING A	Answer
People drink, dance, have street parades with costumes and floats, celebrate and protest.	

B

- This exercise focuses on reading for detail. Students can do the questions individually or in pairs. Encourage them to refer back to exercise **D** on page 12 and use dictionaries to help with unknown vocabulary.
- Check the answers. Encourage students to give more information about each sentence. Prompt them with questions if necessary.

3 READING B	Answers
1 slaves 2 samba schools 3 samba schools 4 members of the samba schools 5 Carnival themes 6 the Roman Catholic Church	

C

- Read out the sentences in turn and ask students to answer orally. Correct the false answers with the class.

3 READING C	Answers
1 False (There are street parades all over the city, but the parade in the Sambódromo is the biggest and most famous.) 2 True 3 True 4 False (The Carnival is becoming very commercial because of sponsorship, television rights and tourists.)	

D

- Make sure that students understand the questions. Students discuss the questions with a partner or in small groups.
- Ask students to report back to the class. Ask students to give reasons for their opinions and encourage students to discuss each other's opinions.

4 LANGUAGE: Adverbs of frequency and manner

- Tell students that they are going to look at adverbs. Check that they know what an adverb is, or in monolingual classes ask students for one or two examples in their own language. Do the following task with the whole class or let students answer the questions in pairs and then have a class feedback.

A

- Students look at the examples. Read out the questions in turn and give students time to think before they answer orally.

4 LANGUAGE A	Answers
usually, often. They go between the subject and the verb. (NB: They can also go at the beginning or end of the sentence, but it is best to avoid teaching this at this stage. Point out or elicit that if there is an auxiliary verb in a sentence such as 'They don't usually watch the parade' that the adverb of frequency goes between the auxiliary and the main verb. Adverbs of frequency also go after the verb *to be*.)	

B

- Students look at the examples and answer the questions.

4 LANGUAGE B	Answers
hard, passionately They go after the verb or after the verb + object.	

C

- Ask students for further examples. Write suggestions on the board in two columns. Underline the endings of the adverbs and elicit how adverbs of manner are usually formed.
- Refer students to the explanation for adverbs of frequency and manner in Workbook Unit 2. They can read the explanation and do the exercises in class or for homework.

5 LISTEN IN — CD1 (Blue) track 2, page 14 SB

Picture / background information

The photos show a British police officer (top right) and a DJ (bottom left) at the Notting Hill Carnival in London. The carnival in London's Notting Hill area started in 1959, after race riots between white gangs and black immigrants from the Caribbean (mainly from Trinidad). They brought with them a tradition of carnival as a celebration of the abolition of slavery. Britain today has a large black Caribbean population, with 60% living in London. However, in recent years the Carnival has become a more multicultural party. About a million people take part. The Carnival is held in August, not at Easter, which is the usual date for carnivals in most countries in order to celebrate the end of the Christian tradition of Lent.

For more information on the Notting Hill Carnival:
www.mynottinghill.co.uk/nottinghilltv/carnival1.htm
www.bbc.co.uk/london/carnival/history.shtml
www.guardian.co.uk/weekend/story/0,3605,774956,00.html
www.guardian.co.uk/uk_news/story/0,3604,1029265,00.html

A

- Predicting the content of a listening text will help students become familiar with the content and give them a framework for listening. This will help make the listening process easier.
- Look at the photos with the class and elicit ideas about the place and what is happening. Prompt students if necessary. Ask: What uniform are the men in the first photo wearing? What's their job? What is the man in the second photo doing? Write all the ideas on the board. Introduce key vocabulary such as *police offer, DJ, sound system.*

B

Tell students they are going to listen to a radio report at the event in the pictures. Students listen for the first time. Make sure they understand they are only listening for the main ideas. (NB: The man and woman interviewed both speak with a typical Caribbean accent.)

- Ask students where and what the event is. Students compare their answers to their ideas from **A** and discuss if they were the same.

5 LISTEN IN B	Answers
The Notting Hill Carnival in London	

C

- Before students listen again, ask them to read through the sentences. Explain any unknown vocabulary.
- Play the CD again. Students listen and match the sentences to the correct speaker.
- Ask students to compare their answers with a partner or, if necessary, play the CD again.
- Check the answers. Ask students if they agree with the last question.

5 LISTEN IN C							Answers
1 M	**2** W	**3** W	**4** W	**5** M	**6** W	**7** W	**8** M

6 YOUR TURN TO SPEAK

A Role play

- Read the task with the class. Help students to prepare the role play by making two lists on the board: the good things about the Notting Hill Carnival and the problems there. Refer students back to the listening and ask them to suggest ideas for both columns.
- Go through the phrases in **LB 3** with the class. If you wish, you can prepare the role play further by asking students for more advice using the phrases given.
- Divide the class into pairs. Students practise the role play. They can take turns to play both parts.
- Ask for volunteers to perform the role play in front of the class.
- To consolidate the language used in this activity, do the exercise in **LB 3** with the class. Alternatively, ask students to review the phrases in **LB 3** at home and do the exercise for homework.

LANGUAGE BANK 3 **Answers to exercise in WB on page 40**

1 should **2** Make sure **3** should
4 Why don't you **5** shouldn't **6** should
7 and **8** *Example answers:*
Why don't you get advice from somebody in the music business?
You should learn a musical instrument.

B Conversation

- Go through the phrases in **LB 4** with the class.
- Students work in pairs and take turns to ask and answer the questions, using **LB 4** to help them.
- To consolidate the language used in this activity, do the exercise in **LB 4** with the class. Alternatively, ask students to review the phrases in the **LB** at home and do the exercise for homework.

LANGUAGE BANK 4 **Answers**

Tom: Hardly ever / Never Lola: How well
Lisa: Really well. Sam: How often

7 YOUR TOPIC

- Read out the points learners have to prepare to speak about. Remind learners to make notes and write key words or ideas on cards rather than writing whole sentences. Also remind them to speak clearly and slowly and make eye contact with members of the audience.
- Students can present their festival to the class or smaller groups if you have a large class. Encourage them to ask questions about each other's presentations and comment on the things they found interesting. If students work in groups, ask them to briefly report back to the class.

Extra activity: A festival poster

Students can work in groups and produce a poster advertising one of the festivals they have presented.
- Students write a brief text with information about the main attractions and practical details.
- They can add their own artwork or design features or use photos printed out from the internet.
- Students produce their poster. Put them on the classroom walls for everyone to read.

8 *MUSIC TECHNOLOGY in English* Page 15 SB

Picture / background information

DJ is the abbreviation for 'disc jockey'. The meaning of the word has changed to include not only people who simply play songs (for example on the radio) but also create new music by mixing and changing songs. The DJ in the picture is using a vinyl disc turntable but DJs also use CD players and an Ipod mixer is in development.
For more information on deejaying and DJ mixing: www.discjockey101.com
For more information on DJ Blakey: www.djblakey.com

A

- Ask students how important music is in their life; allow several students to answer. You might like to tell students how important music is to you.
- Refer students to the photo and the diagram of the DJ's equipment. Ask them if they know anything about deejaying and mixing music and if they like this type of music. Write any ideas or useful vocabulary on the board.
- Students read the text and look at the diagram in detail, then complete the sentences in **A** individually or in pairs.
- Check the answers. Refer back to the text or the diagram if there are any problems with comprehension.

8 *MUSIC TECHNOLOGY in English* A Answers
1 decks **2** (stereo) cables **3** amp (volume)
4 headphones **5** speakers

B

- Read out the definitions. Make sure students can say *rhythm* correctly.
- Ask students to read the text again and find the words which match the definitions.
- Check the answers.

8 *MUSIC TECHNOLOGY in English* B Answers
1 the beat **2** track **3** vocals **4** scratch

C

- Students discuss the questions in pairs.
- Ask students to join up with another pair and tell them briefly what they discussed. Encourage them to comment and discuss the questions further.
- Students report back to the class. Ask students if they prefer to listen to music in their own language or in English or another language. How is music in their own language different to American / British music? Encourage students to tell the class about concerts or musical festivals they have attended. If anyone plays a musical instrument, you could invite them to play for the class in the next lesson.

Optional project A: A favourite song

Ask students (individually or in pairs if you have a large class) to present one of their favourite songs in English to the class.

- Students should find a recording and the lyrics to the song and prepare a short explanation of what the song is about and why they have chosen the song.
- In class, they can give students a copy of the lyrics or use an OHP transparency or Powerpoint. After the student's introduction to the song, the class listens to the song and reads the lyrics. (Do not discuss the meaning of the lyrics in detail.)
- Encourage the class to comment on the song.

Optional project B: A favourite CD

Ask students (individually or in pairs if you have a large class) to compile a CD that includes their favourite songs in English.

- Students list the songs and then give the CD a title. Have them explain why they have put these particular songs together.
- If students have the opportunity, have them burn the CD themselves and present it to the class.

9 PORTFOLIO WRITING

- Tell students that a useful idea to prepare a piece of writing is to write some basic questions to structure their writing. Prepare the profile as an example: brainstorm questions students could answer when writing about their favourite singer or band. For example: When and where was he born? When did he start singing? What does he sing about? What sort of music is it? When did he produce his first album? What is his most famous song?
- Remind students to divide their writing into paragraphs. With students, divide the sentences on the board into three paragraphs. Remind them also to think of a good introductory and closing sentence.
- When students have written their profiles or festival descriptions, ask them to swap with a partner and read their partner's work.

10 *Your answer*

- Finish the unit with a final whole class discussion of ***The BIG Question***: *Why are we celebrating?* Discuss the questions given and then ask two or three students to give their answer to the main question.
- Refer students to the Workbook Unit 2 activities.

Last word

- After doing the workbook activities, students evaluate their performance in the three areas. Check if any students feel they need extra practice in any area.

WORKBOOK answers

Pages 6–7 WB

1 Language: adverbs of frequency and manner

A

(Example answers)

1 I often listen to music.
2 I sometimes listen to songs in a foreign language.
3 I occasionally watch music TV.
4 I never go to concerts or music festivals.
5 I never sing in a group.
6 I always sing in the shower.

B

1 happily
2 uncomfortably
3 hungrily
4 worriedly
5 tiredly

C

(Example answer)
I usually do judo once a week at a sport's club. I sometimes practise at home, too. I can do judo quite well.

2 Vocabulary

A

1 c) carnival
2 g) festival
3 h) floats
4 e) costumes
5 i) music
6 d) parade
7 f) protests
8 a) controversial
9 b) good time

B

DJ equipment: amp, headphones, mixer, deck, cables, speaker
Parts of a song: beat, sound, vocal, scratches

C

(Example answers)
Instruments you play with your hands: keyboard, guitar, violin, drums, piano
Instruments you play with your mouth: trumpet, flute, harmonica, clarinet, saxophone

3 Connections

A

1 of
2 with
3 about

4 Use of English

A

1 has (has got)
2 very / extremely
3 loved
4 very well
5 forgot

5 Portfolio Writing

(Individual answers)

What's new?
Subject: Work, job satisfaction, meetings
Language: Comparatives and superlatives of adjectives
Functions: LB 5 Comparing and contrasting
Pronunciation: Vowels, CD1 (Blue) track 4

1 *The BIG question:* WHAT KIND OF JOB IS BEST FOR YOU?

The theme of this unit is the world of work, and the contrasting satisfaction of high-pressure but supposedly more secure jobs in large firms and corporations, as opposed to the risks but also the pleasures of working on your own. ***The BIG Question*** is: *What kind of job is best for you?* Is job security more important than a challenging job?

Picture / background information

www.businesslink.gov.uk
www.startups.co.uk
www.ivillage.co.uk/workcareer

- Introduce the topic by talking about your job as a teacher with the students. Elicit and write up the advantages and disadvantages of teaching (eg advantages: long holidays, interesting subjects, working with people; disadvantages: taking work home, low pay, administrative frustration).
- Brainstorm as a class and write up the students' own ideal jobs and their positive and negative factors.
- Read the ***The BIG Question*** and the **FACT** box with the class. Are the students' ideal jobs in companies or on their own?
- Discuss setting up your own companies and whether it's easy in your country. Elicit a first list of positive and negative aspects.

2 FOCUS ON…

Words

Picture / background information

More information about jobs generally:
news.bbc.co.uk/1/hi/education/3429767.stm
jobsadvice.guardian.co.uk/rise/story/0,,1257927,00.html
Gardening jobs:
www.hortjobs.com
www.andersplus.com
Ski instructors jobs:
www. basi.org.uk/index/index_noflash.asp
www.psia.org
Jobs in computer programming:
www.en wikipedia/org/
Business studies resources for secondary students:
www.bbc.co.uk/schools/16/business.shtml

2 A 1

- Talk about the photos with the students, making sure they understand the three jobs illustrated.
- Pair the students to do the matching exercise. Encourage them to discuss vocabulary difficulties (eg *software, financial records, advice*) and try to guess the meanings from the context before using their dictionary.
- Check the answers.

2 FOCUS ON…Words A 1	Answers
1 c 2 d 3 e 4 b 5 a	

2 A 2

- Use one of the ideal jobs listed on the board as an example. Ask students to provide a definition from their dictionaries.
- Ask students in pairs to write two, three or four more definitions (depending on time available) for jobs.
- Students read out a definition in turn as the class guesses the name of the job.

2 B

- These business terms may be new to many classes. Read the first exercise aloud to the class, and get them to guess 'sole traders', partnerships', etc. Then use their dictionaries to check their answers.
- Students work through the exercise in pairs.
- Check the answers. Recycle the vocabulary by going over the other advantages and disadvantages of working by yourself, for a small company, or a large one.

2 FOCUS ON…Words B	**Answers**
1 c **2** d **3** b **4** a	

2 C

- Explain the task.
- Students give their own opinions. Then compare their ideas in a class feedback.

2 FOCUS ON…Words C	**Answers**
1 ✓ **2** ✗ **3** usually ✗ **4** ✓ but could be ✗ **5** usually ✓ **6** usually ✓	

2 D

- Students discuss the questions in pairs.
- As soon as a pair seems to have finished, ask them to join another pair and compare their views.
- Ask the groups what were the most interesting reasons they heard for question **1**. For question **2**, focus on the worst kinds of jobs, as ideal jobs have already been discussed.

2 FOCUS ON…

Ideas

- Read out the two questions. Make sure students understand secure and challenging.
- This is a chance to let students start practising the comparative forms. Write some comparative adjectives on the board (eg more / less secure, interesting, challenging, stressful; safer, riskier, healthier, friendlier).
- Students discuss the questions with a partner.
- Ask students to report back to the class.

3 READING CD2 (Red) track 3, page 17 SB

Picture / background information

For more information on ski instructors and plant specialists, see page 16, 2A.

For more information about jobs and training for hotel and hospitality management:
www.studyoverseas.com/hhm/
www.foodreference.com/html/hotel-rest-management.html
www.hospitalitytraining.net/

3 A

- This activity aims to spur students into reading quickly, for gist. Set a fairly short time limit for the first reading (eg one to three minutes, to encourage students to skim the stories in order to choose the best title for each).
- Check the answers and help students formulate reasons for their choices.

3 READING A	**Answers**
1 More friends, less money	
2 Being your own boss	
3 The most beautiful place in the world	

3 B 1

These questions promote reading for specific detail.

- Students complete the table in pairs or as a classroom activity.

3 READING B 1	**Answers**
a) Adriana **b)** Gemma **c)** Franco **d)** Gemma **e)** Franco **f)** Adriana	

3 B 2

- Warn students that some of the expressions may fit more than one category.
- Students work on their own or in pairs. One can fill in 'old job', the other 'new job', and then they compare notes.

3 READING B 2 — **Answers**

	Old job	**New job**
Franco	e) working with computers	f) a healthier lifestyle
Adriana	a) working in a hotel	c) a more challenging job / owning a business
Gemma	d) working for a large company	b) owning a business / a more challenging job

3 C 1

- Read out the questions. Students compare ideas in pairs.
- After that, compare views with the class, helping students to express their reasons for finding some jobs more interesting than others.

3 READING C **Answers**

1 The impression given by the articles is that being your own boss is better for people, making them happier even if not so rich.

4 LANGUAGE

4 A

- Go over the four sentences with the class, reminding them of the rules for comparatives and superlatives (comparatives with two things, superlatives with more than two).
- Ask them to compare the way comparatives and superlatives are used in English and in their own language.
- Elicit the rules for forming superlatives.

4 LANGUAGE A **Answers**

Comparing two things: sentences 1 and 3.
Comparing more than two things: sentences 2 and 4.

4 B / C

- Read out the question. Students answer orally.
- Check the answers. Ask students to find other examples in the texts.
- Elicit the rules for using *-er* (one-syllable words, two-syllable words ending in -y) and *more / less* (most two-syllable words, words with more than two syllables).

4 LANGUAGE B / C **Answers**

-er: friendlier, healthier (smaller, happier, bigger)
more / less: more important, less stressful (more challenging, less secure, more interesting)

- Refer students to the explanation of the form and use of comparatives and superlatives in Workbook Unit 3. They can read the explanation and do the exercises in class or for homework.

5 LISTEN IN CD1 (Blue) track 3, page 18 SB

Picture / background information

The photos show an in-company training seminar by a financial analyst and a freelance reporter. In-house training:
www.rec.UK.com/rec/contacts/development.aspx
Financial analysts:
www.bls.gov/oco/ocos259.htm
Training for journalists:
www.nctj.com/journalist.htm
www.ca.courses-careers.com/journalism.htm
The two speakers in the listening text are both British.

5 A 1

- Encourage students to say as much about the photos as they can. Their first response with the left-hand picture may be to say 'teacher'. Ask them to say more about the kind of instruction shown (eg adults in a business setting).

5 LISTEN IN A 1 **Answers**

financial analyst / business consultant
freelance reporter

5 A 2

- Students speculate about the advantages of the jobs in the photos.

5 LISTEN IN A 2 **Suggested answers**

financial analyst: good pay, job security, working with people
freelance reporter: adventure, excitement, working in different places

5 A 3

- Pre-teach two informal expressions: *geek* (a boring, untrendy person) and *techie* (a person very interested in, or knowledgeable about, technology and especially computers.
- Elicit personal views about the expressions, which may be positive or negative. Encourage students to explain their answers and agree or disagree with other students.

5 B

- Read through the eight phrases with students, making sure they understand *information technology* (IT – the use of computers to store / retrieve / send information) and *adventures* (exciting, sometimes dangerous experiences).
- Play the CD. Students can listen individually or in pairs – one for Lynn and one for Gary.
- Check the answers.

5 LISTEN IN B **Answers**
1 G 2 L 3 L 4 L 5 G 6 L 7 G 8 G and L (both of them want fun in different ways)

5 C

This exercise recycles and reinforces vocabulary and arguments.

- Encourage students to try to remember the arguments they heard in the recording, and to think of ones of their own.

5 LISTEN IN C **Suggested answers**
1 steady routine, can get promotion, get a nice car, can pay your bills on time, don't have to worry about money, don't have to worry about not having enough work
2 see other countries, work with people, adventure, exciting, no routine, own boss / can do what you want

6 YOUR TURN TO SPEAK

A Role play

- Get students to choose a job. It can be one they would like, or the opposite.
- They prepare by making a list of the qualities they have for the job. They then think of reasons why they might not be right for the job and the possible disadvantages of the job (eg danger, low pay etc).
- Circulate and help with vocabulary and ideas.
- Ask students to perform their role play for another pair or the class.
- If there is time, reverse the roles so that each student has the opportunity to be student and advisor.

B Conversation

- Go through the expressions in **LB 5** with the class.
- Ask students to prepare their own answers to the three questions in **1**. They then compare these with their partner.
- Students discuss question **2** together.
- Discuss the questions as a class. You can do a survey of attitudes to work in your class by asking for a show of hands for each one of the questions.
- To consolidate the language used in this activity, do the exercise in **LB 5** in class. Ask students to complete the dialogue and then read it with a partner to check. Alternatively, ask students to review the phrases in **LB 5** at home and do the exercise for homework.

7 YOUR TOPIC

- The topic has been well prepared by the activities in the unit, so students can start immediately making their notes for their talk.
- Circulate while students are preparing, reminding them to structure their talk according to the four questions, and to make notes with key words or phrases rather than whole sentences. Help with language problems.
- Write on the board a list of things they have to remember while giving their talk:
  1) using notes as brief reminders
  2) speaking clearly
  3) making eye contact with the audience
  4) asking for questions and answering them
- Afterwards, ask the listeners to give a positive response to the talk, and perhaps, in supportive classes, to suggest things that could be added, or ways of improving delivery.

Extra activity: A guessing game

- Students choose one job they would really like to do – either a job in this unit or another one (they can use their dictionaries).
- They write one sentence saying one good thing and one bad thing about the job (eg *In my job, I work with people, but I don't make much money.*)
- They read their sentences to the class. The others guess. You can set a maximum of three guesses **OR** students get one point for each wrong guess.

8 *BUSINESS STUDIES in English* Page 19 SB

Picture / background information

This cross-curricular section focuses on good practice in meetings, a recurring topic in business studies. The vocabulary may be new to some students at this level but is undoubtedly useful and connected to their future work.
Resources for business studies:
www.thetimes100.co.uk

Information about running meetings:
www.gsanetwork.org/resources/facilitate.html
www.campusaction.net/activist_toolbox/How%20To/run_good_meeting.htm

- Warm-up: Ask about the students' own experience of meetings – in class committees or school councils, for example. What were the main problems they experienced? Did they enjoy the meetings?
- Work with the picture: elicit explanations for the various jobs represented (get students to use their dictionaries if necessary). Ask for reactions to the arrangement of seats for this meeting. Looking at the seating diagrams underneath to the left, what is the aim of the meeting?
- Ask students to read the text fairly quickly, and underline any problems that they have with expressions or concepts. Go over these with the whole class.
- Elicit a first response to the text. Do students feel that this kind of advice is useful / unnecessary / easy or hard to follow? How many of them look forward to a career in business later on? Would they like this kind of meeting?

8 A

- Ask students to use the context to find the correct words and phrases for the definitions. They can work individually, in pairs, or as a class.
- Check the answers.

8 ***BUSINESS STUDIES in English*** **A**	**Answers**
1 motivate	**2** chairperson
3 the minutes	**4** off track

8 B

- Ask students to discuss the questions in pairs. Alternatively, add a game element by dividing the class into two 'camps' to see which can find more ways to compare English classes with business meetings.
- Discuss the ideas that came up with the whole class.

8 ***BUSINESS STUDIES in English*** **B** **Suggested answers**

1 They are both about communication.
People are supposed to work collaboratively but sometimes don't.
There is an 'agenda' in the form of the unit activities, but perhaps it hasn't been prepared.
Students sometimes go 'off track'.

Optional project: A careers fair

- Students work in groups to collect information, brochures and application forms for as many jobs as possible. Each group focuses on one particular type of job (eg in education, business, television or print journalism, the film industry, hospitality and catering, sports activities, IT jobs etc). Students can use the library or the internet.
- If your school has a careers service, ask students to interview advisors and collect material from them.
- Each group sets up their 'stall' around the classroom, displaying information, brochures etc.
- In turn, one student of the group looks after the stall and answers questions, while others go around looking at other jobs on display and asking questions.
- Possible feedback: ask the groups to prepare and present a short oral report on the jobs they found most interesting.

9 PORTFOLIO WRITING

- This is a formal business letter of enquiry. If students have not written letters of this kind before, you may wish to give some general information about them before they do the exercise.
- Ask students whether they write formal letters in their own language, and what register they would use.
- Point out that there are standard formats for business letters in English. One common one is the following:

Writing model

Your address
…………………
…………………
Date

Name of the person you are writing to.
Address of the person you are writing to.
……………………………
……………………………

Re: the subject you are writing about

Dear Sir or Madam *(when you don't know the person's name)*
OR
Dear Mr / Ms / Mrs Smith, *(when you know the person's name)*

Text of the letter
……………………………………………………………………
……………………………………………………………………
……………………………………………………………………
……………………………………………………………………
Yours faithfully *(when you've written* Dear Sir *or* Madam)
OR
Yours sincerely *(when you've written* Dear Mr / Ms / Mrs Smith)

Your signature *(handwriting)*
Your name *(typed)*

- Tell students that the register of a business letter is formal. Long forms are more usual than short forms (*do not* rather than *don't*). American letters are often more informal than British ones. Americans often use *Yours sincerely* whether they know the person's name or not.
- Students put the expressions for the body of the letter in the right order.
- Check the answers.
- Students write a first draft of their letter. They can then compare with a partner, ask advice, and write a second draft.

9 PORTFOLIO WRITING **Answers**

1 f **2** b **3** d **4** c **5** e **6** a

10 *Your answer*

- Ask students to volunteer answers to the questions and compare their opinions.
- Refer students to the Workbook Unit 3 activities.

Last word

- After doing the workbook activities, students evaluate their performance in the three areas. Check if any students feel they need extra practice in any area.

WORKBOOK answers — Pages 8–9 WB

1 Language: comparatives and superlatives

1 A

1 healthier, more boring
2 harder, the hardest
3 more secure, less interesting
4 the best, the worst

1 B

1 most good – *the best*
2 most democratic – *more democratic*
3 most boring – *the most boring*
4 effectiver meetings – *more effective*
5 careful – *more careful*
6 importantest questions – *the most important*

1 C

(Individual answers)

2 Vocabulary

2 A

(Example answers)

	Good things	**Bad things**
1 as a sole trader:	challenging, (interesting, flexible)	stressful, risky, long hours
2 in a partnership:	friendly, fewer hours, (creative, less stressful)	big responsibility to other partners
3 in a large company:	secure, good money, time for other activities, (chance for promotion)	boring, same routine

2 B

1 computer programmer
2 salary
3 promotion
4 agenda

3 Use of English

1 Working for a large company is *more secure* than being a sole trader.
2 Many young people want *to set up* their own business.
3 The Alps has *the cleanest* environment in the world.
4 It's good to arrive *on time / early* for a meeting.

4 Pronunciation CD1 (Blue) track 4

a) 3 **b)** 2 **c)** 1 **d)** 2 **e)** 1 **f)** 3 **g)** 2 **h)** 3
i) 3 **j)** 3 **k)** 3 **l)** 1 **m)** 2 **n)** 2 **o)** 2

5 Portfolio Writing

(Individual answers)

What's new?

Subject:	Entertainment (television, films)
Language:	*going to* future (WB extra language point: gerunds)
Function:	**LB 6** Expressing likes and dislikes
	LB 7 Talking about future plans and intentions
Pronunciation:	Consonants, CD1 (Blue) track 6

1 *The BIG question:* ARE REALITY SHOWS GOOD TV?

The theme of this unit is entertainment, in particular television and film, and ***The BIG Question***: *Are reality shows good TV?* Is reality TV entertaining or just cheap TV that exploits its participants?

- Start by asking students a few warm-up questions: How often do you watch TV? Do you watch TV when you get up in the morning? Is there 24-hour TV in your country? Do you watch DVDs at home? How often do you go to the cinema?
- Read out ***The BIG Question***. Elicit a few initial reactions and reasons.
- Read through the **FACT** box with students. Ask: Do you know the programme *Survivor*? Are there a lot of reality shows in your country?

British / American English

This unit focuses on some different uses of British English (BE) and American English (AE). The texts in this unit therefore contain many words that are different in British and American English. (Students have already encountered some American English words in Units 1-3.) In addition, the *Reading* texts and the text on the CLIL page use American spelling. This is because the context of this unit is American reality TV shows. Reality TV is a genre (a loan word from French to indicate a type of art) heavily influenced by American shows, and therefore containing many American words. Exercise 3B in the Workbook focuses on both differences in words and spelling. The rest of the unit uses British spelling. The standard for this book is British English in all texts, rubrics and exercises. American English is only used where the context demands, and the authenticity of the text (or the accent in the audio recordings) depends upon it.

Picture / background information

Reality TV:
www.usatoday.com/life/television/reviews/2004-06-10-reality-tv-main_x.htm
news.bbc.co.uk/1/hi/talking_point/3607482.stm
www.dailytargum.com/news/2003/01/30/Opinions/Fox-At.It.Again-355467.shtml
news.bbc.co.uk/1/hi/magazine/4491349.stm

2 FOCUS ON...

Words

Picture / background information

The first photo shows American talk show host Jay Leno and the actor Hugh Grant on Jay Leno's nightly talk show *The Tonight Show*. The second photo shows a news correspondent talking in front of the White House. The third photo shows *ER*, the popular American soap opera about the emergency room of a hospital in Chicago. In British English this section of a hospital is called 'Accident and Emergency', or 'A and E', or 'Casualty'. There is a British soap opera called *Casualty*, about a hospital A and E Department.

2 A

- Read out the types of TV shows and make sure students can pronounce them correctly.
- Ask students to match the TV shows with their definitions. Check the answers.
- Ask students what other types of programmes you can see on TV and make a list on the board (for example: sport, cooking programmes, travel programmes, cartoons and children's programmes, detective and crime series).

2 FOCUS ON...Words A 1 — **Answers**

1 e **2** d **3** f **4** a **5** b

2 B

- Ask students to look at the photos on page 20. Read out the questions in 1.
- If students know the programme in 1 or 3, ask them if they often watch it and if they enjoy it. Ask: How often do you watch the news on TV? Do you prefer to read news in the paper or read news online?

2 FOCUS ON…Words B **Answers**
1 talk show (Jay Leno) **2** the news
3 soap opera (*ER* = Emergency Room)

2 C

- Read out the words in the box and make sure students can pronounce them correctly.
- Ask students to put the words in the box in the correct sentences. They can do this in pairs. Check the answers.

2 FOCUS ON…Words C **Answers**
1 viewers **2** producer **3** series
4 critic **5** Contestants

2 D

- Remind students that it is important to learn words in combination with others.
- Ask students to combine the verbs with the correct nouns. Check the answers.

2 FOCUS ON…Words D **Answers**
1 d **2** e **3** b **4** c **5** a

2 FOCUS ON…

Ideas

A

- Read the task with the class and go through the phrases in **LB 6**. Explain that in spoken language we usually say 'I don't like' rather than 'I dislike'.
- Divide the class into pairs. Students discuss TV shows with a partner.
- Students report back briefly to the class.
- To consolidate the language used in this activity, do the exercise in **LB 6** with the class. Alternatively, ask students to review the phrases in **LB 6** at home and do the exercise for homework.

B

- Read out the questions and make sure students understand the word *harmless*.
- Students discuss the questions in pairs.
- Students report back briefly to the class.

3 READING CD2 (Red) track 4, page 21 SB

Picture / background information

The first photo shows the British actress Kate Winslet (star of films such as *Titanic* and *Eternal Sunshine of the Spotless Mind*). After she heard that a girl on MTV's reality programme *I Want a Famous Face* had plastic surgery on her body to look like her, Kate Winslet told the press she cried. She said many photos of her are digitally changed to make her look thinner and more attractive.

The second photo shows a contestant on *Survivor* walking over hot coals, a regular challenge on the programme.

Further information on *I Want a Famous Face*:
www.mtv.com/onair/dyn/i_want_a_famous_face-2/series.jhtml?_requestid=10399
www.ringsurf.com/info/Entertainment/TV/Reality_TV/Makeover_Reality_TV/I_Want_a_Famous_Face.html
www.admiringkatewinslet.com/SunApril27.htm
Further information on *Survivor*:
www.cbs.com/primetime/survivor/

3 A

- Read out the task.
- Read out the titles of the TV shows and encourage students to link them with the photos and their captions. Ask students what they think the shows are about. Discuss their ideas but don't confirm or deny their ideas at this point.

3 B

- Read out the questions.
- Students read the texts.
- Discuss the questions orally with the class.

3 READING B **Answers**
1 *I Want a Famous Face* is a documentary; *Survivor* is a game show.
2 *(Individual answers)*
3 On *I Want a Famous Face*, young people have plastic surgery to look like their favourite stars. On *Survivor*, people live together on a tropical island and do challenges to survive.

3 C

- Students read the sentences and decide if they are true or false without reading the texts again.
- Students read the texts again and check their answers.
- Check the answers with the class. Ask students to correct the false sentences.

3 READING C **Answers**
1 True
2 False (They say it trivialises plastic surgery and exploits people.)
3 False (They don't actually look like them.)
4 False (There's going to be another series soon.)
5 False (It's a game show.)
6 False (It's the last programme in the series.)
7 False (It's an old show.)
8 False (They are hard but not gross.)

3 D

- Read out each question in turn and discuss them with the class. You could tell the class your opinion, too.

4 LANGUAGE: *going to* future

4 A 1

- Students scan the text and highlight six sentences with *going to*.
- Ask students to read out the sentences. Write them on the board.

4 LANGUAGE A 1 **Answers**
1 **'I'm going to be** Kate Winslet,' she said. (line 4)
2 Tonight on *I Want a Famous Face* **we're going to meet** Jessica. (line 6)
3 **There's going to be** another series soon. (line 21)
4 On tonight's show, the final three contestants **are going to do** their last challenges. (text 2, line 2)
5 All three are going to try and win the million dollar prize. (line 6)
6 **I'm** certainly **going to watch** this one. (line 32)

4 A 2

- Focus students' attention on the examples on the board and read out the question.
- Students answer orally. Ask what time phrases refer to the future (2 *tonight*, 4 *on tonight's show*).

4 LANGUAGE A 2 **Answer**
future activities

4 A 3

- Read out the question. Students answer orally.
- Check that students have understood by asking about their plans and intentions for this evening.

4 LANGUAGE A 3 **Answer**
plans and intentions

4 A 4

- Underline the verbs in the examples on the board. With students' help, write a formula on the board.

4 LANGUAGE A 4 **Answer**
subject + *be* + *going to* + verb

- Ask students to form the negative of the first example *(I'm not going to be Kate Winslet)* and the question form *(Am I going to be Kate Winslet?)*.
- Refer students to the explanation about the *going to* future in Workbook Unit 4. They can read the explanation and do the exercise in class or for homework.
- This unit has an extra language point in the Workbook: gerunds as subject or object and after prepositions. Students can read the explanation in the Workbook and do the exercise for homework, or you can deal with this point in class: draw students' attention to the examples in the text (*having celebrity surgery …*, line 20; *walking over hot coals*, line 6; *viewers who love watching*, line 21; *the most important part is living together)* and explain the form and use of gerunds.

5 LISTEN IN — CD1 (Blue) track 5, page 22 SB

Picture / background information

The two photos show authentic pictures from the American reality shows *The Bachelorette* (a dating show in which a woman chooses the man she wants to marry from people she met on a blind date), and *Extreme Makeover* (a total makeover show involving women undergoing plastic surgery as well as having hair, makeup and clothes style changes).

For more information on *The Bachelorette* and *The Bachelor* (a corresponding show where a man chooses a woman):
abc.go.com/primetime/bachelorette/index.html
abc.go.com/primetime/bachelor/index.html
For more information on *Extreme Makeover*:
abc.go.com/primetime/extrememakeover
The speakers in the listening text give opinions about similar programmes. The speakers in the listening texts are all American.

5 A

- Students look at the photos and read the captions. They discuss what sort of programmes the photos show and whether they would be interested in watching them. They should give reasons for their answers.

5 B

- This section pre-teaches key vocabulary from the listening text. Ask students to find the meaning of the words and phrases in their dictionaries.
- Check the meanings with the class. Make sure students understand that 'dumb' and 'They suck' are American English.

5 LISTEN IN B **Answers**

unattractive = not physically good-looking
beauty queen = a woman who wins a beauty competition
dumb (mainly AE) = stupid, not clever
worms = long thin animals with no legs
humiliate = make somebody look stupid
They suck! (AE) = They're terrible.

5 C

- Tell students they are going to listen to three speakers talking about TV shows. Explain the task and make sure that students know they only have to understand enough to complete this task; they do not have to understand every word.
- Students listen and tick the correct boxes.
- Check the answers with the class.

5 LISTEN IN C **Answers**

Speaker 1: likes reality TV
Speaker 2: likes reality TV
Speaker 3: dislikes reality TV

5 D

- Students read the statements.
- Students listen again more carefully and choose the correct speaker for each statement. Play the CD again if necessary.
- Students compare their answers with a partner.
- Check the answers with the class.

5 LISTEN IN D **Answers**

a) 1 **b)** 2 **c)** 3 **d)** 1 **e)** 3 **f)** 2 **g)** 2

6 YOUR TURN TO SPEAK

A Role play

Picture / background information

A casting call is an advertisement to find participants in TV shows. Most reality shows advertise for contestants on the internet, or sometimes in newspaper and specialist magazines. With each series of programmes, the casting becomes more complex: contestants with handicaps and disabilities, with a particular background (class, rural / urban etc); and not just single contestants but engaged or married couples, relatives and whole families.

- Read the task with the class and ask a student to read out the casting call while the class reads. Make sure they understand.
- Prepare the role play by asking students why somebody would like to take part in a show like this. Write notes on the board. Then ask students why somebody would be against taking part in a programme like this; again make notes on the board.
- Divide the class into pairs. Students practise the role play, using the notes on the board to help them. They can take turns to play both parts.
- Ask for volunteers to perform the role play in front of the class.

B Conversation

- Go through the phrases in **LB 7** with the class.
- Students work in pairs and take turns to ask and answer the questions, using **LB 7** to help them.
- Ask some students to report back to the class.
- To consolidate the language used in this activity, do the exercise in **LB 7** with the class. Alternatively, ask students to review the phrases in **LB 7** at home and do the exercise for homework.

7 YOUR TOPIC

- Read out the points learners have to prepare to speak about. Remind students to make brief notes on each point.
- Students can present their show to the class or smaller groups if you have a large class. Encourage them to ask questions about each other's presentations and say if they know or watch the programme and what their opinion of it is. If students work in groups, ask them to briefly report back to the class.

Extra activity: A new soap opera

Students can write their own soap opera in groups. They should:
- invent characters and give them names
- write a summary of the first episode
- write a scene from the first episode
- present their soap opera and act out their scene to the class.

The class can vote on the best show.

8 *MEDIA STUDIES in English* Page 23 SB

Picture / background information

The screen shot shows one of many websites that list mistakes of all kinds in films. These include:
www.nitpickers.com/
www.imdb.com/Sections/Goofs/
For more information on continuity:
en.wikipedia.org/wiki/Continuity_%28fiction%29
The website www.moviemistakes.com shows stills from many of the films which have mistakes in them.

- Ask students these questions: Would you like to study media studies? Is anyone interested in a career in film or television?
- Draw students' attention to the website. Ask: Have you ever used a website like this? Why do you think there are so many websites about mistakes in films?
- Students read the text. Ask: What is continuity?

8 A

- Read out the definitions. Students read the text again and find the words which match the definitions.
- Check the answers.

8 *MEDIA STUDIES in English* A — Answers

1 plot	**2** the crew	**3** a scene
4 location	**5** the cast	**6** shooting schedule

8 B

- Ask: What is a visual error? What is a plot error? Write the characteristics of each on the board.
- Ask students to read out the mistakes in turn. The class says whether it is a visual or plot error. They should refer to the notes on the board.

8 *MEDIA STUDIES in English* B — Answers

1 visual	**2** visual	**3** plot

8 C

- Students discuss the questions with a partner.
- Discuss the questions briefly with the class. Find out if several people have the same favourite film and if male and female students like the same films.

Optional project: *Your mistakes* website

Tell students the class is going to make a *film mistakes* website.
- Students make lists of mistakes in films they have seen. They decide how to order them by looking at other film mistakes websites (eg by film, by top ten mistakes etc)
- They set up the website alone or with help from the school computer department.
- Students from other classes can add their mistakes to the list.
- Students continue the project for a limited time and observe how often the website is used and added to.

9 PORTFOLIO WRITING

- Find (or ask students to find) film reviews from magazines or the internet. Read out one or two as examples. Point out that film reviews are usually in the present tense.
- Write the structure of the review on the board:
  1) first paragraph: what sort of film, cast
  2) the film plot
  3) opinion of the film
- Read out one of the reviews again. Ask students to take notes about the three items on the board.

Check the answers with students and write them on the board.

- Students prepare their own essay: they make notes using the structure given.
- Students write their review in class or for homework.
- When students have written their reviews, ask them to swap with a partner and read their partner's work.
- Take in the reviews. Read out the best one(s) to the class.

10 *Your answer*

- Finish the unit with a final whole class discussion of the question: *Are reality shows good TV?* Discuss the questions given and then ask two or three students to give their answer to the main question.
- Refer students to the Workbook Unit 4 activities.

Last word

- After doing the Workbook activities, students evaluate their performance in the three areas. Check if any students feel they need extra practice in any area.

WORKBOOK answers — Pages 10–11 WB

1 Language: *going to* future

1 A

1 are we going to see **2** 's going to watch
3 'm not going to see **4** are you going to do
5 'm not going to do **6** is going to come
7 're not going to see **8** 'm not going to go

1 B

(Example answers)

1 *Shopping* is my favourite activity.
2 I love *playing tennis.*
3 I'm interested in *studying to be a doctor.*
4 I'm good at *speaking English.*

2 Use of English

1 I'm not keen on watching TV.
2 Reality TV is harmless.
3 That show is the worst show in the world.
4 I always watch *Survivor*.
5 Game shows are my favourite programmes.

3 Vocabulary

3 A

1 c **2** e **3** b **4** d **5** a

3 B 1

a gross **b** dumb **c** They suck!
d mom **e** movie

3 B 2

a program **b** favorite **c** trivialize
d neighbor **e** color

3 C

1 cast **2** location **3** shooting schedule
4 crew **5** scenes **6** plot
7 continuity

4 Pronunciation — CD1 (Blue) track 6

4 B 1

a) dead **b)** very **c)** sink
d) bit **e)** class **f)** choke

5 Portfolio Writing

(Individual answers)

What's new?

Subject:	Shops and shopping
Language:	Adverbials of quantity (WB extra language point: quantifiers)
Function:	LB 8 Complaining LB 9 Quantifying

1 *The BIG question:* DO SHOPS RIP YOU OFF?

The theme of this unit is shopping, in shops and online, and ***The BIG Question:*** Do shops rip you off? Do customers get the right quality of service? Is shopping enjoyable?

- Look at the title of the unit. Ask students: What is a *shopaholic*? (a person who can't stop shopping / is addicted to shopping. Compare 'alcoholic' and 'chocoholic'). Ask: Are any of you shopaholics?
- Read out ***The BIG Question***. Explain the verb *rip off* (to cheat somebody – informal).
- Read through the **FACT** box with students. Make sure students understand *faulty goods*: give or elicit examples. Ask students what they understand by *sales methods* (the way sales assistants try to sell things).

2 FOCUS ON...

Words

Picture / background information

In Britain and the USA, there are many large shopping centres (US: shopping malls) outside towns and cities. There are also many large chain stores with shops in lots of different places (in Britain these are often called 'high street stores'). This means many small independent or family shops are forced to close because of price competition; in Britain some people think this is destroying shopping culture in towns.
In Britain and the USA, most people pay in shops with credit cards (so they can pay the bank later) or a debit card (which takes money directly out of the cardholder's bank account). In some shops in Britain you can also get 'cash back': you can ask for cash at the till (US: check out), so you don't have to go to the bank, or to a cash machine.

Most British shops have store cards (credit cards for a particular shop). Picture 4 shows a store card for Boots, a big chemist and beauty products chain.

Shopping tips for the UK and London:
www.ukstudentlife.com/Life/Shopping.htm#Introduction
www.visitlondon.com/choose_site/?OriginalURL=/city_guide/shopping/
Shopping tips for the USA:
www.usatourist.com/english/tips/shopping.html
Shopaholics:
observer.guardian.co.uk/uk_news/story/0,6903,403121,00.html

2 A 1

- Look at the table with students and check that they understand the task. Students work individually and add three more items to each list.
- Write the shops as headings on the board and elicit lists of items from the class. Alternatively, you can use consumer items (eg a handbag, an electronic item like an iPod, a sports item like trainers) you have brought from home to prompt students.
- Brainstorm a list of other shops on the board with the class. Students work in pairs and make a list of items for one or two shops on the board.
- Students report back to the class. Add items to the shops on the board.

2 FOCUS ON...Words A 1 Suggested answers

Department store: furniture, beauty products, bags and luggage, toys, electrical items, sports equipment
Electronics shops: computers and computer equipment, phones, music players, CDs and DVDs
Newsagent: newspapers, sweets, cigarettes, stamps, stationery (cards, paper, pens etc)
Sport shops: sports clothes, trainers, football boots, tennis rackets, table tennis / cricket bats, knee pads, helmets
Other shops and items:
Bakers (bread, cakes, sandwiches); butchers (meat, sausages, chicken); chemists (bandages, sun cream); florists (flowers, plants); jewellers (watches, necklaces, rings); supermarket (food, drinks, cleaning products); toy shop (toys, books, games)

2 A 2

- Read out the questions. Students work in pairs and answer the questions.
- Students report back to the class.

2 B 1

- Look at the words in the box with the class. Point out that the same words can have different meanings in British and American English (eg *purse*).
- In pairs or individually, students match the photos with the words in the box.
- Check the answers. Make sure students understand that in British English a purse is usually for women and that wallets are usually for men. Check that students understand what a store card is.

2 FOCUS ON...Words B 1 **Answers**

1 c 2 e 3 g 4 h 5 d 6 b 7 a 8 f

2 B 2

- Make two lists on the board: *ways to pay* and *places to keep money*. With the class, complete the lists using the words in exercise **1**.

2 FOCUS ON...Words B 2 **Answers**

Ways to pay: cash, cheque, credit card, store card
Places to keep money: purse, backpack, handbag, wallet

2 B 3

- Read out the question and elicit answers from the class. Ask: At what age can you get a credit card? When do people usually use cheques / cash / credit cards?
- Use the information in the background information box to discuss how ways of paying when shopping are different in the students' country to Britain and the USA.

Extra activity: What's in my bag?

- Tell students they have to guess what is in your handbag / backpack. Make sure you have a combination of 'normal' items such as keys, wallet, pens, books etc and a few more unexpected items.
- If they guess correctly, take out the items and put them on your desk.
- Prompt them with definitions and hints so they can guess difficult items.

2 C

- Students do the task individually or in pairs.
- Check the answers.
- Ask: Is it easy to get refunds or exchange things in shops here? Are sales assistants usually helpful?

2 FOCUS ON...Words C **Answers**

1 a 2 a 3 b 4 b 5 a

2 FOCUS ON...

Ideas

- Read out the statements. Explain or elicit the meaning of *pushy* (in this instance, trying hard to sell something) and customer service (help and good advice).
- In pairs, students discuss the statements.
- Students report back to the class.

3 READING CD2 (Red) track 5, page 25 SB

Picture / background information

Customer service in Britain and especially in the USA is generally very good: most shops will exchange goods or give refunds if you have a receipt; a few shops even exchange things without a receipt, particularly if the goods are the shop's own brand. Big chain stores will often also exchange or refund items bought in different towns.

In the last few years, store cards have become a big business, leading to debt problems for some customers, particularly young people.

Store cards:
www.oft.gov.uk/Consumer/Store+cards/default.htm
news.bbc.co.uk/1/hi/business/2963394.stm
www.hero.ac.uk/uk/studying/archives/2003/house_of_cards5465.cfm

3 A

- Look at the magazine page with students. Ask: Do you like reading readers' letters in magazines? Do you ever write letters to magazines or newspapers?
- Look at the pictures with the class. Ask: What do you think the letters are about?
- Read out the task. Students read the letters quickly and answer the question. Tell students not to worry about words that they don't understand; they just need to find the answer to the question.

- Check the answer with the class. Ask: Who is the other letter from? (someone who was a shop assistant); Did he like the job? Why? / Why not?

3 READING A	**Answer**
The last letter / Laurence's letter	

3 B

- Students read the sentences. Check that they understand them.
- Students read the letters again and decide which people (or none of them) did the things in the sentences.
- Check the answers.
- Check that students understand the meaning of the following words. Encourage them to look at the text and the pictures to explain the meaning.

  Letter 1: *down* (sad), *shut somebody up* (make somebody stop talking), *afford* (have enough money for), *interest* (extra money you pay when you borrow money)
  Letter 2: *mosquito* (an insect), *bargain* (cheap), *discount* (money off the price)
  Letter 3: *criticise* (say bad things about), *approach* (go to), *target* (a certain number)

3 READING B	**Answers**
1 L **2** R **3** L **4** A **5** N **6** R **7** A **8** L **9** A **10** N	

3 C

- Read out and discuss the questions with the class.

3 D

- Students tell the class about their experiences.

Optional project: A letters page for a class magazine

Tell students they are going to create their own readers' letter page.

- The class decides on a name for their class magazine. Decide who is going to put the letter's page(s) together (ie be the editors).
- Ask students to write a letter about a shopping experience they have had.
- Students write their letters and send them by email to the editors.
- The editors produce a letters page or pages for everybody to read.

4 LANGUAGE: Adverbials of quantity

4 A

- Look at the example sentences in turn with the class. For each sentence, elicit the meaning. For example, for sentence **1**: read out the sentence and ask: Did the clothes suit them? (No); Did the clothes look bad or very bad? (Very bad).
- Explain that the symbols represent how much people like or do something. Ask students to match the meanings of the adverbials of quantity in the example sentences with the correct positive or negative symbol.
- Check the answers.

4 LANGUAGE A	**Answers**
1 – – **2** + + **3** – **4** +	

- Refer students to the explanation for adverbials of quantity in Workbook Unit 5. They can read the explanation and do the exercises in class or for homework.
- This unit has an extra language point in the Workbook which is linked to the main language point: revision of *quantifiers*. Students can read the explanation in the Workbook and do the exercise for homework, or you can deal with this point in class.

5 LISTEN IN — CD1 (Blue) track 7, page 26 SB

5 A

- Students look at the photo and the illustration. Ask them what they think the listening text is about (a customer is complaining on the telephone about an order).
- Ask students if they often complain and if they find it difficult.

5 B

- Read out the task.
- Play the CD. Students listen and answer the question.
- Check the answer.

5 LISTEN IN B	**Answer**
Lucy lives in Brighton, but there is another Lucy Smith in Manchester. Lucy got the Manchester order.	

5 C

- Students read the sentences and try to complete them.
- Play the CD again. Students check or complete their answers.
- Check the answers.

5 LISTEN IN C — **Answers**

1 Customer **2** website **3** CD **4** pink handbag
5 birthday **6** manager **7** faulty **8** keep

5 D

- Discuss the sentences with the class.

5 LISTEN IN D — **Answer**

1 Lucy was angry. She shouted because the order was wrong and Debbie wasn't very helpful.

6 YOUR TURN TO SPEAK

A Role play

- Read the task with the class. Make sure they understand. Check the meaning of *exchange* and *credit note*.
- Go through the phrases in **LB 8** with the class.
- Ask students to complete the dialogue in pairs from the exercise **LB 8** and then read it together. Check the answers.
- Divide the class into pairs. Students practise the role play, using **LB 8** to help them. They can take turns to play both parts.
- Ask for volunteers to perform the role play in front of the class.

B Conversation

- Go through the phrases in **LB 9** with the class.
- Students work in pairs and take turns to ask and answer the questions, using **LB 9** to help them.
- Ask some students to report back to the class.
- To consolidate the language used in this activity, do the exercise in **LB 9** with the class. Ask students to read out their answers. Alternatively, ask students to review the phrases in **LB 9** at home and do the exercise for homework.

7 YOUR TOPIC

- Read out the points learners have to prepare to speak about. Remind students to make brief notes on each point. You can ask students to bring in the items they bought if they are portable.
- Students can present their best or worst buys to the class, or to smaller groups if you have a large class. Encourage them to ask questions about each other's presentations and comment on what they say. If students work in groups, ask them to briefly report back to the class.

8 *CONSUMER RIGHTS in English* Page 27 SB

Picture / background information

Online shopping has become very popular in Britain and many other countries. Most British high street stores and also many small shops provide online shopping services. There are also many online-only shopping websites. One report says that more than one in twenty online shoppers has been a victim of online fraud. As more and more people also do their banking online, there have been many cases of 'identity theft' in which people find that their various online accounts have been used by criminals to buy things or to steal money.

Consumer rights:
www.oft.gov.uk/Consumer/Your+Rights+When+Shopping/default.htm

The online shopping tips text is based on information from the UK Office of Fair Trading website:
www.oft.gov.uk/Consumer/Your+Rights+When+Shopping+From+Home/Online+shopping/default.htm

Other online shopping tips:
www.imrg.org/8025696F004581B3/pages/toptentips

Online shopping fraud:
www.e-consultancy.com/newsfeatures/156668/uk-online-shopping-fraud-reaches-one-million-people.html?keywords=online+shopping

- Look at the photo and read out the first line of the text. Ask students to compare the popularity of online shopping in the UK with their country. Ask: How popular is online shopping? What age group mostly shop online? Do your parents use the internet to shop?

8 A

- Students read the text and find words or phrases to match the definitions. Tell them to use the text to help them.

- Students check their answers with a partner.
- Check the answers with the class.

8 *CONSUMER RIGHTS in English* A	**Answers**
1 postal address	**2** secure
3 privacy statement	**4** consumer rights
5 confirmation	**6** order
7 cancel	**8** credit card statement

8 B

- Read out the questions.
- In pairs, students discuss the questions.
- Students report back to the class.

8 C

- Read out the questions in turn. Elicit answers from the class.
- Ask: Has anybody had a bad experience when shopping online?

Optional project: Shopping websites research

Tell students they are going to do some research on the websites of British high street stores.

- Students work in pairs or groups and study the website of one of these companies: Blockbusters (CDs, videos, games), Boots (beauty products), Debenhams (department store), Harrods (luxury department store), Holland and Barrett (health products), Marks and Spencer (clothes and food), Next (clothes), Thorntons (chocolates), Topshop (clothes), Waterstones (books).
- Students should find the web address of the company and find out what they sell. They should check if the website contains a postal address and if the website has a privacy statement and secure way of paying.
- Students report back briefly to the class.

9 PORTFOLIO WRITING

- Read the task with the class.
- Discuss what to write in the subject bar of the email (faulty camera / broken lamp etc). Then discuss how to start and end the email: *Dear* with a name (if available) and *Yours sincerely* OR with *Dear Sir or Madam* and *Yours faithfully*.
- Write up the parts of the email on the board:
  1) what you bought and when
  2) what the problem is
  3) what you want the company to do
- Elicit phrases from the class for each section of the email (eg *I bought / ordered a … from your website on … . It's faulty / doesn't work / has got a hole in it. I'd like a refund / a new …*)
- Tell the class that *I look forward to hearing from you soon* is a good closing phrase for the end of the email.
- Students write their emails in class or for homework.
- Collect the emails and check them.

10 *Your answer*

- Finish the unit with a final whole class discussion of ***The BIG Question***: *Do shops rip you off?* Discuss the questions given and then ask two or three students to give their answer to the main question.
- Refer students to the Workbook Unit 5 activities.

Last word

- After doing the workbook activities, students evaluate their performance in the three areas. Check if any students feel they need extra practice in any area.

WORKBOOK answers — Pages 12–13 WB

1 Language: adverbials of quantity; quantifiers

1 A

1 Maria enjoys spending money a lot.
2 She doesn't stay at home much.
3 She goes out with boyfriends a lot.
4 She doesn't watch TV at all.
5 She listens to music a little.
6 Jimmy doesn't like going out much.
7 He plays computer games a lot.
8 He doesn't read much.
9 He doesn't enjoy shopping at all.
10 He shops on the internet a little.

1 B

1 many	**2** How much	**3** a lot of
4 a few	**5** How many	**6** How much
7 a little	**8** much	

2 Vocabulary

2 A

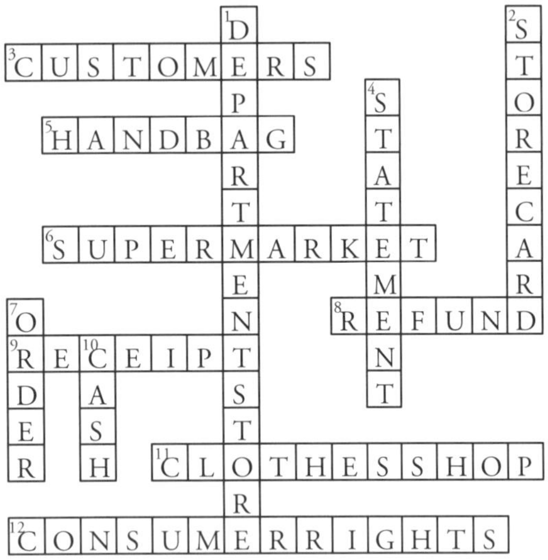

3 Word Building

3 A

Adjective	Noun
angry	anger
a *faulty*	fault
private	**b** *privacy*
c *secure*	security
shocking	**d** *shock*
e *useful*	use

Verb	Noun
to explain	**f** *explanation*
g to *criticise*	criticism
to pressurise	**h** *pressure*
i to *produce*	product
to complain	**j** *complaint*
k to *cancel*	cancellation

4 Use of English

4 A

1 I can't *afford* it.
2 I don't have *much* time.
3 The sales assistant was *rude* to me.
4 Can you please send me *confirmation* of my order?
5 They don't like shopping *at all*.
6 I'm *going* shopping later.

5 Portfolio Writing

(Individual answers)

What's new?

Subject:	Food
Language:	Connecting words: *and*, *but* and *because*
Functions:	**LB 10** Giving reasons
	LB 11 Making and replying to requests
Pronunciation:	Word stress, CD1 (Blue) track 9

1 *The BIG question:* MUST WE KILL TO EAT?

The theme of this unit is food, in particular vegetarianism, and ***The BIG Question*** is: Must we kill to eat? Is vegetarian food healthy? Is it tasty? Is it better for our environment?

- Tell students that they are going to talk about food. Ask: Is the taste of food the most important thing for you? Or is how healthy the food is?
- Read out ***The BIG Question***. Elicit initial reactions.
- Read through the **FACT** box with students. Make sure students understand what a *vegetarian* is (somebody who doesn't eat meat or fish). Ask students if they think the number of vegetarians is similar in their country. Ask: Is vegetarian food popular here?

2 FOCUS ON…

Words

2 A

- Look at the pictures with students and check to see that they understand the task. Students work individually or in pairs and add as many words to each list as they can. Ask students to do this in the form of a mind map. They can use the items in the pictures as prompts.
- Ask a student to draw his / her mind map on the board. Elicit other words from students and add them to the mind map or let individual students come to the board and add items themselves.

2 FOCUS ON…Words A **Suggested answers**

1 Vegetables: lettuce, carrots, onions, tomatoes, mushrooms, cabbage, broccoli, leeks, cucumber, radishes, potatoes
2 Dairy produce: milk, butter, cheese, cream, yoghurt
3 Meat: lamb, beef, pork, chicken, turkey
4 Fish: salmon, plaice, cod, haddock, squid
5 Fruit: oranges, apples, pears, bananas, grapes, pineapple, melon, peaches, plums, apricots

2 B

- Read out the words in the box. Ask students to repeat and check that they can pronounce the words correctly.
- Make two lists on the board. Read out each word in turn again and ask students if the word is positive or negative. Write the words in the correct lists. Explain or elicit the exact meaning of each word. (*bland* = doesn't taste of anything, *delicious* = tastes very good etc).

2 FOCUS ON…Words B **Answers**

Positive: delicious, fantastic, healthy, tasty, mouthwatering
Negative: bland, disgusting, horrible

2 C

- Read out the questions and check that students understand them.
- In pairs, students discuss the questions.
- Students briefly report back to the class.

2 D

- This exercise deals with words from the text (which contains quite a lot of difficult vocabulary). Go through the definitions with the class and check that these are clear.
- Tell students to first try to match the words with their definitions. Then ask them to use their dictionaries to check their answers.
- Check the answers.

2 FOCUS ON…Words D **Answers**

1 b 2 d 3 e 4 h 5 a 6 f 7 c 8 g

2 FOCUS ON…

Ideas

- Read out the questions and make sure students understand them.

- Students discuss the questions with a partner. Alternatively, they can work in small groups. Give students help with learning the vocabulary and expressing their opinions.
- Ask students to report back to the class.

3 READING CD 2 (Red) track 6, page 29 SB

Picture / background information

The photos show sheep in a truck ready to be taken to the slaughterhouse. Many animals die while they are being transported because of overcrowding, or because they get too hot or too cold, or do not have enough water.
www.ciwf.org.uk/

Australia is the largest exporter of live animals (about 4 million sheep a year). There have been many campaigns against shipping live animals to Asia and the Middle East.
www.animalsaustralia.org/

The second photo shows an area that was rainforest and that is now used for cattle. The 'rainforestweb' website says that 5m^2 of rainforest is destroyed for every quarter pound of hamburger made from rainforest cattle. See:
www.rainforestweb.org/Rainforest_Destruction/Cattle_Ranching/

The information in the Reading article is based on a brochure by the Vegetarian Society UK (www.veg-soc.org/news/2000/21cv/basic-facts.html). See also:
www.vegsoc.org/info/goingveg.html
www.vegsoc.org/health

Further arguments can be found on the website of the International Vegetarian Union:
www.ivu.org/religion/articles/argument3.html
Statistics and further information:
www.all-creatures.org/articles/ar-anag2003.html

3 A

- Look at the photos and the captions with the class. Explain the captions if necessary. Ask students: How do you feel when you look at the pictures?
- Read out the question. Students then read the text quickly and answer it.

3 B

- Read through the questions with the class and check that they are clear.
- Students read the article again and answer the questions.
- Check the answers.

3 READING B **Answers**

1 Vegans don't eat or wear any animal products: they don't eat dairy produce, eggs or honey and they don't wear leather shoes.
2 About ten billion.
3 They produce lots of methane gas.
4 We can use the land to grow vegetables instead of meat.

3 C

- Ask students to find the figures in the text and what they refer to. Make this into a mini-game: Which student can find the answers the fastest?
- Check the answers.

3 READING C **Answers**

35: the number of animals per person that die each year for meat in the USA.
25%: the amount of methane gas livestock produce in the UK.
114: the amount of beef half a hectare of land can produce.
100,000: the amount of water it takes to produce 900 litres of water.

3 D

- Discuss the questions with the class.
- When students have expressed their ideas, explain that the text is based on an article by the UK Vegetarian Society so that the aim is obviously to show that it is better not to eat meat. The writer perhaps wants to make readers feel guilty about the cost of eating meat.

4 LANGUAGE: Connecting words *and, but* and *because*

- Read through the example sentences with the class.
- Read out the questions in turn. Students answer orally.

4 LANGUAGE **Answers**

A because **B** and **C** but

- Refer students to the explanation about connecting words in Workbook Unit 6. They can read the explanation and do the exercises in class or for homework.

5 LISTEN IN CD 1 (Blue) track 8, page 30 SB

Picture / background information

The photo shows some young people enjoying a very large cheeseburger at a fast food restaurant. One in four Americans goes to a fast food restaurant every day and every month more than 90% of the children in the United States eat at McDonald's (www.media-awareness.ca/english/resources/educational/handouts/advertising_marketing/food_facts.cfm). However, most American fast food restaurants also sell salads and fruit juice and there are many new healthier fast food restaurants. See www.usatoday.com/money/industries/food/2002-09-29-fast-food-1acover_x.htm
Arguments against vegetarianism:
www.whyveg.co.uk/argumentsagainst.htm
GM crops:
pbs.org/wgbh/harvest/exist/
The speakers in the listening text are both American.

There has been a lot of debate about the effects of fast food on health and the environment. Eric Schlosser's books *Fast Food Nation* and *Chew on this* and Morgan Spurlock's film *Supersize Me* have been amongst the most influential. See www.supersizeme.com.

5 A

- Look at the photo with the class. Ask them what they can see.
- Discuss question **1** with the class. Make a list of positive and negative ideas on the board. Discuss if fast food is as popular in the students' country as in the USA.
- Read out question **2.** Elicit answers from different students. Encourage them to explain what they like about their favourite restaurant or café. Do different students in the class like the same places?

5 B

- Read out the task and the words in the box. First make sure students can pronounce the words correctly (for example, silent 'r' in *iron* [ˈaɪən]; soft 'g' in *genes* [dʒiːnz]).
- Students check the words in their dictionaries.
- Check the meanings of the words with the class. Alternatively, ask them to give you an example sentence using the word: students often find this easier and it shows more clearly that they have understood the meaning.

5 LISTEN IN B **Answers**

iron = a metal (chemical symbol: Fe) which you can find in some foods and in our blood.
genetically modified food = food in which scientists have changed the genes
vitamins = you find these in some foods; they are important for a healthy body
cruel = very unkind; causing pain
care about = be interested in / have a good opinion of
genes = they determine what people, plants and animals are like

5 C

- Read out the task.
- Play the CD. Students listen for the general meaning and answer the question.
- Check the answer.

5 LISTEN IN C **Answer**

Dan is angry with Ellen because she has decided to become a vegetarian and he thinks this is silly.

5 D

- Read through the sentences with the class and check that students understand them.
- Play the CD. Students listen and tick the arguments Dan mentions.
- Students compare their answers with a partner.
- Check the answers.

5 LISTEN IN D **Answers**

1, 4, 5, 9, 10

5 E

- With the class, summarise Dan's arguments for eating meat on the board.
- Brainstorm other ideas and add them to the arguments on the board.

- Ask students briefly what they think of the arguments but do not discuss them in depth as this is done in sections **6** and 7.

5 F

- Discuss the question with the class. Ask students to explain their answers.

6 YOUR TURN TO SPEAK

A Conversation

- Go through the expressions in **LB 10** with the class. Point out or elicit that we use *because* before a clause and *because of* before a noun; *That's why* comes at the beginning of a sentence.
- Check that students understand the questions. As these questions are fairly difficult, give prompts. Ask:
  Question 1: Do you think plants can feel? Is killing plants as bad as killing animals?
  Question 2: What happens to the land where we keep animals for food? What about water? How can we use land better? (Refer students back to the reading text on page 29 if necessary.)
  Question 3: Why do farmers want to grow GM crops? How do scientists change GM foods?
- Students work in pairs and discuss the questions using **LB 10** to help them.
- Discuss the questions briefly with the class.
- To consolidate the language used in this activity, do the exercise in **LB 10** with the class. Students can do the exercise orally in pairs and then report back to the class. Alternatively, ask students to review the phrases in **LB 10** at home and do the exercise in writing for homework.

B Role play

- Ask students to read the last part of the listening script with the class where Dan orders some fast food. Ask: What does Dan order? (a cheeseburger and fries); What does Ellen order? (nothing).
- Read out the task and go through the expressions in **LB 11** with the class. Look at the menu with the class and ask two or three students what they would like to order.
- In pairs, students role play ordering food using the menu. They can swap roles.
- Ask one or two pairs to do their role plays in front of the class.
- To consolidate the language used in this activity, do **LB 11** with the class. Students can complete the exercise individually and then check it by reading it with a partner. Alternatively, ask students to review the phrases in **LB 11** at home and do the exercise in writing for homework.

7 YOUR TOPIC

- Read out the task and the points learners have to prepare to speak about. Students find a partner and decide who is going to present the advantages of eating meat and the advantages of vegetarianism.
- Students make brief notes on each point according to the aspect they have chosen. They can work individually or with the corresponding partner from another pair.
- Students work in pairs and present their arguments to each other. Their partner asks questions.
- Ask one or two pairs to demonstrate their presentations to the class.

8 *NUTRITION in English* Page 31 SB

Picture / background information

A study in 2004 showed that junk food (eg sweets, soft drinks, hamburgers, pizza and potato chips) makes up about one third of calories in the American diet.
www.berkeley.edu/news/media/releases/2004/06/01_usdiet.shtml
www.epha.org/a/1279
www.lauralee.com/news/junkfoodintake.htm
www.guardian.co.uk/usa/story/0,12271,1185457,00.html

The Food Guide Pyramid was created by the U.S. Department of Agriculture and the U.S. Department of Health and Human Services and gives guidelines for a healthy diet. The text in this section is adapted from original material about the pyramid (www.nal.usda.gov/fnic/Fpyr/pmap.htm).

The U.S. Department of Agriculture has also developed new diet guidelines which focus on the foods and amounts suitable for individuals. See *MyPyramid* at www.mypyramid.gov/. Students can use this website to calculate what they should eat (according to sex, age and amount of physical exercise). The Food and Nutrition Information Center (www.nal.usda.gov/fnic/) gives further advice on nutrition.

8 A

- Look at the diagram of the Food Guide Pyramid with the class. Ask: Have you seen this or something similar before? Where? What does it show? Discuss if students have seen this diagram in other books or on the backs of food packets, in brochures etc.
- Students read the text and look at the diagram and find words or phrases to match the definitions. Tell them to use the context to help them.
- Students compare their answers with a partner.
- Check the answers.

8 *NUTRITION in English* A **Answers**

1 sparingly	**2** serving	**3** diet
4 calories	**5** weight	**6** saturated fat
7 food groups	**8** health	

8 B

- Read out the questions. Students read the text again and answer the questions.
- Check the answers.
- Ask: Do you eat foods from all groups? Do you pay attention to a healthy diet? Are you and the people in your family healthy eaters? Discuss with the class.

8 *NUTRITION in English* B **Answers**

1 This group is at the top of the pyramid, the smallest part, because people should only eat small amounts of these foods.
2 The bread and pasta group is at the bottom because people should eat a large amount of foods from this group.
3 Because each food group provides different nutrients and we need all the different nutrients for good health.

8 C

- Read out the question and refer students to the Food Guide Pyramid. Discuss the question with the class.

8 *NUTRITION in English* C **Answer**

A vegetarian diet is a healthy diet if vegetarians follow the rules of the food pyramid. That means they should eat something else from the 'meat' group (beans, eggs or nuts), eat lots of servings from the other four bottom food groups and only small amounts from the fats, oils and sweets group.

A vegetarian diet isn't a healthy diet if it doesn't include food from all groups or if it includes too many sweets or too much fat.

Optional project: Healthy food

Tell students they are going to hold a healthy food café. Agree on a time (in their next English class, outside lessons etc).

- Students can work individually or with a partner. They should think of a (simple) healthy dish or find a recipe for one (from their family, from a cookbook, or from the internet). Some students could make interesting healthy drinks.
- Students should write a list of the ingredients in English and the amounts of each. Then they should use a calorie counter (on the internet, for example) and calculate the number of calories for each ingredient and then the total number of calories for the dish and per 100g.
- Students prepare their dish at home.
- Each student (or pair of students) should display their dish with the list of ingredients and calories. Students walk round the 'café' and taste the dishes and drinks.
- Discuss the foods with the class. How difficult was it to prepare them? What foods did they like best? You could take a class vote on the best dish and award a small prize to the best cook/s.

9 PORTFOLIO WRITING

- Read the task with the class.
- Remind the class to divide their essay into logical paragraphs: an introduction; a healthy diet; a comparison between a meat and a vegetarian diet; a conclusion.
- Discuss how to write an introduction. Ask: What is important in the first sentences (to explain the topic, get people's attention, give one or two interesting facts or ask a question). Elicit possible opening sentences for the essay.
- Discuss how to write a conclusion. Ask: What is important in a conclusion? (summarising arguments, giving a final opinion). Elicit suitable sentences for writing a conclusion. You could teach the sentence beginnings: *In conclusion …*, *To sum up …*, *Finally ….*
- Students write their essays for homework.

- Students swap their essays with another student and read them.
- Check the essays. Read out the best one in class.

10 *Your answer*

- Finish the unit with a final whole class discussion of ***The BIG Question***: *Must we kill to eat?* Discuss the questions given and then ask two or three students to give their answer to the main question.
- Refer students to the Workbook Unit 6 activities.

Last word

- After doing the workbook activities, students evaluate their performance in the three areas. Check if any students feel they need extra practice in any area.

WORKBOOK answers — Pages 14–15 WB

1 Language: connecting words *and, but* and *because*

1 A

1 because **2** but **3** and **4** but **5** because

1 B

(Example answer)
My boyfriend and I went to a restaurant yesterday **and** (we) had a meal for his birthday. The restaurant was very busy **and** it was very noisy, too. My boyfriend wanted fish **but** there was no fish on the menu. So we had chicken **because** we both like that. It tasted okay **but** it wasn't anything special. The wine was good **but** it was too warm. We waited twenty minutes for the bill **and** then (we) complained. We complained again when we got the bill **because** it was wrong. It wasn't a very good birthday!

1 C

(Individual answers)

2 Use of English

2 A

1 My boyfriend eats quickly.
2 Fries are *worse* for you than chocolate.
3 We're *going* to eat out on Friday.
4 There aren't *many* vegetarians in the USA.
5 The food *didn't* taste very good.

3 Vocabulary

3 A

1 cheese **2** potatoes **3** fries
4 aubergine **5** oranges **6** bread

3 B

1 963 **2** 4,335 **3** 672,000
4 200,450 **5** 1,500,000

3 C

1 Eight hundred and forty-one
2 Seventy-eight thousand, six hundred and fifteen
3 One hundred and fifty-seven thousand
4 Nine hundred and ninety-nine thousand, nine hundred and eighty-seven
5 Three million, seven hundred and sixty thousand, two hundred and three

3 D

1 diet **2** calories / weight **3** Health
4 fat **5** Nutrients

4 Pronunciation — CD1 (Blue) track 9

4 A 2

Noun	Adjective
environment	environmental
accident	accidental
misery	miserable
knowledge	knowledgeable
geography	geographic
economy	economic

4 A 3

miserable, knowledgeable (the words ending in *-able*)

4 B 2

Verb	Noun
produce	produce
increase	increase
decrease	decrease
export	export
research	research

4 B 3

The stress is on the last syllable of the verbs and the first syllable of the nouns.

5 Portfolio Writing

(Individual answers)

What's new?

Subject:	Diaries, blogs, self-exposure
Language:	Present perfect with *ever, never, just*
Functions:	**LB 12** Talking about events in the indefinite or recent past
Pronunciation:	Strong and weak forms, CD1 (Blue) track 11

1 *The BIG question:* WHAT DO YOU KEEP PRIVATE?

The theme of this unit is blogging; that is, posting a personal diary on the internet to record everything that happens to you and your feelings about it. With the rising trend in blogging, the distinction between private and public is becoming ever more blurred. ***The BIG Question*** is therefore: What do you keep private? Is the increase in the public display of feelings and private information to be welcomed or not? The issue is a controversial one and gives students the opportunity to express different viewpoints.

- Read out ***The BIG Question***. Make sure students understand the word *private*. Ask them what the opposite of *private* (public) is.
- Introduce the topic of blogs by discussing the **FACT** box with students. Ask students: What is a blog? (an online diary). Invite a first reaction to the rise of blogs: Do any of the students read blogs, or write a blog themselves?

Picture / background information

Blogs are diaries and personal writing on websites that can be read by anyone. The fact that any writer can now publish their work instantly and free for a world-wide readership is changing the way people think about journalism and the media. Now anyone can be a journalist and publish their own news and opinions. This does not mean that the writing is good, or the facts reliable, or the opinions worth reading. But it makes freedom of speech and democratic access to the media available to all. It also means that traditional media and having to take account of this very personal, immediate and often eye-witness form of reportage. The law is still working out how to apply important principles like libel, privacy, decency and preventing people from preaching hatred on the internet.

General information on blogs:
en.wikipedia.org/wiki/Weblog
History of weblogs:
www.rebeccablood.net/essays/weblog_history.html
How to blog and make money:
www.washingtonpost.com/wp-dyn/articles/A43241-2005Jan27.html
www.microsoft.com/smallbusiness/resources/marketing/online_marketing/how_to_make_money_from_your_blog_5_tips.mspx
Design of weblog page:
www.globeofblogs.com/
Self-exposure:
eserver.org/zine375/exposure.html

2 FOCUS ON...

Words

2 A

- Before students do the activity, read out the words to express emotions in the box, making sure they understand all the words.

Optional warm-up activity

- Give students a list of circumstances, and ask them to write down what they feel at those times. For example: a) first thing in the morning.... b) when you've just finished a really good book.... c) on Monday morning, when you haven't done your homework over the weekend d) when you've just got your exam results.... e) when you've quarrelled with a friend or a parent.... etc. (Note this is an opportunity to introduce the present perfect for very recent events.)
- Students compare lists with a partner or in small groups (depending on how friendly the class is and how at ease they are with each other).
- Students report back to the class: ask students to say whether their answers were mostly similar or not.

- Pair the students up to do the exercise.
- Check the answers. Ask about any differences in the lists. For example, *proud* could be considered a good or bad feeling. Ask whether the students can say when the feelings could be good or bad.

2 FOCUS ON...Words A	Answers
Good feelings: happy, excited, proud, relieved **Bad feelings:** sad, depressed, angry, upset, lonely, scared	

Picture / background information

The photos represent things done in public or private.
The woman crying is a painting of the face of Mary Magdalene from the 'Crucifixion' fresco by the Italian Renaissance artist Ercole de Roberti (c. 1453-96).
The dancer is by the French artist Edgar Degas (1834-1917). He called this work of art, done in pastel, the 'Pink Dancer'.
www.ibiblio.org/wm/paint/auth/degas/ballet/degas.classe-danse.jpg

2 B 1

- Look at the table and discuss the visuals with the class. Let students express differences of opinion.
- Individually, students add more activities to the lists. Help with words or expressions.

2 B 2

- In pairs, students compare their lists and answer the questions.
- Discuss students' answers with the class. Ask students to put activities on the board under the two headings. Ask them to try to explain the reasons for saying that an activity is public or private.

2 C

- This is a pre-reading exercise, also designed to enrich vocabulary.
- Check the answers. Ask students which of the four words they think is most important for them.

2 FOCUS ON...Words C	Answers
1 c 2 d 3 b 4 a	

2 D

- In this exercise students encounter some of the vocabulary in the reading text. Encourage students to have a first go without their dictionary
- Ask students to compare their answers with a partner.
- Check the answers.

2 FOCUS ON...Words D	Answers
1 c 2 d 3 a 4 b	

2 FOCUS ON...

Ideas

- Go over the two statements with the class. The vocabulary has been prepared by the previous activities.
- Put students in pairs and invite them to give a first response, both to what students feel about the internet, and what they feel about privacy.
- Discuss briefly as a class. Encourage differences of opinion and attempts to justify them. The issue will be further discussed and students will be able to add reasons as they work through the unit.

3 READING CD2 (Red) track 7, page 33 SB

Picture / background information

Baghdad Blogger: Salam Pax, the Baghdad Blogger, wrote a blog in English on a website called 'Where is Raed?' during the war in Iraq in 2003. He started his blog six months before the war to keep in touch with his friend Raed who had moved to Jordan. His eye-witness reports during the war were very popular with the western press. He later wrote a column for the *Guardian* newspaper in London and his blog was published in book form as *The Baghdad Blog* (2003, Atlantic Books).
dear_raed.blogspot.com/
www.thebaghdadblog.com/home/
Many blogs are written by people interested in particular subjects (Fashion, Travel). Many also contain photographs, or may be online photo albums. Links to other blogs are a common feature of these sites.

3 A

- The first general question asks students to read quickly for one type of contrastive information.

- Check the answers and write them on the board in lists.

3 READING A **Answers**

In the past, diaries were usually private, often published a long time after events; blogs are public, posted immediately on the internet; blogs are also interactive – the blogger gets immediate feedback from readers.

3 B

- These questions promote a second reading to deepen understanding and find detail. Students can answer them in pairs or you can do the exercise as a class activity.

3 READING B **Answers**

1 Emma Brown **2** Kelly **3** Tom Grant
4 Salam Pax, the Baghdad Blogger

3 C

- This task asks students to respond personally to the text. Make sure students know the expression *to propose* (to ask someone to marry you).
- Students compare and discuss their ideas in pairs.
- Compare views with the class. There are no 'correct' answers here, and the point is to encourage discussion of different feelings.
- Note the use of the present perfect with *ever* in question **3**. In the class feedback, extend practice by using questions with *ever* and answers with time expressions (eg *once, twice,* or *never*).

4 LANGUAGE: The present perfect with *ever, never, just*

4 A

- Read the four sentences with the class. Students answer orally. Ask students what the tense is in sentences **2** and **4** (simple past). Explain that the tense in sentences **1** and **3** is the present perfect.
- Ask students to extract the time expressions in the four sentences:
  1) ever (an expression which means anytime up to now)
  2) during the Iraq War in 2003 (we are no longer in 2003)
  3) just (a very recent event)
  4) last month (a definite time marker – an event that is definitely in the past).

4 LANGUAGE A **Answers**

Actions at a definite time in the past: sentences 2 and 4.
Actions at an indefinite time in the past: sentences 1 and 3.

Optional follow-up activities

- Ask students to think about how they would say the four sentences in their own languages. Is there a difference in verbs that refer to definite or indefinite time in the past?
- Ask students to reread the text and pull out all the past tense verbs, listing them in two columns: definite time / indefinite time.
- Refer students to the explanation for the present perfect with *ever, never, just* and its relation to the simple past in Workbook Unit 7. They can read the explanation and do the exercises in class or for homework.

5 LISTEN IN

CD1 (Blue) track 10, page 34 SB

Picture / background information

The two speakers in the listening text are both American.

5 A

- Look at the photos with the class. Encourage students to describe the two couples in the photos in as much detail as possible.
- Invite speculation about the couple on the left. Are they in disagreement about something? What could it be? Have they just had an argument? What are frequent causes of arguments among young couples? Are they sad because they have to part?
- Elicit imaginative descriptions of the happy couple on the right. What makes a couple happy? Are they in love? Have they been successful at something?
- Move the conversation on to the question of how much couples should tell other people about what they're feeling. Ask: Should couples keep arguments private? Should they tell the world when they're in love?

5 B

- Ask students if the four words in the box are familiar to them. Can they guess *self-centred* from their previous work on words with *self*?
- Students look up the words and make up sentences using them.

5 LISTEN IN B **Answers**

self-centred: selfish; always thinking about yourself.
rubbish: one meaning of 'rubbish' is waste material to be thrown away. Here, *it* is used as an exclamation to mean: *Nonsense!* Or *I don't agree!*
nerd: this is a slang word meaning a boring and unfashionable person. It is sometimes used for people who are so interested in computers and online matters that they have no time for anything or anyone else.
properly: well, correctly

5 C

- Ask students to read the five sentences before they listen. Make sure students understand them.
- Ask students to guess whether the sentences are True (T) or False (F) before they listen. Then play the CD. Students listen and check their answers.
- Check the answers quickly with the class.

5 LISTEN IN C **Answers**

1 F **2** F **3** F (according to Josh) **4** T **5** T

5 D

- Explain the task.
- If you feel the class needs it, play the conversation again before they do the exercise. Alternatively, ask students to do the exercise; then play the conversation afterwards to confirm.
- Check the answers.

5 LISTEN IN D **Answers**

Lizzie's reasons against blogs:
– just self-exposure
– our lives should be private, not public
– you shouldn't write about people without making sure their feelings will not be hurt
– blogs are just boring rubbish
– people who blog have no self-control; their writing is not edited and therefore not controlled
– blogs are not real communication
– we all spend too much time on the internet

5 E

- This is an opportunity for students to express their own opinions and feelings about the internet and about keeping online diaries online. Students work in pairs or small groups and discuss the questions.
- Students report back to the class. Encourage students to ask each other reasons for their views and to justify their own views. This prepares the role play and the conversation which follow.

6 YOUR TURN TO SPEAK

Picture / background information

Blogs are increasingly used in education. There are many websites for information or resources on educational blogging, including:
www.educause.edu/ir/library/pdf/erm0450.pdf
www.washingtonpost.com/ac2/wp-dyn/A25305-2005Mar10?language=printer

A Role play

- Set the scene by asking students if they would like to have a website on which they could express their ideas about their classes. Get them to discuss this in groups first. Then have a class feedback.
- Write reasons for or against in columns on the board. Accept all views.
- Students separate into pairs for the role play. Circulate and help with vocabulary and ideas.
- Students perform their role play for another pair.
- Reverse the roles, or put students into pairs with new partners.

B Conversation

- Go through the expressions in **LB 12** with the class.
- Point out the two uses of the present perfect that this unit focuses upon: actions at an indefinite time (the verb is used with *ever* or *never*, or frequency expressions like *once, twice*) and actions in the very recent past that can be said to be almost present (used with *just*).

- Students discuss the questions with a partner using **LB 12** to help them.
- Students join another pair and compare their ideas.
- Students report back to the class.
- To consolidate the language used in this activity, do the exercise in **LB 12** with the class: students complete the sentences and then read them out to a partner and discuss them. Alternatively, ask students to review the phrases in **LB 12** at home and do the exercise in writing for homework.

Extra activity

- Start by giving students examples of questions starting with *Have you ever….*? (eg Have you ever been sailing / camping etc?) Write a few on the board, and write a follow-up question: *When was that*? with some possible answers: *last week, last summer during the holidays* etc.
- Ask students to write four questions of their own on a slip of paper, each one starting with *Have you ever…* ? They don't show their questions to others. Help with suggestions or language needed.
- Students go around the class, asking one student at a time their question. When another student answers *yes*, they ask the second question: *When was that*? and they write the name of the student + the time details on their slip of paper.
- The first student to get '*yes* answers' for all four questions is the winner. He or she has to report back to the class by saying sentences using the correct tense (eg 'Julie went sailing in July last year' or 'Julie has been sailing once only. She went with her family during the last summer holidays.')

7 YOUR TOPIC

- The topic invites the students to use the present perfect and the emotion vocabulary they have worked with in the unit.
- Circulate while students are preparing their topic, reminding them to make notes using key words and to structure their talk logically.
- After students have talked about their experi-ences, ask the rest of the class to respond positively and suggest improvements.

8 *CREATIVE WRITING in English* Page 35 SB

Picture / background information

The cross-curricular page in this unit is on writing skills. The tips on writing cover the whole process from planning to revising and editing, and are undoubtedly useful for writing in the students' own language as well as in English.
For more information on creative writing:
www.belhaven.edu/Academics/Divisions/Humanities/Creative_writing/Creative_Writing.JPG
www.britishcouncil.org/mozambique-creative-writing-workshops-330.jpg
For more information about Neri and 'The Writer'
www.guardian.co.uk/arts/features/story/0,,1463927,00.html

Giancarlo Neri is an Italian sculptor, originally from Sicily who once played professional football. His gigantic sculpture, 'The Writer' has been shown in large the public parks of the Villa Ada in Rome and on Hampstead Heath, London. Being so big and so simple, the sculpture gives an idea of the loneliness of the writer, someone whose art needs only a table and chair.

8 A

- One way of proceeding with this page is to start with task **B**. Ask students to think about their last writing assignment in English and to make notes about the four sections of question **1**.
- Students discuss the questions in groups and compare their responses. Have a class feedback.
- On the board, list some of the main problems that have come up in the discussion.
- Ask students to read the three texts quickly, by themselves or with a partner.
- Refer to the problems listed on the board. Is there any advice in the three texts for the problems?
- Invite an initial reaction to the texts – just a general impression because they are going to review the tips in task **B**, numbers **2** and **3**.
- Ask students to reread the general questions at the top of the page and the three texts and find words for the definitions in **A**.

8 *CREATIVE WRITING in English* A Answers

1 improve **2** brainstorm **3** a bullet point
4 make an outline **5** attention-getter
6 spot mistakes

8 B

- This task can be done individually, in pairs, or with the whole class.
- Feedback: ask students to choose the three top tips for them, and rank them in order of importance, 1, 2, and 3.
- Compare choices with the class.

8 C

Look at the photos and the captions with the class. Ask them for their reactions.

- Ask students to think of at least one reason for thinking that creative writing is best done alone, and one for thinking it's good to do it in a group. Discuss their ideas with the class.
- Invite students to share their experiences of creative writing groups or classes they've attended.

Optional project A:

If students are interested in blogging and have access to online websites:

- In groups, students go online and find a blog that they find interesting. They make a summary of it and write a report for the class. Ask them to download visuals and to give their views about the chosen blog.
- Pin up the reports and get students circulating and talking about them.
- Alternatively, students can access a blog in their own language. In their groups, they then work on a short oral report in English to tell the class about it.

Optional project B:

For students who are interested in creative writing:

- In groups, students research the writing habits of a writer they admire. It can be an English writer or one from their own country. They can use the library, encyclopaedias, online information (eg from Wikipedia).
- They prepare a short account of how one writer actually writes, what they find difficult, what particular strategies they used to get started, how they managed to get published. They prepare a colourful poster with pictures and short texts.

9 PORTFOLIO WRITING

- Ask students to work in pairs. Each one chooses his or her own topic. Then, individually, they brainstorm ideas in bullet points.
- The pairs read each other's outline and comment. Is the plan interesting? Are there points that could be added?
- The students each write their 'diary' of 120–150 words. The pairs read each other's work and comment on it by answering the questions in 'While writing'.
- The pairs revise, then read their diary out loud to each other, suggest improvements, and ask their partner to check spelling and grammar.
- Check the diaries. If students wish to do so, they can put their diaries on a class website for everyone to read.

10 *Your answer*

- Finish the unit with a final whole class discussion of ***The BIG Question***: What do you keep private? The three questions review the main areas of controversy explored by the unit. Students can work in groups before a general class feedback.
- Refer students to the Workbook Unit 7 activities.

Last word

- After doing the workbook activities, students evaluate their performance in the three areas. Check if any students feel they need extra practice in any area.

WORKBOOK answers **Pages 16–17 WB**

1 Language: the present perfect with *ever, never, just*

1 A

1 've been **2** 've just read **3** has been
4 've never wanted **5** 've had **6** 've just sent
7 've just checked **8** 's dumped

1 B

(Example answers)

1 a) I've written projects.
b) I've done an online search.
2 a) I've never been to the USA.
b) I've never played football.
3 a) I've just completed / finished this unit.
b) I've just had a cup of coffee.

1 C

1 Have you ever written **2** read **3** sent
4 has just started **5** 've never had **6** had

2 Vocabulary

2 A

1 d **2** a **3** b **4** f **5** c **6** e

2 B

1 c **2** b **3** a **4** d **5** g **6** e **7** h **8** f

3 Pronunciation

CD1 (Blue) track 11

3 C

1 W **2** S **3** W **4** S

4 Use of English

4 A

1 I've *just finished* my piece of writing.
2 The first sentence is a real *attention-getter*.
3 She's a full-time *writer*.
4 I like the blog *because* it's interesting.
5 My life is a *private* thing.

5 Portfolio Writing

(Individual answers)

What's new?

Subject: Fashion
Language: Articles
Functions: **LB 13** Talking on the phone
LB 14 Talking about preferences

1 *The BIG question:* ARE YOU A FASHION LEADER?

The theme of this unit is fashion, in particular the importance of electronic accessories such as mobile phones, and the question of where our clothes come from. ***The BIG Question*** is: Are you a fashion leader? Is fashion important to you? How often do you change your mobile phone? Who makes our clothes?

- Look at the title of the unit with the class. Explain or elicit what a *fashionista* is (somebody who is a passionate follower of fashion). Ask: How important is fashion in your life?
- Read out ***The BIG Question*** but do not discuss it at this stage.
- Read through the **FACT** box with students. Make sure students understand *luxury* (beautiful and expensive, not necessary for daily life). Ask students why they think this fact is true.

Picture / background information

The information in the **FACT** box is from:
www.tucsonshowguide.com/stories/nov04/fashion2.cfm.
This article suggests that Japanese people like to wear designer brand labels to be part of a group and identify with other people.
Asia as a style leader:
www2.agsm.edu.au/agsm/web.nsf/Content/News-MediaReleases-DrGianaEckhardtAsianconsumersfuturefocus

2 FOCUS ON...

Words

Picture / background information

The large picture shows young people in the Harajuku area of Tokyo wearing their own styles of street fashion. The Harajuku area is where teenagers hang out to show off the latest fashions, or trends that they hope will become fashions. Since the 1990s this area has become a laboratory for the newest trends in fashion and music, with bands playing on the street corner between the station and the park.
For information on Japanese Street Fashion:
www.onatoko.com/
japanesestreets.com/
www.ringsurf.com/info/Culture/Japanese_Cool_/Japanese_Movements/Japanese_Fashion.html
www.metamorphose.gr.jp/english/index.html
The smaller pictures show Chinese Communist leader Mao Zedong on the face of a fashion watch and style icon David Beckham wearing POLICE brand sunglasses.

2 A 1

- Students brainstorm as many clothes words as they can.
- Students compare their list with a partner. They explain any words their partner doesn't have.
- One pair of students writes their list on the board. Ask other students to call out additional items and add these to the list.
- Categorise some of the words. Ask: Which of these clothes do you wear in hot weather? And in cold weather? What do you wear on your feet? What do you wear on your head / hands / legs? etc.

2 A 2

- Explain the task. Read out the words in the box and the categories in the table. Make sure students can pronounce them correctly (eg necklace [ˈnekləs], jewellery [ˈdʒuːəlri]). Point out that in American English a mobile phone is a 'cell phone'.
- Students work individually or in pairs and complete the table.
- Check the answers.

2 FOCUS ON...Words A 2 **Answers**

Jewellery: bracelet, earrings, necklace, watch
Electronics: mobile phone, music player (watch)
Other accessories: bag, hat, scarf, sunglasses

2 B 1

- Students match the adjectives to the correct pictures using their dictionaries.
- Check the answers.
- Ask: Who's wearing something spotted / patterned / plain / striped / checked?

2 FOCUS ON…Words B 1 **Answers**

1 b 2 c 3 e 4 d 5 a

2 B 2

- Students match the adjectives with the correct definitions using their dictionaries.
- Check the answers.

2 FOCUS ON…Words B 2 **Answers**

1 e 2 d 3 c 4 a 5 f 6 b

2 B 3

- Look at the photos on this page with students. Ask individual students to describe them using the words from this page and then give their opinion of the styles. Other students agree or disagree.

2 FOCUS ON…Words B 3 **Suggested answers**

Big picture: the girl on the left is wearing a plain cardigan and sports shoes, a flamboyant, patterned dress and trousers, brown sunglasses and a scarf.

The person next to her is wearing a plain red coat, a red and white hat and red sunglasses. She is also wearing a baggy, patterned dress and carrying a plain orange plastic bag.

The next girl is wearing a patterned hat, dress and shoes. She is wearing sunglasses.

The person on the right is wearing a striped cardigan, a plain white T-shirt with a long necklace, black and white striped trousers and plain black shoes. She is wearing white sunglasses.

Smaller pictures: In the first picture a person is wearing a red watch. There is a picture of the Chinese Communist leader Mao Zedong or 'Chairman Mao' on it. In the second picture David Beckham is wearing a tight T-shirt and black sunglasses. These are the Police brand which he promotes.

Optional project A: Fashion magazines

- Students bring in pages from fashion magazines which show interesting or flamboyant fashions.
- In class or small groups, each student holds up a picture and gives a brief description of what the model is wearing. The rest of the class / group gives their opinion of the fashion. Have the students rate the outfits they see on a scale from 1 to 10 and give reasons for their ratings.

Optional project B: Fashion show

- Each student brings in items of clothing from home (their own clothes, clothes belonging to parents or other family members).
- Half the class are models. They choose items of clothing and dress up in them. The idea is to look as interesting / silly as possible.
- The models do a classroom catwalk parade. The remaining students give a catwalk commentary on what the models are wearing.

2 C

- Students ask and answer the questions with a partner.
- Ask students to briefly report back to the class.

2 FOCUS ON…

Ideas

- Read out each question in turn and discuss it with the class.

3 READING CD2 (Red) track 8, page 37 SB

Picture / background information

Clothes and social identity:
www.tucsonshowguide.com/stories/nov04/fashion.cfm
Brands:
www.gsb.stanford.edu/community/bmag/sbsm0008/faculty_research_brand.html
Fashion trends:
www.style.com/
www.fashionwindows.com/fashion/default.asp

The artworks are by a Japanese artist in the Manga style. The word means 'comic' in Japanese, but it has become the general name given to a particular style of drawing that is now very popular in western media as well in Japan. Originally, Japanese Manga stories were sometimes associated with violence, but now the style is used for many popular magazines and comic books, similar to the American 'graphic novel' type of picture story book.

3 A

- Students read the descriptions quickly and decide which fashions they like best.
- Ask students to briefly report back to the class.

3 B

- Explain the task. Point out that they can write more than one name for some categories.
- Students read the descriptions again and write the names of the correct fashionistas.
- Check the answers.

3 READING B	Answers
a) Ms Individual, Ms Eco	
b) Mr Brand, Mr Hip-Hop, Ms Professional	
c) Ms Eco	
d) Ms Fashion Slave, Mr Brand, Mr Hip-Hop, Ms Professional	
e) Ms Fashion Slave, Mr Brand, Ms Gothic	
f) Mr Strong Man	

3 C

- Students decide if any of the descriptions apply to them. If not, they should write a short description in the same style and read it out to the class. The class can help find a good name for the new type of fashionista.

3 D

- Read out the questions and check that students understand them.
- In small groups or in pairs, students discuss the questions.
- Discuss the students' opinions with the class.

4 LANGUAGE: Articles

4 A

- Read out the example sentences in turn. Ask students to find the examples in the descriptions and say which fashionista they refer to. (a and b = Ms Fashion Slave; c = Mr Brand; d = Mr Hip-Hop).
- Students answer the questions.
- Check the answers. Explain that these are basic general rules. Refer students to the explanation for articles in Workbook Unit 8 and go through it with the class. Students can do the Workbook exercises in class or for homework.

4 B

4 LANGUAGE B	Answers
1 d c **2** a d **3** b	

5 LISTEN IN — CD1 (Blue) track 12, page 38 SB

Picture / background information

With the very wide spread of mobile phones, the traditional function of the phone has changed. We now use our phones for various different modes of communication – speech, text, photo, video, email. Notice in the three photos how phone technology can be used to communicate in a variety of ways. The attraction of mobile phones is often not just their convenience but also their suitability to the user's preferred mode of communication.

Phone fashion:
www.thefeature.com/article?articleid=15726
semperaptus.com/news/ns_020203.shtml
www.compukiss.com/populartopics/moneyworkhtm/article1024.htm
Text messages:
news.bbc.co.uk/1/hi/sci/tech/1926272.stm
Reading novels on mobile phones:
www.msnbc.msn.com/id/7232995/
web-japan.org/trends/lifestyle/lif040310.html

5 A

- Look at the photos. Ask: What are the people in the photos doing? (The man in picture **1** is sending a text message on his mobile phone, in picture **2** somebody is taking a photo of two divers and in picture **3**, a man is talking on his mobile.) Give help with vocabulary as necessary.
- Ask: What do you use your mobile phone for? Again, give help with vocabulary if necessary.

5 B

- Explain the task. Read through the reasons for using mobile phones and check that students understand them. Read out the list of names.

- Play the CD. Students listen and match the correct speakers to the reasons.
- Students compare their answers with a partner.
- Check the answers.

5 LISTEN IN B					Answers
1 e	**2** c	**3** f	**4** a	**5** d	**6** b

5 C

- Read through the sentences with the class. Students try to remember or guess what the missing words are.
- Play the CD again. Students listen and complete the sentences.
- Check the answers.

5 LISTEN IN C		Answers
1 text	**2** matches	**3** girlfriend
4 download	**5** message	

5 D

- Read out the questions and discuss them with the class.

6 YOUR TURN TO SPEAK

A Role play

- Read the task with the class and check that it is clear.
- Go through the phrases in **LB 13** with the class.
- Ask students to put the telephone dialogue from the exercise in **LB 13** in the correct order and then read it in pairs. Check the answers.
- In pairs, students practise the role play, using **LB 13** to help them. They can take turns to play both parts.
- Ask for volunteers to perform the role play in front of the class.

B Conversation

- Go through the phrases in **LB 14** with the class.
- Students work in pairs and talk about the clothes and accessories, using the list of points and **LB 14** to help them.
- Ask some students to report back to the class.
- To consolidate the language used in this activity, do the exercise in **LB 14** with the class.

Ask students to write the questions with a partner and then read out the questions and answers in pairs. Alternatively, ask students to review the phrases in **LB 14** at home and do the exercise for homework.

7 YOUR TOPIC

- Read out the points learners have to prepare to speak about. Remind students to make brief notes on each point.
- Students can present their items of clothing or accessory to the class, or to smaller groups if you have a large class. Encourage them to ask questions about each other's presentations and comment on what they say. If students work in groups, ask them to briefly report back to the class.

8 *GLOBALISATION in English* Page 39 SB

Picture / background information

Globalisation:
www.guardian.co.uk/globalisation/story/0,7369,823274,00.html
www.guardian.co.uk/globalisation/story/0,7369,823097,00.html
www.guardian.co.uk/globalisation/story/0,7369,1368818,00.html
Sweatshops:
en.wikipedia.org/wiki/Sweatshop
Cotton farming:
www.panda.org/about_wwf/what_we_do/freshwater/problems/agriculture/cotton/index.cfm
Sustainable development:
www.ptree.co.uk/oc_campaign.html

8 A

- Look at the title of the section and the photos with the class. Ask: What do you think the text is about?
- Read out the first line of the text. Encourage students to look at the labels in their clothes and say where they come from. Ask: Why do you think these clothes are made there?
- Students read the text and find words or expressions in the text that match the definitions in **A**.
- Check the answers.

8 *GLOBALISATION in English* A			Answers
1 suppliers	**2** factories	**3** sustainable	**4** exploit

8 B

- Read out the questions.
- Students discuss the questions in pairs.
- Discuss the questions with the class.

8 C

- Read out the YOU CAN list. Check the meaning of *organic cotton* (cotton from farms that don't use chemicals), *fair trade companies* (companies that pay a good price for products from developing countries), *locally* (from your area) and *second-hand* (not new).
- Ask: Which of these things do you do? Then ask students to explain why or why not.

Optional project: Behind the brand

Students work in small groups. They choose a well-known brand of clothing – check that groups have chosen different brands. Students then find out as much as they can about their brand. They could consider these points:
- Who makes the clothes and where?
- Who buys the clothes?
- Does the company have a fair trade policy?

Each group should make a poster about the brand they have chosen and display it for the class to read. Ask students to comment on each other's posters in a short group discussion session.

9 PORTFOLIO WRITING

- Read out the two tasks.
- Revise how to start and end an informal email.
- For the first email, elicit reasons from the class why organic cotton is better (better for the environment – no chemicals, also better for your skin; better for cotton farmers – they get a good price for their cotton.)
- For the second email, ask the class what the latest fashions are. Tell them to think about what items, shape, pattern and colours.
- Students choose their task and write their email in class or for homework.
- Collect the emails and check them.

10 *Your answer*

- Finish the unit with a final whole class discussion of ***The BIG Question***: *Are you a fashion leader?* Discuss the questions given and then ask two or three students to give their answer to the main question.
- Refer students to the Workbook Unit 8 activities.

Last word

- After doing the Workbook activities, students evaluate their performance in the three areas. Check if any students feel they need extra practice in any area.

WORKBOOK answers — **Pages 18–19 WB**

1 Language: articles

1 A

1 Paris, **the** beautiful capital on **the** Seine in **France**, has always been **the** world's centre of haute couture fashion.
2 Fashion for **dogs** is a new trend in **the** USA. **The** fashion hasn't reached **Britain** yet.
3 Kate Moss is **a** fashion model. When she is at **work**, she earns about $10,000 **a** day.
4 London Fashion Week takes place twice **a** year in **the** UK's capital. You can see **the** latest clothes from **the** most important British designers.
5 People are starting to name their children after **brands. The** most popular names from **the** world of fashion are Armani for **girls** and Timberland for **boys**.

1 B

1 a **2** a **3** – **4** The **5** an **6** – **7** the / a **8** the
9 a **10** – **11** The **12** a **13** the **14** – **15** –

2 Vocabulary

2 A

(Example answers)
Footwear: shoes, trainers, sandals, boots
Outerwear: jacket, coat, hat, scarf, gloves
Sportswear: shorts, T-shirt, trainers, socks
Underwear: socks, pants, bra, tights

2 B

1 loose **2** plain **3** jewellery **4** flamboyant
5 sunglasses

2 C

(Example answer)
I'm wearing tight blue jeans, a patterned pink and green T-shirt and a plain pink cardigan. I'm also wearing cool trainers.

2 D

1 b **2** e **3** a **4** d **5** c **6** f

3 Word Building

3 A

dis-	in-	im-	un
disorganised	inexpensive	impolite	uncomfortable
dissatisfied	informal	impossible	unfashionable

4 Use of English

4 A

1 I've *never* been to a fashion show.
2 I *prefer* buying shoes to buying clothes.
3 He was *unhappy* with his new trainers.
4 I *didn't* take my sunglasses with me.
5 I don't *care* about fashion.

5 Portfolio Writing

(Individual answers)

What's new?
Subject: Fame and success
Focus: Reading an online interview

1 *The BIG read:* AROUND THE WORLD IN 71 DAYS, Ellen MacArthur

There are two Extended Readings in QSE 1, both of which are outside the structural progression of the book (ie the texts contain structures which are unknown to students but which are not focused on in exercises). The texts are primarily a chance for students to read longer, authentic texts for pleasure and develop their reading and discussion skills.

This extended reading deals with fame and success as experienced by the British sailor Ellen MacArthur after her record-breaking solo voyage around the world in 2005.

- Look at the photo of Ellen MacArthur and ask: Do you know anything about her? What is she famous for?
- Students read the factfile on Ellen MacArthur. Ask: How old was she when she first went sailing? (four); How old was she when she bought her first boat? (12).

Picture / background information

Ellen MacArthur grew up in the British countryside but started sailing as a small child with her aunt who owned a boat. In a BBC poll in 2005, 52% of people said she was Britain's greatest sporting hero. The photograph shows her sailing her trimaran (3-hulled sailing boat) in the English Channel at the end of her voyage. The trimaran was painted with the name of her sponsors, B&Q on one side and Castorama on the other. These are DIY and hardware chain stores that belong to the same company. B&Q operates in Britain and Castorama in France.

Ellen MacArthur has written two books about her experiences: *Taking on the world* (2003) and *Race against time* (2005).
www.ellenmacarthur.com/
www.time.com/time/europe/hero2004/mcarthur.html
www.penguin.co.uk/nf/Author/AuthorPage/0,,0_1000000093,00.html
http://www.spiegel.de/fotostrecke/0,5538,PB64-SUQ9NTQzMCZucj0x,00.html

This last website has dramatic pictures of Ellen on her trimaran. Search *Google* images for more pictures.

2 READING CD2 (Red) track 9, page 41 SB

Picture / background information

This interview is from the English-language service of the German magazine *Spiegel* Online:
service.spiegel.de/cache/international/spiegel/0,1518,344748,00.html (The original interview has been cut and slightly adapted in places.)

Ellen MacArthur set sail on 28 November 2004 from France and arrived in Falmouth, England on 7 February 2005. On her trip she faced icebergs, gale force winds and other dangers. Ellen MacArthur's trimaran was specially built for her in Australia. It contained the latest technology such as an autopilot (a computer which steers the boat) and technology to provide complex weather data. She was in constant contact with her base on shore, reporting progress in a daily blog.
www.solarnavigator.net/dame_ellen_macarthur.htm
sport.guardian.co.uk/sailing/story/0,10087,1408340,00.html

2 A 1

- Look at the photo with the class. Ask: Can you imagine sailing alone around the world in a small boat like that? What problems do you think Ellen MacArthur had? Discuss with the class.
- Read out the questions in **A**. Students read the text quickly and answer the questions. Check the answers.

2 READING A 1 **Answers**

1 She did it because she loves sailing and being out on the sea.
2 No, because she shared her experiences with lots of people using modern communications such as email.

2 B

- This exercise practises working out the meaning of unknown words from the context. Do the first word together with students as an example. Ask them to find the word *bucket* in the text (line 3). Read out the three definitions and ask students to see which definition best fits the context.
- Students read the text again and choose the correct meaning for the other words by finding the words in the text and using the context. Check the answers.

2 READING B	**Answers**
1 a **2** a **3** b **4** c **5** c **6** a	

2 C

- Read out the sentences and the alternatives in turn. Students choose the correct alternative orally.

2 READING C	**Answers**
1 extraordinary **2** dangerous **3** very different from	

2 D

- Read out the questions.
- Individually or in pairs, have students answer the questions.
- Check the answers. Discuss the third question with the class. Ask: Do you think she is happy with her life? Is there anything missing? Could you live like this?

2 READING D **Answers**

1 She sails because she just wants to sail.
2 Dangerous things include hitting icebergs and other ships at night. The most important thing is survival.
3 Nothing.

2 E

- Explain the task.
- Individually students make notes on the points given.
- Students compare their answers with a partner.
- Check the answers. Make notes on the board under the headings *eating, sleeping, washing*.

2 READING E **Answers**

1 freeze-dried food mixed with hot water; she ate because it was necessary and not for pleasure
2 in as many short naps as possible; whenever she had the chance and the weather let her
3 in a bucket or in the rain because she had no shower on board the boat; not very often

3 YOUR TURN TO SPEAK

3 A

- Read out the questions and make sure students understand them. Explain the second question more fully: many people have criticised Ellen for not being a proper sailor because her boat has too much technology. 'Real sailors' in the past sailed in small wooden boats without any help to navigate or forecast the weather and had to deal with being completely alone, with no contact to the outside world. In the past, sailing was also connected with adventure and discovery: some people say Ellen's trip was simply a selfish desire for fame.
- Students discuss the questions in pairs or small groups.
- Ask students to report back to the class.

3 B

- Students work in pairs or small groups and discuss the points.
- Ask students to report back to the class. Did they have similar ideas?

3 C

- Read out the questions. Elicit opinions and reasons from the class and encourage other students to agree or disagree.

Optional portfolio writing

Write this optional writing task on the board and ask students to do it for homework. Imagine a situation when either you had to use all your mental and physical strength, or you were alone for a long time.

- Make notes about where, when and why the situation happened.
- Write five adjectives that describe your feelings at the beginning, during and at the end.
- Describe how the situation ended.
- Write a blog or diary entry of up to 150 words describing the situation.

WORKBOOK Progress check 1

The Progress Check 1 after Unit 8 in the Workbook does not correspond directly to the Extended Reading in the Student's Book but revises the vocabulary and structures from the first half of the Student's Book (Units 1–8).

- Give the students the pages to do for homework and when checking the answers with the class, discuss and explain any unclear points.
- Alternatively, if you think your students need more support, revise word fields and structures with the class before students do the exercises either in class in pairs or at home.

WORKBOOK answers Pages 20–21 WB

Progress check 1 (Units 1–8)

1 Language

1 A

1 c **2** e **3** d **4** b **5** a **6** f

1 B

(Individual answers)

1 C

1 won **2** became **3** have won **4** have achieved **5** have competed **6** defeated **7** beat **8** did **9** are (the sisters) going to do **10** is going to be

1 D

(Example answers)

1. Hip hop is *cooler* than pop.
2. Alicia Keys is *the most interesting* singer around at the moment.
3. The Rio Carnival is *more famous than* the Notting Hill Carnival.
4. The Live 8 concert was *the best* concert I've ever seen.
5. DJ mixing is *less creative* than writing songs.
6. *Learning the violin is harder than learning the guitar.*
7. *Going to concerts is more exciting than listening to music at home.*

1 E

1 – **2** – **3** The **4** a **5** the **6** the **7** the **8** – **9** the **10** – **11** an **12** – **13** the **14** an **15** a

1 F

1 c **2** a **3** b **4** c **5** c

2 Vocabulary

2 A

Food: g) dairy produce, h) fruit, p) meat, m) vegetables (fish/bread/rice)
Jobs: a) accountant, c) computer programmer, l) editor, f) reporter (teacher/manager/ski instructor)
Sports injuries: b) bruise, d) cut, k) sprained knee, o) swollen ankle (cracked rib/broken ankle/injured leg)
TV programmes: e) documentary, j) series, i) soap opera, n) viewers (producer/the news/talk show)

2 B

1 delicious **2** dangerous **3** baggy **4** controversial **5** plain

2 C

1 customer **2** shirt **3** receipt **4** sale **5** refund **6** jackets **7** store card **8** pay **9** cash **10** wallet

2 D

Festivals *(suggested answers)*

– floats	– music	– dancing
	– sound systems	– DJs, bands
– carnival	– Lent	– religion
– parade	– celebrate	– event to celebrate
	– make a protest	– controversy
	– have a good time	– have a bad time
– dancers	– costumes	– feathers
– decorations	– flags	
– violence	– big crowds	– alcohol, drugs, knives
	– police	– criminals

Computers *(suggested answers)*

- internet
  - blogs – self-exposure
  - no editors – freedom
  - websites – shopping, information
  - chat rooms – meet new people
  - danger of strangers
  - emails – keep up with friends
- creative writing
- letters
- prevent real communication – friends and family

2 E

1 head **2** neck **3** eyes / nose / face **4** feet
5 neck **6** wrist / arm **7** feet **8** face

2 F

1 an online diary
2 the increasing temperature of the Earth's atmosphere
3 an extreme sport where people jump out of planes
4 for example, necklaces, bracelets and rings
5 buying things from websites
6 getting money for an event for advertising something
7 the person who leads a meeting
8 the growing importance of world markets and culture

What's new?

Subject:	Rules and regulations
Language:	Modals of obligation and necessity: *must, have to, need to*
Function:	**LB 15** Expressing obligation and necessity
Pronunciation:	Stress on auxiliary verbs, CD1 (Blue) track 14

1 *The BIG question:* WHO NEEDS RULES?

The themes of this unit are rules in daily life and laws in different countries. ***The BIG Question*** is: Who needs rules? Are rules and laws for our good? Or are they just a way to control people?

- Read out ***The BIG Question***. Ask: Are rules a good thing or a bad thing? Ask for a quick show of hands for *yes / no* without giving students the chance to qualify their opinion. Explain that you are going to look more deeply at the question in the course of the unit.
- Read through the **FACT** box with students. Make sure students understand *restrictions* (limits on things you can do). Ask students if they agree personally with this opinion. Ask: Do you think a similar number of people in your country would have the same opinion?

Picture / background information

The information in the **FACT** box is from a survey entitled *Mapping Britain's Moral Values*, Nestlé Family Monitor 8, March 2000. For a summary, see: www.mori.com/polls/1999/nfm7.shtml

2 FOCUS ON...

Words

2 A 1

- Read out the phrases in the box. Make sure students can pronounce words such as *fraud* and *graffiti* correctly.
- Go through the task with students and check that they understand it.
- In pairs, students complete the table with the things from the box, using their dictionaries to help them.
- Check the answers. Write the headings for the table on the board and complete the lists with the students. There might be some answers which students disagree on. Ask them to explain their answers.
- Elicit other things which are illegal or not allowed and add them to the correct list. Make sure all students understand any new vocabulary which comes up.

2 FOCUS ON...Words A 1 **Answers**

(Suggested additions in brackets)

Always illegal: fraud, murder, shoplifting (selling drugs, living in a foreign country without permission, rape, cheating in exams)

Sometimes not allowed: drinking alcohol, dropping litter, using mobile phones, taking photos, smoking, talking, graffiti (eating snacks, wearing casual clothes, carrying a rucksack)

2 A 2

- Read out the questions. Refer to the list on the board from exercise **2** and discuss the questions with the class.

2 FOCUS ON...Words A 2 **Suggested answers**

Drinking alcohol: at school, at work in working hours, everywhere in some countries; in a public place in some countries, at a pub outside pub opening times

Dropping litter: in the street, in public buildings

Using mobile phones: at school, in cinemas, on public transport, in libraries, on planes

Taking photos: in some museums and art galleries

Smoking: at school, in some places of work, public buildings, on public transport and planes, some restaurants

Talking: in exams, in the library, during lectures and talks

Graffiti: on objects or buildings without permission

2 B

- In pairs, students discuss the questions.
- Students discuss their opinions with another pair.
- Ask students to report back to the class. Encourage students to agree or disagree with each other and to explain their opinions.

Optional activity:

- Ask students to work in pairs or small groups and make up new rules for their school or workplace.
- Each pair or group should make a 'rules' poster and present it to the class.
- Discuss the rules and decide on the best ones.

2 C

- Look at the photos with the class. Ask: What is the police officer doing in picture **1**? What is the man doing in picture **2**? Where is the man in picture **3**?

2 FOCUS ON…Words C **Answers**

1 b **2** a **3** c

2 D

- Explain that the nouns in the boxes and some of the verbs are in the text.
- Individually or in pairs, students decide which verb in each group cannot be used with the noun.
- Check the answers. Remind students to learn verbs and nouns in combination.

2 FOCUS ON…Words D **Answers**

(✗ indicates incorrect use)
✗ do rules ✗ develop possessions
✗ collect freedom ✗ risk a commune

2 FOCUS ON…

Ideas

- In pairs, students discuss the questions.
- Read out each question in turn and discuss it with the class.

3 READING CD2 (Red) track 10, page 43 SB

Picture / background information

The picture shows followers of the Indian guru Bhagwan Shree Rajneesh greeting him as he drives past in one of his 93 Rolls Royce cars at his commune in Oregon, USA. Bhagwan Shree Rajneesh was born as Rajneesh Chandra Mohan Jain in 1931 in India and was later also known as 'Osho'.The Sanskrit word *Bhagwan* means 'Blessed one' and *Shree* means 'spiritual wealth'. After his arrest in the USA, Rajneesh was given a suspended sentence and ordered to leave the country. He returned to India where he died in 1990. See:
en.wikipedia.org/wiki/Rajneesh
The reading text is based on reviews of Tim Guest's book *A Life in Orange* (published by Granta, 2004) in which he explores his childhood in a commune.
www.timguest.net/orange.htm
www.amazon.com/exec/obidos/tg/detail/-/015603106X/002-8555647-7588044?v=glance
www.guardian.co.uk/india/story/0,12559,1120263,00.html

3 A

- Look at the photo with the class. Ask them what they can see and what they think is happening. If necessary, prompt them with questions: What does the man in the car look like? Where do you think he's from? What sort of car is he driving? Who is watching him? What are they doing with their hands? Who do you think they are?
- Elicit as many ideas as possible and write any keywords or important vocabulary on the board (eg Indian guru, followers, Rolls Royce).

3 B

- Explain the task to the class.
- Students read the article quickly and choose the best title. If you wish, play the article on the CD while students read. (Note: This is the first recording on CD 2.)
- Check the answer. Tell students that *A Life in Orange* is the name of a book which Tim Guest has written about his childhood.

3 READING B **Answer**

A Life in Orange

3 C

- Go through the sentences with the class. Check that they have understood *strict* and *forgiven*.

- Students read the article again and decide if the sentences are true or false. Alternatively, students can decide in pairs if the sentences are true or false and then read the article again to check.
- Check the answers. Ask students to say why the false sentences aren't correct.

3 READING C **Answers**

1 False. His followers didn't have to obey many rules.
2 True.
3 False. He was very lonely although he liked the freedom.
4 False. He was angry with his mother and he drank and took a lot of drugs.
5 False. Today he defends his mother.

3 D

- In pairs, or in small groups, students discuss the questions. Help students with vocabulary as necessary.
- Read out each question in turn and discuss it briefly with the class.
- Ask: Would you like to live in a commune?

4 LANGUAGE: Modals of obligation and necessity: *must, have to, need to*

4 A

- Read out each example in turn. Draw students attention to the verbs in bold and ask students to say if it is an example of obligation or necessity or no obligation or necessity.
- Write *obligation* on the board and the two verbs *must* and *have to*. Elicit the form we use for lack of obligation (*don't have to*). Point out, for example, that the opposite of *I must* go is *I don't have to go*. If necessary, tell students that the form *mustn't* has a different meaning (prohibition, for telling somebody not to do something).

4 LANGUAGE A **Answers**

1 a **2** a **3** b **4** a

4 B

- Look at example sentence **3** with the class and point out or elicit that this is the negative past form of *have to / must*, showing lack of obligation in the past.
- Ask: What is the past form of *have to* and *must?* Tell them to find examples in the article.
- Check the answer.
- Revise or teach the form of *have to* and *must* as appropriate.

4 LANGUAGE B **Answers**

Examples of *had to:*
All Bhagwan's followers had to wear the colours of the sun. (line 6)
For the next six years Tim had to wear orange clothes. (line 25)
The kids had to share their parents as well as their toys. (line 41)
He says she had to do it. (line 67)

- Refer students to the explanation about modals of obligation and necessity in Workbook Unit 9. They can read the explanation and do the exercises in class or for homework.

5 LISTEN IN CD1 (Blue) track 13, page 44 SB

Picture / background information

For more information about New York's clean-up campaign:
observer.guardian.co.uk/international/story/0,6903,1120526,00.html
Strange laws in Turkmenistan:
www.mirror.co.uk/news/allnews/tm_objectid=14147820&method=full&siteid=50143&headline=barmy-leader-bans-gold-teeth-and-beards-name_page.html
Banning of English words in France:
www.guardian.co.uk/online/news/0,12597,1002708,00.html
The speakers in the listening text are both British.

5 A

- Look at the photos and the captions with the class. Elicit reasons from students why people might ban these things and write the ideas on the board.

5 B

- Read out the task and the list of places.
- Play the CD. Students listen and write what each place has banned.

- Students compare answers with a partner.
- Check the answers.

5 LISTEN IN B	**Answers**
a) France: English words (such as the word *email*)	
b) Halifax: perfume or products with a strong smell	
c) New York: drinking alcohol in public places, smoking in restaurants, feeding pigeons	
d) Turkmenistan: gold teeth	
e) Tokyo: using mobile phones on the train	

5 C

- Students read through the sentences from the listening text. Check that they understand them.
- Play the CD again. Students listen and choose the correct words.
- Students check their answers in the listening script.
- Check the answers quickly with the class.

5 LISTEN IN C	**Answers**
1 a **2** a **3** b **4** b **5** a **6** b	

5 D

- Students discuss the laws in the radio programme in small groups or as a class.

6 YOUR TURN TO SPEAK

A Role play

- Read the task with the class. Make sure they understand.
- Divide the class into groups. Groups role play the situation and decide on three things they would like to ban.
- The groups present their laws and the reasons for them to the rest of the class. Encourage students in other groups to ask questions and make comments.

B Conversation

- Go through the phrases in **LB 15** with the class.
- Students work in pairs and take turns to talk about the things given in the task, using **LB 15** to help them.
- Ask some students to report back to the class.
- To consolidate the language used in this activity, do the exercise in **LB 15** with the class. Ask students to work in pairs and complete the dialogue and then read it together. Alternatively, ask students to review the phrases in **LB 15** at home and do the exercise for homework.

7 YOUR TOPIC

- Read out the task and the points learners have to prepare to speak about. Remind students to make brief notes on each point.
- Students can present their laws to the class, or to smaller groups if you have a large class. Encourage them to ask questions about each other's presentations and to comment on what each other says. If students work in groups, ask them to briefly report back to the class.

8 *EUROPEAN CITIZENSHIP in English* Page 45 SB

Picture / background information

The first photo shows the flag of the European Union with its twelve stars, representing twelve member states (Belgium, France, Netherlands, Germany, Italy, Luxembourg, Denmark, Ireland, UK, Greece, Portugal and Spain). Austria, Finland and Sweden joined in 1995, and in 2004 Cyprus, Malta, Hungary, Poland, Czech Republic, Slovak Republic, Slovenia, Estonia, Latvia and Lithuania also joined, bringing the total number of countries to 25. Bulgaria, Romania and perhaps Turkey are also expected to join. The second photo shows the European Parliament in Strasbourg.

History: The European Economic Community (EEC) was founded in 1957, focussing on economic cooperation and peace in Europe. In 1993 the EEC became the European Union (EU) and expanded its areas of economic and political cooperation.

European Union:
www.bbc.co.uk/schools/citizenx/internat/eu/lowdown/eu_basics_1.shtml
wordiq.com/definition/European_Union
europa.eu.int/abc/index_en.htm

- This is quite a difficult topic, but certainly an invaluable one for students in European Union countries. If you teach students outside the European Union, you might prefer to deal with the topic of the EU very briefly and concentrate on the wider question in section **C**. On the other hand, you may prefer to give students extra information on the make-up, function and history of the EU.

- Look at the photo of the EU flag with the class. Elicit from students what it represents – you could take this opportunity to revise the names and pronunciation of European countries.
- Look at the second photo and discuss it with the class. Ask: What does it show? Where is it?
- Go through the diagram with students and make sure they understand it.
- Students do the EU quiz. They take it in turns to read out a question and then agree on an answer. They should use dictionaries to help them.
- Check the answers to the quiz with the class.

8 *EUROPEAN CITIZENSHIP in English* **Answers to quiz**

1 c
2 b (Note: some countries in the EU still have passport controls)
3 a, c, and e (Note: one point for all the correct countries together)
4 b
5 a
6 a

- After checking the answers, ask students to put up their hand for the following four groups of answers and read out the relevant part of the key in turn:

6 correct answers:	You're an EU expert! Well done!
4–5 correct answers:	Good! Are you an EU citizen?
2–3 correct answers:	Mmm, you need to study some information about the EU.
Less than 2 correct answers:	Oh dear, try the quiz again!

8 A

- Focus on vocabulary: look at exercise **A** with the class and read out the definitions.
- Students look at the quiz and diagram again and find the words for the definitions in the quiz.
- Check the answers.

8 *EUROPEAN CITIZENSHIP in English* A **Answers**

1 citizens **2** elect **3** propose **4** reject **5** union

8 B

- Read through the incomplete sentences with the class.
- Students complete the sentences, referring back to the quiz and the diagram if necessary.
- Check the answers. Make sure students understand them.

8 *EUROPEAN CITIZENSHIP in English* B **Answers**

1 member states **2** single market
3 European currency **4** customs, passport
5 Parliament, Commission

8 C

- Read out the questions and discuss them with the class.

Optional project: The EU for beginners

- Ask students to make an information brochure about the EU. It should give basic information about what the EU is and what it does in a simple way.
- Students should work in small groups and produce the brochure together. They can add diagrams, drawings or photos as they wish.
- Display the brochures for everyone to read. The class should decide which one is the best brochure.

9 PORTFOLIO WRITING

- There are two alternatives here: students who do not live in the EU area or weaker students may prefer to do the second task which is more personalised and which has already been prepared in speaking tasks in the unit.
- *The EU article:* prepare this thoroughly with students in class. Write two headings on the board: good idea and bad idea. Elicit good and bad aspects of the EU from the class, giving them help with vocabulary and prompting as necessary.

9 PORTFOLIO WRITING **Answers**

Good ideas:
- peace between EU member states
- strong economic market (against competition from USA / Asia)
- richer countries help poor countries
- citizens can travel easily between countries
- it's possible to live and work in different countries one currency: easy to compare prices and buy things in different countries, easy to travel

Bad ideas:
- culture becomes the same, countries lose their national identity (dress, food, customs)
- countries can't make some of their own laws
- prices have gone up since the Euro was introduced

- Look at a possible structure for the essay and write it on the board. For example: first paragraph = introduction (What is the EU?); second paragraph = good things about the EU; third paragraph = bad things about the EU; final paragraph = summary and students' own opinion.
- You might like to give students some linking words, focussing on contrasting ideas, for example: *but, although, however, on the one hand … on the other hand.* Revise phrases for summarising and giving opinions.
- The rules article: discuss a possible structure for this article with the class. For example:
  first paragraph: introduction; something about the place
  second paragraph: description; what the rules are and why they exist
  third paragraph: students' opinion of the rules
  fourth paragraph: summary
  Again, for this article, revise phrases for summarising and giving opinions.
- Students write their articles for homework.
- Ask students to swap their essays with a partner: first to read and comment, and a second time to focus and correct any mistakes or unclear parts.
- Check the articles and then ask students to write a clean draft.

10 *Your answer*

- Finish the unit with a whole class discussion of ***The BIG Question:*** *Who needs rules?* Do this by focussing on the questions given in the instruction.
- Refer students to the Workbook Unit 9 activities.

Last word

- After doing the Workbook activities, students evaluate their performance in the three areas. Check if any students feel they need extra practice in any area.
- Ask students to swap their essays with a partner: first to read and comment, and a second time to focus and correct any mistakes or unclear parts.

WORKBOOK answers — Pages 22–23 WB

1 Language: obligation and necessity: *must, have to* and *need*

1 A

1 have to pay **2** have to pass **3** have to pay
4 has to be **5** don't have to buy
6 doesn't have to charge

1 B

1 don't have to **2** had to **3** need to **4** must
5 didn't need to

2 Connections

2 A

do: an English course, your homework, what you want, a test, the shopping
make: a decision, a phone call, a mistake, laws, dinner

3 Vocabulary

3 A

1 b **2** a **3** c **4** e **5** d

3 B

1 b My cousin Vinny *breaks* the law regularly.
2 e Last week Vinny *committed* another crime.
3 a The manager of the shop *called / phoned* the police.
4 c The police came and *arrested* him.
5 d Vinny *is* in prison again now.

4 Pronunciation

CD1 (Blue) track 14

4 A

1 phone **2** smoke **3** remember / wash
4 breaking **5** get out

4 B

We don't usually stress auxiliary verbs.

4 C

1 have **2** don't / must **3** can't **4** can
5 need to **6** have to

5 Use of English

5 A

1 You *don't need to have/don't have to have* a ticket for the museum.
2 It's *dishonest* to copy your friend's homework.
3 Smoking in restaurants is against *the law* here.
4 You *don't have to / need to* shout.
5 You should *obey* laws.

6 Portfolio Writing

(Individual answers)

What's new?

Subject: Future developments
Language: *will* future for predictions
Functions: **LB 16** Giving and following instructions
LB 17 Informing about and predicting the future

1 *The BIG question:* WHAT WILL CHANGE THE WORLD NEXT?

The theme of this unit is future developments. ***The BIG Question*** is: What will change the world next? Have we invented everything important? Are new developments always positive? Does the future look good?

Picture / background information

Thomas J. Watson (1874–1956) reportedly said this in 1943. It is possible that this is in fact a misquote – he may never have said it. However, at that time nobody could predict computers would ever become so cheap, so powerful and so essential to every aspect of life and business. Watson was the founder of International Business Machines (IBM), which made the mass-produced PC available throughout the world and at one time was the most important computer company in the world. It has now become more of a business services company. In 2004 IBM sold its PC business to a Chinese company, Lenovo.
en.wikipedia.org/wiki/Thomas_J._Watson

- Read out ***The BIG Question***. Elicit a few initial reactions.
- Read through the **FACT** box with students. Ask: Have you heard this before? Are you surprised? Why do you think he said this?

2 FOCUS ON...

Words

Photo and background information

The photo of the wheel shows the first recorded picture of a wheel on a Sumerian tablet. The wheel was made of wood. Originally from southern Iraq, the tablet was found in a large grave and dates from 2600 to 2400 BC. Referred to as the Standard of Ur, it now resides in the British Museum in London.
www.zyworld.com/Assyrian/Inventing_the_wheel.htm

The telephone was invented by Alexander Graham Bell. He was born in Scotland in 1847. He went to America before he started his career as an inventor. He died in 1922. The picture shows Bell inaugurating the New York-Chicago telephone on 18 October 1892. The mobile telephone was invented in 1946.
sln.fi.edu/franklin/inventor/bell.html
The printing press was invented in the West by Johannes Gutenberg (1397-1468). However, the art of printing was invented in China much earlier.
www.gutenberg.de/english/erfindun.htm
en.wikipedia.org/wiki/Printing_press
Information on other inventions:
corporate.britannica.com/press/inventions.html
library.christchurch.org.nz/Childrens/FactSheets/WhoInventedIt.asp
Funny inventions:
www.totallyabsurd.com/archive.htm

2 A 1

- Look at the pictures and the captions with the class. Ask students if they know anything else about these inventions.
- Brainstorm five or more inventions with the class on the board. Students can use a dictionary to help them.

2 A 2

- Have students work with a partner to discuss the inventions on page 46 and also those on the board. Which ones have had the most effect on the world?
- Students then report back to the class. Ask them to explain their choices and encourage other students to agree or disagree.

2 FOCUS ON...Words A 2 Suggested answers

computer, the internet, television, mobile telephone, camera

2 B 1

- Students label the picture with the words in the box.
- Check the answers with the class.
- Ask: Does this plug and this socket look like the ones you use? How are they different?
- Ask: Can you change a plug? Do you like doing things like that?

2 FOCUS ON…Words B 1	Answers
(from left to right) switch, socket, plug, cable	

2 B 2

- Read out the verbs in the box. Illustrate the meaning (or ask students to illustrate the meaning) by using electrical items in the classroom (eg switch the light on and off).
- Students complete the sentences. Check the answers.

2 FOCUS ON…Words B 2			Answers
1 Switch off	**2** plug in	**3** switch on	**4** Press

2 C

- Tell students they are going to read a story about the future. Read out the words from the text. Check that students can pronounce them correctly.
- Ask students to match the words with the correct definitions. Check the answers.

2 FOCUS ON…Words C				Answers
1 d	**2** c	**3** e	**4** b	**5** a

2 D

- Read through words in the boxes to check that students understand them.
- Ask students which time words are largest and which are smallest. Write these on the board. Then ask students to organise them from smallest to largest using the scale 1–8.
- Check the answers.

2 FOCUS ON…Words D			Answers
1 second	**2** minute	**3** hour	**4** day
5 month	**6** year	**7** decade	**8** century

2 FOCUS ON…

Ideas

- Read out the questions and make sure students understand them.
- Students discuss the questions in pairs. They should give reasons for their answers.
- Students report back briefly to the class.

3 READING CD 2 (Red) track 11, page 47 SB

Picture / background information

The text is an extract from a science fiction book called *Eager* by Helen Fox (Hodder Children's Books, 2004). The photo shows the cover of the book with a picture of Eager the Robot. Eager is a new type of robot that can think and feel. In the book, a group of robots threaten humans. The book has a sequel called *Eager's Nephew* (Hodder Children's Books, 2005). There is a third book in the series called *Eager and the Mermaid*.
www.madaboutbooks.com/index.asp?url=authordetails.asp&author=23496
www.kidsreads.com/reviews/0385746725.asp

3 A

- Read out the task.
- Look at the picture of Eager with the class. Ask them to describe him and say what they think is special about him.
- Note students' ideas on the board. Give help with vocabulary where necessary.
- Play the CD while students read.
- Check if the students' ideas about Eager were correct.
- Discuss students' first impression of their reading of the extract. Ask: Did you enjoy reading it? Why? / Why not?

3 B

- Students read the extract again more carefully and answer the questions.
- Check the answers.

3 READING B — **Answers**

1 At Professor Ogden's house.
2 He is trying to find them a new robot.
3 They can see, hear, reason and move around.
4 He learnt it.
5 They will teach him about life: about feelings and right and wrong.

3 C

- Read out the quotes. Ask students to find them in the text and underline them. What is the professor referring to when he says these sentences? (The door that can see; Eager).
- Discuss the questions about the quotes with the class. Encourage them to give reasons for their answers.

3 READING C	**Suggested answers**
1 Some people think that things they don't understand are 'magic'. But there is usually a technological or scientific explanation for how things work. **2** They're a dream because they can do lots of jobs people do, make everyday life a lot easier and save a lot of money. But thinking robots can also be dangerous and harm people or destroy things.	

- Ask students if they enjoy reading science fiction. Discuss why students like or dislike this type of fiction. Ask students who enjoy science fiction to tell the class about a good book they have read.

4 LANGUAGE: *will* future for predictions

4 A

- Read out the examples and the question. Check that students understand the word 'predictions'. Students answer orally.
- Ask: Which form do we use for definite plans and intentions? (*going to*). Write examples on the board which contrast the use of both forms. For example: *I'm going to see a new comedy film tonight (definite plan). I think the film will be good* (prediction, but it isn't certain that the film will be good).
- Ask students for more examples of *will* and *going to*. Write them on the board in columns.

4 LANGUAGE A	**Answer**
predictions	

4 B

- Read out the questions. Ask students to find examples in the text.
- Check the answers.

4 LANGUAGE B	**Answers**
Short form: 'll *Examples*: We*'ll* find out if it can do all the things we think it can (line 2 ; You*'ll* be its family (line 68). Negative form: will not / won't. *Example*: You *won't* be its teachers. (line 67)	

- Refer students to the explanation about the *will* future in Workbook Unit 10. They can read the explanation and do the exercises in class or for homework.

5 LISTEN IN — CD1 (Blue) track 15, page 48 SB

5 A

- Look at the photos and captions with the students. Point out the remote control and give or elicit the name of this in English. Ask students if these appliances are something most people have in their country. Ask: Do you have these things? How important are they?
- Write the words on the board under the heading 'machines and appliances in the home'. Ask students if they can add the names of other machines and appliances. You could also prompt them with pictures cut from magazines, catalogues or advertising brochures.
- Read out the questions in **A**. Students answer orally.

5 B

- Tell students they are going to listen to a conversation between Leo, an American teenager, and his father. Read out the questions. Remind students they are only listening for the answers to these questions and not to understand every word.
- Play the CD. Students listen and answer the questions.
- Check the answers.

5 LISTEN IN B	**Answers**
Leo's dad has a new computer and it isn't working. Leo notices that his dad hasn't plugged the computer into the socket and switched it on.	

5 C

- Read out the sentences and check that students understand them.
- Play the CD again. Students listen and write the correct names.
- Check the answers or ask students to check their answers in the listening script.

5 LISTEN IN C					Answers
1 D	**2** D	**3** D	**4** B	**5** D	**6** L

5 D

- Students read the sentences in **5C** again and discuss them with a partner.
- Discuss students' opinions with the class. Is the class generally positive or negative about technology? Ask: Do you think older people are more negative about technology than younger people?

6 YOUR TURN TO SPEAK

A Role play

- Read the task with the class and make sure they understand.
- Look at the phrases in **LB 16** with the class. Check that their meanings are clear.
- Divide the class into pairs. Students each choose an appliance (but don't tell their partner) and make notes on how it works.
- Students give instructions, using their notes to help them. Their partner guesses the appliance.
- Ask for volunteers to give instructions in front of the class so that the class can then guess the appliance.
- To consolidate the language used in this activity, do the exercise in **LB 16** with the class. Alternatively, ask students to review the phrases in **LB 16** at home and do the exercise for homework.

B Conversation

- Go through the phrases in **LB 17** with the class.
- Students work in pairs and take turns to make predictions, using **LB 17** to help them. Their partner should comment on their predictions.
- Ask some students to report back to the class.
- To consolidate the language used in this activity, do the exercise in **LB 17** with the class. Alternatively, ask students to review the phrases in **LB 17** at home and do the exercise for homework.

7 YOUR TOPIC

- Read out the points learners have to prepare to speak about. Remind students to make notes about each point.
- Ask students to bring photos, pictures or diagrams to illustrate the development they are talking about.
- Students can present their development to the class or smaller groups if you have a large class. Encourage them to ask questions about each other's presentations and say if they also think it is an important development. If students work in groups, ask them to briefly report back to the class.

8 *INFORMATION TECHNOLOGY in English* Page 49 SB

Picture / background information

Sony's QRIO robot:
www.sony.net/SonyInfo/QRIO/
www.newscientist.com/article.ns?id=dn4845
Honda's ASIMO robot:
world.honda.com/ASIMO/
electronics.howstuffworks.com/asimo.htm
Robots with personalities:
www.guardian.co.uk/life/science/story/0,12996,1403780,00.html?gusrc=rss
How robots work:
electronics.howstuffworks.com/robot.htm

- Look at the photos with the class. Ask: Are you surprised that robots can do these things?
- Students read the text quickly. Ask: What other activities can robots do? (talk, walk upstairs, dance and conduct an orchestra).

8 A

- Read out the definitions. Students read the text again and find the words which match the definitions.
- Check the answers.

8 *INFORMATION TECHNOLOGY in English* A		Answers
1 software	**2** hardware	**3** process
4 program	**5** data	

8 B

- Ask students to read the sentences and decide if they are true or false.
- Students check their answers in the text and correct the false sentences.
- Check the answers. Discuss any answers where students have differing opinions.

8 *INFORMATION TECHNOLOGY in English* B **Answers**

1 True
2 True
3 False. Some computers can solve problems but in a different way to humans.
4 False. They can only communicate with humans on a simple level.
5 False. A Korean professor says his software will give robots personalities and feelings in the future.

Optional project: Robots

- Students work in small groups. They find out more information about ASIMO, the QRIO robot or another interesting robot. They should concentrate on its special features and what it can do.
- Each group makes a short presentation to the class. They should show photos if possible.

9 PORTFOLIO WRITING

- Remind students of their discussion about thinking robots (page 47). Ask students to give their opinion on the developments in robotics. Make brief notes on the board in two columns: positive and negative ideas.
- Look at the phrases to express opinion with the class. Encourage students to use these in their emails.
- Students write their emails in class or for homework.
- When students have written their emails, ask them to swap with a partner and read their partner's work. Do they agree with their partner?
- Collect the emails. Select a few to read out to the class.

10 *Your answer*

- Finish the unit with a final whole class discussion of ***The BIG Question***: *What will change the world next?* Discuss the questions given.
- Refer students to the Workbook Unit 10 exercises.

Last word

- After doing the workbook exercises, students evaluate their performance in the three areas. Check if any students feel they need extra practice in a particular area.

WORKBOOK answers — Pages 24–25 WB

1 Language: *will* future for predictions

1 A

In five years, I'll live in London.
I'll be a teacher.
I'll travel a lot.
I won't be rich.
I won't have my own flat.
I won't be married.

1 B

1 will happen **2** won't take
3 won't discover **4** will probably happen
5 will take place **6** will get
7 won't be **8** will be / 'll be

1 C

(Individual answers)

1 D

1 'm going to buy **2** Are you going to see
3 will develop **4** won't change
5 're going to do

2 Vocabulary

1 f **2** d **3** c **4** b **5** e **6** a

2 B

1 b **2** b **3** a **4** b **5** b

2 C

1 d **2** b **3** c **4** e **5** a

2 D

1 d **2** e **3** c **4** a **5** b

3 Word Building

3 A

1 invention **2** develop **3** information
4 solve **5** communication **6** scientific
7 technology **8** optimistic **9** magic
10 ignorant

4 Use of English

4 A

1 I *don't think* intelligent robots will ever exist.
2 Futurists make *predictions* about the future.
3 Everybody will *definitely* have wireless technology soon.
4 Alexander Bell invented the telephone *X years* ago. [depending on the current year]

5 Portfolio Writing

(Individual answers)

What's new?

Subject:	Travel and transport
Language:	Present perfect with *for* and *since*
Functions:	**LB 18** Stating the duration of events
Pronunciation:	Consonant clusters 1, CD1 (Blue) track 17

1 *The BIG question:* WILL AIR TRAVEL COST THE EARTH?

The theme of this unit is travel and transport and, in particular, cheap air travel. ***The BIG Question*** is: Will air travel cost the Earth? Is cheap air travel increasing the risk to our environment? What can we do to help?

Picture / background information

FACT box source: *Aviation and Global Climate Change*, Friends of the Earth: www.foe.co.uk

- Start by asking students a few warm-up questions: Do you like travelling? How often do you travel? Do you usually travel to other parts of your country or do you travel to other countries?
- Read out ***The BIG Question***. Explore the double meaning of the question with the class. Explain that 'to cost the Earth' means to 'be very expensive'. Ask: What other meaning does this question have? (= Will air travel destroy our planet / our environment?)
- Read through the **FACT** box with students. Elicit reactions. Ask. Why do you think this will happen?

2 FOCUS ON...

Words

Picture / background information

The photos show methods of air, sea and land travel. The plane in the photo is a European Airbus 380, the biggest passenger plane in the world that has two decks and 550 seats. Its first flight was in April 2005.
events.airbus.com/A380/seeing/indexminisite.aspx
www.airliners.net/info/stats.main?id=29
The car in the photo is a hybrid vehicle which has both an electric motor and a petrol engine. It uses less fuel than normal petrol cars and produces less CO_2 and other gases which harm the environment.
app.nea.gov.sg/cms/htdocs/article.asp?pid=699
Diesel-powered ferries produce a lot of pollution. They are a bigger danger to the environment and public health than cars or buses.
www.bluewaternetwork.org/campaign_ss_ferries.shtml

2 A 1

- Look at the photos with the class. Write the word *eco-friendly* on the board. Practise the pronunciation [iːkəʊ ˈfrendli] and elicit the meaning. Ask students how eco-friendly they think the forms of transport in the pictures are.
- Look at the table and the examples with the class. Brainstorm other types of transport with students. Write them in the table. Prompt students if necessary by using definitions or magazine pictures.

2 FOCUS ON...Words A 1 — Suggested answers

Land: car, van, lorry, taxi, train, underground, tram, bike, motorbike, rickshaw, horse, camel
Sea: boat, ship, raft, ferry, hovercraft, yacht, jetski, power boat, sailing boat
Air: plane, helicopter, parachute, hot air balloon

2 A 2

- Read out the task.
- Students complete the sentences with the correct prepositions.
- Check the answers.
- Work out some rules with the class:
  - to travel **by** + transport (BUT: on foot)
  - to get **in** or **into** / **out of a** car, taxi
  - to get **on** / **off** a bike, a horse, a train, plane

2 FOCUS ON...Words A 2 — Suggested answers

a) by	**b)** into (in)	**c)** on
d) off	**e)** in	

2 A 3

- Read out the question. Students discuss it with a partner.
- Students report back briefly to the class. Ask them to say when they use these methods of transport.

2 B

- Read out the words to the class. Check that students can pronounce them correctly.
- Look at the example together. Students match the adjectives with their opposites.
- Check the answers.

2 FOCUS ON...Words B	Answers
1 c 2 e 3 a 4 f 5 d 6 b	

2 C

- Write these headings on the board: *plane, train, car, boat.*
- Ask students: What are the advantages and disadvantages of travelling by plane? Elicit one advantage and one disadvantage and write it on the board.
- Students work in pairs. Ask students to find more advantages and disadvantages for the methods of transport on the board. They should try to use the adjectives in **B**.
- Check their answers.

2 FOCUS ON...Words C — **Suggested answers**

Plane: very quick for long distances, can be cheap, convenient if you live near an airport; very polluting, can be expensive, can be dangerous, inconvenient if you don't live near an airport
Train: eco-friendly, relaxing, usually safe; expensive, slow for very long distances, can't travel over oceans
Car: convenient, quick for short distances, can be cheaper than public transport; stressful, dangerous, polluting
Boat: relaxing, fairly safe (depending on boat), sometimes only way to reach certain remote places; slow, can be polluting

2 D

- Tell students they are going to read an article about air travel. Read out the words from the text. Check that students can pronounce them correctly.
- Ask students to match the words with the correct definitions.
- Check their answers.

2 FOCUS ON...Words D	Answers
1 d 2 f 3 e 4 b 5 h 6 a 7 c 8 g	

2 FOCUS ON...

Ideas

- Read out the statements. Check the meaning of *luxury*.
- Students discuss the statements in pairs. They should give reasons for their answers.
- Students report back briefly to the class.

3 READING — CD2 (Red) track 12, page 51 SB

Picture / background information

The first photo shows aircraft pollution in the form of vapour trails (*contrails* in American English). These are trails of jet exhaust gasses that trap heat and contribute to global warming.
atschool.eduweb.co.uk/kingworc/departments/geography/nottingham/atmosphere/pages/vapourtrails.html
earth.jsc.nasa.gov/EarthObservatory/Contrail_Web_over_the_Central_Rhone_Valley,Eastern_France.htm
www.newscientist.com/article.ns?id=dn2926
The second photo shows a typical overcrowded airport.
www.independenttraveler.com/resources/feature.cfm?AID=597&category=20
Climate change:
www.foe.co.uk/campaigns/climate/issues/climate_change/index.html
en.wikipedia.org/wiki/Kyoto_Protocol
www.greenhouse.gov.au/science/faq/page5.html
Cheap air travel:
www.guardian.co.uk/comment/story/0,,1192157,00.html

3 A

- Look at the photos with the class. Ask students: Do the photos give a positive or negative picture of train travel? How often do you travel by plane? Do you enjoy travelling by plane?
- Read the task with the class. Check that students have understood and remind them to only look for this information.

- Students read the article quickly and find five environmental problems.
- Check the answers with the class.

3 READING A	Answers
Planes cause air pollution, noise and climate change. Airports destroy countryside and create traffic problems.	

3 B

- Students read the extract again more carefully and answer the questions.
- Check the answers.

3 READING B	Answers
1 cheaper (and) cheaper	**2** increase
3 stress (and) heart problems	**4** carbon dioxide
5 global warming	**6** fuel
7 Environmental groups	**8** eco-friendly

4 LANGUAGE: present perfect with *for* or *since*

4 A

- Read out the examples and the questions. Illustrate the expressions 'period of time' and 'starting point in time' by drawing diagrams on the board.
- Students answer the questions orally.

4 LANGUAGE A	Answer
1 for	**2** since

4 B

- Read out the task. Make two lists on the board with the headings *for* and *since*. Add the time expressions from the examples with the help of the class.
- Students work in pairs and make a list of further examples.
- Check the answers. Complete the lists on the board.

4 LANGUAGE B	Suggested answers
for the last ten years, many years, five weeks, two days, three months, ages, a long time	
since the 1960s, 2001, September 11, last week / month / year, yesterday, Christmas, my birthday	

- Ask: How long have you been a student / worked at ...? and / or other questions relevant to your students.
- Refer students to the explanation about the present perfect with *for* and *since* in Workbook Unit 11. They can read the explanation and do the exercises in class or for homework.

5 LISTEN IN

CD1 (Blue) track 16, page 52 SB

Photo / background information

The first photo shows tree planting in Scotland. The second photo shows a child in a glade dwarfed by enormous trees in Argyll on the west coast of Scotland. The Caledonian forest once covered a large part of Scotland, but today less than 1% of it remains. www.treesforlife.org.uk/

The listening text is a conversation between two Scottish men. They are discussing the benefits and disadvantages of a cheap flight to London. One of the possibilities is to calculate the carbon emissions from flights and then plant enough trees to offset or neutralise the carbon.

Carbon offset:
www.carbonneutral.com/calculators/index_shop_calculator.asp
climatecare.trinomics.net/index.cfm
news.nationalgeographic.com/news/2004/08/0809_040809_travelwatch_air_travel.html
www.sundayherald.com/42829

5 A

- Look at the photos with the students. Ask: What is happening in the first photo? What can you see in the second photo? What is the link with air travel?
- Read out the words and phrases in the box. Ask students to find their meaning using a dictionary.
- Check the answers.

5 LISTEN IN A	Answers
travel broadens the mind = travel provides new experiences, makes you see things differently, makes you more tolerant to plant = to put a plant or tree in the ground so it grows to calculate = to find out something using numbers I'm not with you = I don't understand, I can't follow what you're saying So what? = That's not important; Why does that matter? celebrities = famous people	

5 B

- Tell students they are going to listen to a conversation between Nick and Angus. Read out the sentences and check that students understand them.
- Play the CD. Students listen and write the correct names.
- Play the CD again. Students listen and check their answers.
- Check the answers with the class.

5 LISTEN IN B	Answers
1 N 2 A 3 A 4 A 5 N 6 A 7 N	

5 C

- Ask students to give their own personal opinions on the ideas in the listening text. Read out the two questions in turn and discuss them with the class. Ask: Has anybody paid money to plant trees? Do you know anybody who has done this?

Optional activity: Calculations

1 Students use the carbon neutral calculator on www.carbonneutral.com/calculators/index_shop_calculator.asp
or a similar website to calculate the carbon dioxide for a flight from their area to another part of the country or to a popular place abroad. Is the answer surprising?
2 Students calculate the cost of being a 'carbon neutral citizen' – they should see how many trees are necessary each year to make them eco-friendly citizens of their country. They can then compare their carbon dioxide output with other parts of the world.

5 D 1 / 2

- Read out the fact. Elicit reactions. Ask: Do you leave your mobile phone on overnight? Do you always switch it off when it has charged? What other appliances do you leave on standby overnight, using electricity unnecessarily – video machine / DVD, television, computer?
- Say: Saving energy is one way to reduce carbon dioxide. What else can we do? Discuss with the class.

5 LISTEN IN D 2 — **Suggested answers**

Use clean forms of energy (eg solar power, wind power).
Use eco-friendly methods of transport: cycle or walk for short journeys, take the train for longer journeys; use public transport or share cars.
Reduce rubbish and recycle it.

6 YOUR TURN TO SPEAK

A Role play

- Read the task with the class and make sure they understand.
- Prepare the role play by revising the arguments for and against tree planting programmes in the listening text. Write notes on the board.
- Divide the class into pairs. Students decide who the boss is.
- Students practise their role play. They can swap roles and do the role play again.
- Ask for volunteers to act out their role play in front of the class.

B Conversation

- Read the task with the class.
- Go through the phrases in **LB 18** with the class.
- Divide the class into pairs. Students write two more questions for their partner using *How long ...?*
- Students ask and answer the questions.
- Ask some students to report back to the class.
- To consolidate the language used in this activity, do the exercise in **LB 18** with the class. Students ask and answer the questions orally in pairs and note down their partner's answers. Alternatively, ask students to review the phrases in **LB 18** at home and do the exercise for homework.

7 YOUR TOPIC

- Read out the points learners have to prepare to speak about. Remind students to make notes about each point.
- Students can bring in photos or brochures to support their presentation.
- Students can present their trip to the class or smaller groups if you have a large class. Encourage them to ask questions about each other's trips. If students work in groups, ask them to briefly report back to the class.

8 *BIOLOGY in English* Page 53 SB

Picture / background information

More information about the text in this section can be found at:
www.sciencemadesimple.com/leaves.html
www.bbc.co.uk/schools/ks3bitesize/science/biology/plantpro1_1.shtml
See also:
en.wikipedia.org/wiki/Photosynthesis
rivapprod2.riverdeep.net/portal/page?_pageid=336,207152&_dad=portal&_schema=PORTAL

8 A

- Write the word *Photosynthesis* on the board: Look at the diagram with students and ask if they have dealt with photosynthesis in other classes. Ask: What things do trees take in? (carbon dioxide, water). What do they produce? (glucose and oxygen).
- Read out the definitions. Make sure that students understand words such as *breathe* and *flat*. Demonstrate them with actions and objects.
- Students read the text and find the words which match the definitions.
- Check the answers.

8 *BIOLOGY in English* A — Answers

1 oxygen	**2** roots	**3** leaves
4 cell	**5** glucose	**6** sunlight

8 B

- Students complete the sentences with a partner.
- Students check their answers in the text.
- Check the answers.

8 *BIOLOGY in English* B — Answers

1 carbon dioxide; oxygen **2** glucose; water

8 C

- Read out the questions. Students answer orally, referring back to the text if necessary.

8 *BIOLOGY in English* C — Answers

1 Trees take in carbon dioxide which pollutes the air and causes global warming. Trees also produce oxygen. We need this to breathe.
2 Young trees grow more quickly and take in more carbon dioxide. They therefore produce more oxygen.

Optional project: Autumn leaves

- Students work in small groups and find out the answers to the question: *Why do leaves change colour in autumn?* They can use the internet and reference books to find information.
- Choose one group to present their findings to the class. Other groups add or correct information.

9 PORTFOLIO WRITING

- Read out the task and check that students have understood it.
- Copy the essay plan on the board. Expand the notes into a mind map with the help of the students. Add notes to the advantages and disadvantages given and add new positive and negative arguments.
- Elicit from students phrases to express opinion. Remind students to use these in their final paragraph.
- Students write their essay in class or for homework.
- Take in the essays. Read out the best one(s) to the class.

10 *Your answer*

- Finish the unit with a final whole class discussion of ***The BIG Question***: *Will air travel cost the Earth?* Discuss the questions given.
- Refer students to the Workbook Unit 11 exercises.

Last word

- After doing the workbook exercises, students evaluate their performance in the three areas. Check if any students feel they need extra practice in any area.

WORKBOOK answers Pages 26–27 WB

1 Language: present perfect with *for* and *since*

1 A

1 for	**2** since	**3** since
4 since	**5** for	**6** for

1 B

1 I have liked horseriding for a long time.
2 Cheap airlines have been popular since the 1980s.
3 We have used the Channel Tunnel since it opened.
4 My boyfriend and I have had a motorbike for two years.
5 I have flown three times since the beginning of the year.

1 C

1 has been	**2** started	**3** has only become
4 took place	**5** decided	**6** became
7 have just started	**8** haven't agreed	

2 Vocabulary

2 A

1 relaxing	**2** transport	**3** on	**4** by
5 on	**6** eco-friendly	**7** boat	**8** airlines
9 flights	**10** tax		

2 B

1 f **2** c **3** a **4** g **5** b and d **6** e

3 Use of English

1 How long *have you had* your scooter?
2 I'm sorry, that's very *inconvenient.*
3 I got my car *XX years* ago. (depending on the current year)
4 We can't *afford* to go on holiday.
5 Planes *pollute* the air.

4 Pronunciation **CD1 (Blue) track 17**

4 B

1 smart	**2 str**eet	**3 sp**end	**4 sl**edge
5 screen	**6 sm**ell	**7 spr**ing	**8 st**ar

5 Portfolio Writing

(Individual answers)

What's new?
Subject: Money
Language: Modals of certainty and uncertainty: *will* and *might; too* and *enough* (WB)
Functions: LB 19 Using telephone banking
LB 20 Expressing certainty and uncertainty

1 *The BIG question:* HOW HONEST ARE YOU?

The theme of this unit is money and the question of honesty in particular situations. ***The BIG Question*** is: How honest are you? Does honesty depend on the situation? How important is money?

Picture / background information

The information in the **FACT** box is from a survey entitled *Mapping Britain's Moral Values*, Nestlé Family Monitor 8, March 2000. For a summary see: www.mori.com/polls/1999/nfm7.shtml

- Write this saying on the board: *Money makes the world go around*. Ask: What does this saying mean? (eg We need money to live; money is important etc.). Is it true? How important is money? Can we live without it?
- Read out ***The BIG Question*** and check that students understand the word 'honest'.
- Read through the **FACT** box with the class. Draw attention to the two different statistics. Ask: Why do young people think honesty is less important? What do you think? Do you think honesty is the most important quality?

2 FOCUS ON...

Words

Picture / background information

Banking in the UK:
www.qck.com/banking.html?searchsite=business data&sourcekey=banking
Banking in the USA:
www.foreignborn.com/self-help/banking/index.htm
Most high-street banks provide 24-hour telephone and internet banking.

2 A

- Ask students a general question to get an overview of how familiar they are with banks and banking services: Do you use banks?
- Look at the banking words with students. Look at the example together and do the next word as another example together.
- Students match the rest of the words with the definitions.
- Check the answers.

2 FOCUS ON...Words A	Answers
1 e **2** c **3** a **4** f **5** b **6** d	

- Ask students: Do you have a bank account? (If so …) Do you use cashpoints? How do you check your bank balance?

2 B

- Ask students: When are the banks open in your country? Is telephone banking popular? What do you have to tell the bank assistant when you use telephone banking?
- Look at the dialogue in **LB 19** with students. Ask two students to read it out to the class. Ask: What does the bank assistant ask the customer so she can check he really is that person? (his mother's maiden name); How much is his bank balance?
- Students read the dialogue with a partner.
- Students role-play a new dialogue using their own information. First they should invent a bank account number and a bank balance. Students take it in turns to play the customer. The bank assistant should note down the information.
- Ask one or two pairs to act out their dialogue in front of the class. Check that other students in the class can spell their name correctly. Revise the alphabet if necessary.

2 C

- Look at the pictures with the class. Ask: What can you see in the pictures?
  Picture 1: a woman with a dog is sitting on the street in a town; she's playing a flute; there's a bowl in front of her; she wants money
  Picture 2: a girl is talking to her mum; behind her back she is holding a purse; she's taking some money out of the purse
  Picture 3: there's a pig / a piggy bank with some money in it
- Read out words 1–8 in the box. Ask students to choose the correct word for each picture. Students answer orally.

2 FOCUS ON...Words C	Answers
Picture 1: beg **Picture 2:** steal **Picture 3:** save	

- Ask: In picture **1**, the girl is playing music. Is that begging? Do people beg for money in your town / area? How do you feel about that? What about picture **2**? Is it wrong to take money from your parents? Is this really stealing? Picture **3**: Is it a good idea to save money like this? What other ways are there to save money?
- Check the meaning of the other words in the box.

2 D

- Students read the sentences and complete them with the correct words from exercise **C**.
- Check the answers.

2 FOCUS ON...Words D	Answers
a) invest **b)** win **c)** spend **d)** earn **e)** borrow	

- Ask: Do you think it's a good idea to play the lottery? Do you know anybody who has won a lot of money in a lottery?

2 E

- Read through the questions with the class and check that students understand them. As money can be a sensitive issue, give students the option not to answer questions if they wish. Teach them the phrase 'No comment' but point out this isn't just an excuse for laziness!
- Students work in pairs and ask and answer the questions.
- Ask the class who has a job. Find out what the jobs are and how many hours they work. Ask where other students get their money from.

2 FOCUS ON...

Ideas

- Read the questions out and check that students understand them.
- Students work in pairs and discuss the questions.
- Discuss the questions briefly with the class.

3 READING

CD 2 (Red) track 13, page 55 SB

Picture / background information

The two photos show people using cashpoints. These are called ATMs (Automatic Teller Machines in Australia). Cashpoint fraud is a big problem in many countries, with organised gangs using skimming devices on machines which copy card details and also tiny cameras which record PIN numbers.
www.genesisgroupuk.com/news/index.shtml
www.proximalconsulting.com
The articles in this section concern cases where people receive 'free' money from cashpoints by chance. The names of places and people have been changed in the articles, but both stories are true cases. See:
www.telegraph.co.uk/news/main.jhtml?xml=/news/2003/01/16/ncash16.xml
www.washtimes.com/upi-breaking/20040428-124811-9774r.htm

3 A

- Look at the photos and article headings with the class. Ask students: What do you think the articles are about? Elicit ideas.
- Read out the task. Ask students to read the articles quickly to answer the questions. Remind them they are reading only for this general information; they shouldn't worry about details at this stage.
- Check the answers.

3 READING A	Answers
In both articles cashpoints make mistakes and give people 'free money'. The first story has a happy ending.	

3 B

- Read through the sentences with the class and check students understand them.
- Students read the articles again and answer the questions. Check the answers.

3 READING B — **Answers**

1 B **2** 2 **3** 1 **4** B **5** 1 **6** 2

3 C

- Read out the questions and check students understand them.
- Students work in pairs and discuss the questions.
- Discuss the questions with the class. What is the opinion of the majority?

Optional activity: Cashpoint fraud

- Discuss the problems of cashpoint fraud and security with the class. Help them if necessary or ask students to research the topic for homework (also in their own language).
- Students work with a partner or a small group and make a security poster to be put up near a cashpoint, warning people of the dangers of credit card fraud. For example:
  - *Be careful when you put in your PIN number: don't let people watch you.*
  - *There might be a camera in the machine. Look at it carefully.*
  - *Does the machine have an extra part? Don't use it!*
  - *Make sure you get your card back!*
  - *Put your money away carefully.*
- Students look at each other's posters. Who has the most effective ideas?

4 LANGUAGE: Modals of certainty and uncertainty

will and *might*

4 A

- Look at the use of the modals *might* and *will*. Tell students that *might* and *will* can both be used to talk about predictions for the future. Read out the examples and ask students to find them in context in the text.
- Read out each question in turn and make sure the words *certain* and *uncertain* are clear. Students answer orally.
- Ask: Which modal verb do we use when we are certain about a future action? (*will*) Which modal verb indicates uncertainty? (*might*)

4 LANGUAGE A — **Answers**

1 Many of their neighbours *will* join them there.
2 It *might* be your lucky day.

4 B

- Look at the form of the modals with the class. First look at the examples in **A** again and ask: What type of verbs comes after *might* and *will*? Prompt students if necessary.
- Ask: What other modal verbs do you know? (eg *can, should*). Ask for examples and write them on the board. Point out that all these modals are also followed by the infinitive without *to*.
- Ask students what the negative and question forms of *will* and the modals on the board are (eg *can't, can I; shouldn't, should I*). Elicit or point out that we don't use 'do' to form these negatives and question forms.
- Ask: What are the negative and interrogative forms of *might*? Students answer using the 'rule' to help them and then find examples in the text.

4 LANGUAGE B — **Answers**

The infinitive without *to* comes after *might* and *will*.
Negative and interrogative forms of might: might not (mightn't); Might I / you / he, etc.?
Examples:
The bank might not notice the mistake.
Might you do the same thing?

- Refer students to the explanation about *might* and *will* in Workbook Unit 12. They can read the explanation and do the exercises in class or for homework.
- The Workbook also contains an extra grammar point: *too* and *enough*. Students can read the explanation and do the exercise at home or you can deal with this point in class.

5 LISTEN IN — CD 1 (Blue) track 18, page 56 SB

5 A

- Read out the question and discuss it with the class. Ask students to give reasons for their answers.

5 B

- Look at the quiz with the class. Make sure students understand the questions. Check, for example, *change* in question **3** and *immediately* in question **5**.
- Students work in pairs. One student reads out the question and notes his / her partner's answers. The other student answers the questions. Then they swap roles.

5 C

- Tell students they are going to listen to Leanne and Kirsty doing the honesty quiz. Play the CD. Students listen and tick the correct answers for Leanne.
- Play the CD again. Students listen and check their answers.
- Check the answers with the class.

5 LISTEN IN C — **Answers**

1 b **2** a **3** a **4** b **5** a

5 D

- Ask students to compare their answers with Leanne's. Go through each question and discuss if students agreed or disagreed with Leanne and why.
- Say: Leanne had three a)'s and two b)'s. The magazine said: 'You're quite honest – but only in some situations. Remember: taking something that isn't yours is always stealing.' Do you agree?
- Ask students to count up their partner's a)'s and b)'s. Ask students to put their hands up for their score and read out the relevant part of the key below. Ask students if they think the key fits. If not, ask them to write a new one.

5 LISTEN IN QUIZ — **Answers**

5 a)'s and **0** b)'s:	Wow, congratulations! Honesty must be your middle name! (But are you sure you answered truthfully??)
4 a)'s and **1** b):	Good, you're an honest person – but not 100%. Why did you make a mistake?
3 a)'s and **2** b)'s:	You're quite honest – but only in some situations. Remember: taking something that isn't yours is always stealing.
2 a)'s and **3** b)'s:	Oh, dear! Didn't your parents teach you right and wrong?
1 a) and **4** b)'s:	Terrible! Haven't you heard of honesty?
0 a)'s and **5** b)'s:	Sorry, but you're a thief!

Optional project: A new class quiz

- Students work with a partner and write another quiz question about honesty, similar to the ones used in the honesty quiz.
- Students test their questions on another pair.
- Students report back to the class about the other pair's question. Put the five best questions together as a new quiz.
- Students write the key for the quiz. They can work in pairs or groups and write one part of the key each.
- Make copies of the quiz and ask students to do it. Alternatively, the quiz can be given to another class.

6 YOUR TURN TO SPEAK

A Role play

- Read the task with the class and make sure students understand it.
- Divide the class into pairs. Students decide who is the 'friend'.
- Students do their role play. They can swap roles and do the role play again.
- Ask for volunteers to act out their role play in front of the class.
- With the class, discuss the advice that students gave their friend.

B Conversation

- Read the task with the class.
- Go through the phrases in **LB 20** with the class. Make sure that the level of certainty of each expression is clear (eg *probably* is less certain than *definitely* / *certainly*).
- Divide the class into pairs. Students discuss the questions.
- Ask some students to report back to the class.
- To consolidate the language used in this activity, do the exercise in **LB 20** with the class. Students ask and answer the questions orally in pairs and

note down their partner's answers. Alternatively, ask students to review the phrases in **LB 20** at home and write their answers for homework. They can then compare their answers with a partner in the next lesson.

7 YOUR TOPIC

- Read out the points learners have to prepare to speak about and check that the points are clear.
- This presentation should be done in groups as the content is quite challenging. Divide students into small groups. In their groups, students brainstorm ideas and make notes for each point.
- Students decide who is going to present each point.
- Each group presents its talk to another group. Encourage students to ask and answer questions.
- Ask each group to briefly report back to the class about the other group's presentation.

8 *MATHS in English* Page 57 SB

Picture / background information

The dollar ($), made up of 100 cents, is the currency of the USA. The dollar is the most important reserve currency in the world (held by governments and used for buying products on the global market such as oil and gold) because of the size of the US economy (although the euro is becoming increasingly important as a reserve currency). The dollar can be used in many countries as payment in shops or hotels. There are coins for 1 cent to $1. Many coins have common names: 5 cents is a 'nickel', ten cents is a 'dime', 25 cents a 'quarter' and one dollar is a 'buck'. Banknotes are from $1 to $100 and show the pictures of US presidents.

Ecuador replaced its currency (the sucre) with the US dollar in 2000. In Panama the US dollar is the official paper currency; the country does have its own currency (the balboa) but it is only used for coins.
en.wikipedia.org/wiki/Dollar
www.secretservice.gov/money_history.shtml
www.bep.treas.gov/section.cfm/4

The euro (€), made up of 100 cent, is the common currency of the Eurozone. It came into being as part of the European Economic and Monetary Union, as agreed in the 1992 Maastricht Treaty. The euro is administered by the European System of Central Banks that is the European Central Bank (ECB) in Frankfurt and the banks of the member states. The ECB is responsible for monetary policy and the banks of the member states for printing and minting the notes and coins. Coins have the same design on the side that shows the value and a different design on the national side: this shows the national monarch or a national symbol. Notes have the same design on both sides. There are coins for one cent to €2; banknotes are €5 to €500. The official plural forms are *euro* and *cent*, but the plurals *euros* and *cents* are also sometimes used in spoken and written language.
en.wikipedia.org/wiki/Euro#Towards_a_multi-cultural_name_for_the_currency
www.ecb.int/bc/html/index.en.html

Yen (¥) has been the official currency of Japan since 1871. It was formerly divided into Sen and Rin but these have not been used since 1954. There are coins for ¥1–¥500 yen; banknotes are from ¥1,000 to ¥10,000.
en.wikipedia.org/wiki/Japanese_yen
www.boj.or.jp/en/money/money_f.htm

Pound sterling (£) is the currency of the United Kingdom. The name comes from the fact that the pound was originally the value of one pound weight of sterling silver. It is still called the Pound Sterling and it dates back over 900 years as the only currency of England. For most of that period it was divided into 12 shillings and 240 pence. Decimalisation of the pound (transfer to a decimal system) took place in 1971. Shillings disappeared and there are 100 pence (generally known as 'p') to the £. The pound is used in England, Wales, Scotland and Northern Ireland. In Scotland and Northern Ireland banks print their own banknotes and they have a different design to English banknotes. There are coins from 1p to £2 and notes from £5 to £50.
en.wikipedia.org/wiki/Pound_Sterling
www.bankofengland.co.uk/banknotes/index.htm

8 A 1

- Look at the title of the page and the photos with the class. Ask: What is foreign exchange? (changing money from one country into another country's money). Explain that the word for a country's money is *currency*. Ask: What is the currency of our / your country? What are the most important currencies in the world? (dollar, yen, euro)

- Refer students to the photos. Ask: What is the value of each note? Make sure that students use the plural forms correctly: euro (see above) / yen / dollars / pounds.
- Ask students if they know what the smaller units of currency are for each country. For example, one euro is a hundred …? (euro / cent; yen: no smaller units any more; dollar / cents; pound / pence – one penny).

8 *MATHS in English* A 1 **Answers**

one hundred euro; fifty euro, five euro
one thousand yen
fifty dollars, ten dollars
ten pounds

8 A 2

- Ask students: What countries use the currencies in the photos? Discuss each currency individually.
- Depending on your students' interests and experience, you might like to give them, or elicit from them, more information about the currencies, for example, the history of the euro, the importance of the dollar or slang names for US coins (see **Background information**).

8 *MATHS in English* A 2 **Answers**

€: (16 members, 2006–2009): Austria, Belgium, Cyprus, Finland, France, Germany, Greece, Ireland, Italy, Luxembourg, Malta, Netherlands, Portugal, Slovakia, Slovenia, Spain. **¥**: Japan; **$**: USA; **£**: UK

8 B

- In this exercise students practise using a foreign exchange chart and find out (approximate) exchange rates. Look at the foreign exchange chart with the class. Explain that this is an example of a chart showing foreign exchange rates (how much money you can get for the same amount in another currency) and that the rates are NOT current.
- Do the first question with the class as an example. First look at the formulation and explain that this means 'How many yen can you get for one US dollar?' Ask students to find the column in the chart with the heading *US dollar* and then move down the column until they find *yen*. The figure shown is the equivalent to $1.
- Students work individually or with a partner and do the remaining questions.
- Check the answers.

8 *MATHS in English* B **Answers**

(according to the chart – today's exchange rate may be different)

1 100.511 **2** 1.1033 **3** 1.3323

8 C

- In this exercise students practise calculations using foreign exchange rates. Look at the foreign exchange chart again with the class. Ask students to find the column in the chart with the heading *Euro* and find out the exchange rate for pounds (0.9061. Write £5 X €0.9061 on the board and ask students to calculate it. The answer is £4.5305 (rounded down £4.53). Make sure that the process is clear. Repeat if necessary.
- Students work individually or with a partner and do the remaining questions.
- Check the answers.

8 *MATHS in English* C **Answers**

(according to the chart – today's exchange rate may be different)

1 £4.5305 **2** ¥5025.5 **3** $147.00

8 D

- Read out the questions in turn and discuss them with the class. Check the exchange rate of your currency against the dollar before the class or ask students to find this out for homework. If your currency is in the chart on page 57, compare the current rate against the dollar to the example rate in the chart.

Optional project: Planning a holiday

Students work in small groups. They should imagine they are going on holiday together and need to work out how much money they need. They should:

- choose a holiday destination and decide how long their holiday will be;
- find out the currency of their holiday country, if prices are generally high or low, (they could also find out the VAT rate for that country) and the foreign exchange rate;

- calculate how much money they will need for food and general spending money and calculate how much foreign currency they might need.

Each group should choose one student to present their ideas to the class.

9 PORTFOLIO WRITING

- Read out the task and check that students have understood it. Again, as money might be a sensitive issue with students, emphasise that the essays are only for your eyes.
- Write the title of the essay on the board: *Are you good with money?* Work out a possible paragraph plan with students: look at the questions asked and elicit examples for the content of each paragraph. For example:
  Paragraph 1: where you get your money (parents, job etc) and how often; if you think this amount is enough or not.
  Paragraph 2: what you spend money on, how much you save and how.
  Paragraph 3: if you think you are good with money; how your situation might change in the future / what you hope will change in the future.
- Elicit from students phrases to express opinion. Remind students to use these in their final paragraph.
- Students write their essay in class or for homework.
- Take in the essays and check them. Give individual feedback either in written form or orally.

10 *Your answer*

- Finish the unit with a final whole class discussion of ***The BIG Question***: *How honest are you?* (if you think the question can produce further discussion). Otherwise, ask several students to quickly sum up their own opinion.
- Refer students to the Workbook Unit 12 activities.

Last word

- After doing the workbook activities, students evaluate their performance in the three areas. Check if any students feel they need extra practice in any area.

WORKBOOK answers

Pages 28–29 WB

1 Language: modals of certainty and uncertainty: *will* and *might*

1 A

1 won't **2** might **3** might not / mightn't
4 will / 'll **5** won't **6** might not
7 will / 'll **8** might

1 B

(Example answer)
I'll definitely buy lots of new clothes. And I'll definitely give my parents some money.
I might buy my own house. And I might go on a really nice holiday.

1 C

1 good enough **2** too generous **3** enough money
4 too many

2 Vocabulary

2 A

1 bank account **2** earn **3** exchange rate
4 bank balance **5** cashpoint **6** currency
7 note **8** borrow **9** save
10 steal **11** beg

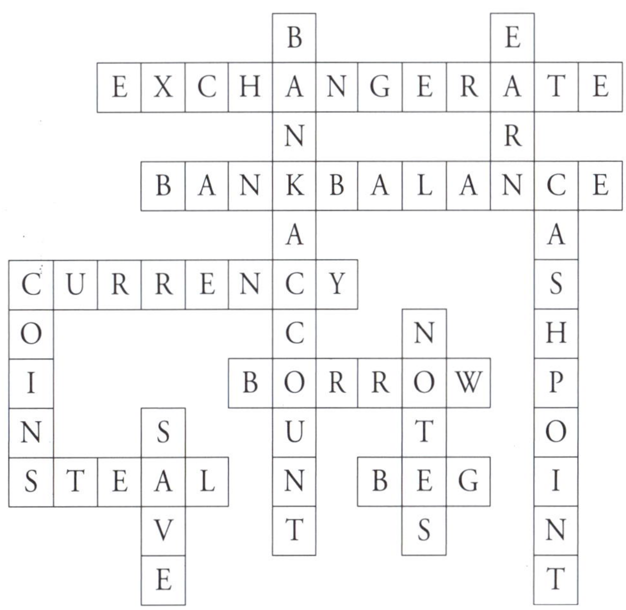

3 Connections

3 A

1 from **2** on **3** in **4** for **5** into

3 B

1 dishonest **2** lend **3** poor **4** strong

4 Use of English

1 The company is looking for *investors.*
2 The bank *might* close down.
3 The assistant gave me £20 change *instead of* £10.
4 The bank's opening hours aren't *long enough.*
5 The customers were very *surprised.*

5 Portfolio Writing

(Individual answers)

What's new?

Subject:	Cars and bicycles
Language:	Infinitive of purpose; order of adjectives
Functions:	**LB 21** Expressing intention and purpose
Pronunciation:	Consonant clusters 2, CD1 (Blue) track 20

1 *The BIG question:* DO CARS RULE OUR LIVES?

The theme of this unit is cars and bicycles. ***The BIG Question*** is: Do cars rule our lives? Are cars a great or terrible invention? Are bicycles better?

- Read out ***The BIG Question***. Ask for brief initial reactions.
- Look at the **FACT** box with the class. Ask students if these figures mean anything to them. If not, tell students that the world population is about 6,500 million (2005). Ask them to work out how many people there are for each car (approximately 12 people per car globally). It is estimated that there will be 1 billion cars in the world by 2020.

Picture / background information

Global car use: with 550 million cars in the world, it means that globally there are about twelve people for every car. And 81 per cent of cars are used in developed countries: in 2003, there were 196 million drivers and 231 million cars in the USA (for a population of 296 million people). However, the number of cars in developing countries is growing significantly, especially in China, India, East and Southeast Asia.
www.people.hofstra.edu/geotrans/eng/ch3en/conc3en/carprodfleet.html
www.newscientist.com/popuparticle.ns?id=in36
www.fhwa.dot.gov/policy/ohim/hs03/htm/dlchrt.htm
Car drivers by gender: In 2003, the number of male licensed drivers and the numbers of female licensed drivers in the USA was approximately the same.
www.fhwa.dot.gov/policy/ohim/hs03/htm/dl1c.htm
In 2004, 61 per cent of women in Great Britain held a full car driving licence, compared with 81 per cent of men. (In 1975, only 29 per cent of women had a licence, versus 69 per cent of men.)
www.statistics.gov.uk/cci/nugget.asp?id=1093
Driving ages:
www.2pass.co.uk/ages.htm
History of the car:
www.si.edu/resource/faq/nmah/earlycars.htm
www.loc.gov/rr/scitech/mysteries/auto.html
www.inventors.about.com/library/inventors/blcar.htm

2 FOCUS ON...

Words

2 A 1

- Tell students the words in the box are parts of bicycles and cars. Read out the words and ask students to repeat them. Point out the silent 'h' in *wheel* (which students met in Unit 10) and *exhaust*.
- Look at the photos and the example with the class.
- Students match the rest of the words with the correct parts of the cars or bicycles.
- Check the answers.

2 FOCUS ON...Words A 1 **Answers**
Car picture: helmet, steering wheel, exhaust pipe
Bike: helmet, handlebars, saddle, pedal

2 A

- Read out the first question. First ask for a show of hands to see how many students have a bike. Then ask several students to describe their bike and when they use it. How many students come to college / English classes by bike?
- For the second question, point out the example answers. Ask: What else is important? Then collect any other ideas on the board (for example, 'It's big / small / cheap / expensive / new / old'; 'It doesn't use much fuel'; 'It's eco-friendly'). Establish if there is any difference between girls' and boys' answers.
- Teach the word *driving licence* (US: *driver's license*). Discuss how old you have to be to have a driving licence in your country and compare this

with other countries (GB, Ireland, Poland: 17; most other European countries, eg France, Germany, Spain, Italy: 18; USA: 16 in most states, but 14 or 15 in some states; New Zealand: 15, Australia: 16–17, most other countries in the world: 18). Talk about how important car ownership is in your country compared to public transport and what most people use their cars for (short or long distances).

- If relevant in your class, ask: Does anybody have a driving licence? How long have you had it? Does anybody already have a car? What is your car like?

2 B

- Read out the words on the left. Make sure students can pronounce *vehicle* correctly.
- Look at the example with the class. You might like to ask students what this is in their own language.
- Students match the rest of the words to the definitions using a dictionary.
- Check the answers.

2 FOCUS ON…Words B	Answers
1 e **2** d **3** a **4** g **5** b **6** f **7** c **8** h	

Optional activity: Traffic collocations

- Write the words in exercise **B** on the board.
- Go through each word in turn with students and try and find verbs and/or prepositions which go with the nouns. For example:
  1 drive on the motorway
  2 drive a vehicle
  3 stop at the traffic lights
  4 stop at / turn right or left at a junction
  5 drive around a roundabout
  6 be in / get stuck in a traffic jam
  7 increase / reduce your speed
  8 have an accident
- Prompt students as necessary.
- You could ask students to write example sentences for homework.

2 C

- Read out the words in the box. Illustrate their meaning with actions or pictures on the board.
- Read out each sentence in turn and ask students to answer orally.
- Alternatively, ask students to complete the sentences individually or in pairs and then check the answers with the class.

2 FOCUS ON…Words C	Answers
1 brake **2** park **3** crash **4** overtake **5** accelerate	

2 FOCUS ON…

Ideas

- Read out the questions in turn and discuss them with the class. Do not go into too much detail as the next pages offer more material on these topics.

3 READING CD2 (Red) track 14, page 59 SB

Picture / background information

The top photo shows a popular American SUV (sport's utility vehicle) called a Hummer. Hummers (which are derived from a military vehicle) and other SUVs have been criticised for being dangerous and also bad for the environment due to high fuel consumption. In British English SUVs are usually known as 4-wheel drives (all four wheels are powered).
www.suv.org/environ.html
www.twincities.indymedia.org/feature/display_printable/16588/index.php
www.suvoa.com/press/042004/index.cfm
The bottom photo shows a motorway accident on the M25 which is the ring road around London. At 118 miles long it is the longest city ring road in the world. Because it is so congested it is sometimes known jokingly as the longest car park in the world.
Road rage:
www.dol.wa.gov/ds/roadrage.htm
www.news.bbc.co.uk/1/hi/wales/south_west/4105353.stm
www.cbsnews.com/stories/2000/11/14/48hours/main249419.shtml
www.sptimes.com/2005/03/10/Hillsborough/Bumper_sticker_evokes.shtml
www.newsvote.bbc.co.uk/mpapps/pagetools/print/news.bbc.co.uk/1/hi/uk/3146781.stm
www.drivers.com/article/462

3 A

- Look at the photos with the class. Look at the first photo and elicit or explain the meaning of SUV. Ask students: What is special about this type of car? What do you know about SUVs? Look at the second photo and ask students what they can see. Ask: How do you feel when you see photos like this?
- Read out the tasks and check that students understand them. Remind students to read the article quickly.
- Check the answers.

3 READING A **Answers**

1 Road rage is when a driver uses his or her car like a weapon in order to harm another driver.
2 Paragraph 1: Angry drivers use cars as weapons
Paragraph 2: Road rage driver shoots woman
Paragraph 3: Traffic jams cause stress
Paragraph 4: Military-style vehicles
Paragraph 5: Speed kills

3 B

- Read out the true / false statements and check that students understand them.
- Students work individually or in pairs. They read the article again and decide if the statements are true or false. Ask students to say why.
- Check the answers.

3 READING B **Answers**

1 False (It has been a problem for a long time. Road rage is a new problem.)
2 False (It is mostly a problem among young men but women and older people also commit road rage attacks.)
3 True (They are stressed because there are too many cars on the roads.)
4 True (It is easy to frighten other drivers with a big SUV.)
5 False (More people die in road accidents.)

3 C

- Read out the first two questions in turn and discuss them with the class.
- Read out question **3** and refer students to the prompts. With the class, brainstorm ideas on the board for making our roads safer. If your class is interested in the topic, discuss the ideas in more detail. Alternatively, they can do the optional project below.

Optional project: Safer roads brochure

- Ask students to work in pairs or small groups.
- Students research road death statistics in their country and possible reasons.
- Students think of ways to make the roads safer in their country, using the information they have found and the ideas discussed in exercise **C**.
- Students make a brochure for drivers about safe driving. They can add pictures or photos.
- Students read each other's brochures and vote for the best one.

4 LANGUAGE: Infinitive of purpose

4 A

- Refer students to the example sentences and read out the question.
- Students read the example sentences and answer the question.
- Check the answer. Discuss what function the infinitive with *to* has in the other sentence.

4 LANGUAGE A **Answer**

Sentences 1, 2 and 4. (In sentence 3 *to* is part of the verb *have to*).

- In addition, you might like to teach students how to use *so that* to express purpose. Reformulate the first sentence and write it on the board: *They brake suddenly so that they annoy other drivers*. Elicit the structure of the *so that* clause from students and write that on the board (*so that* + subject + verb). Reformulate the two other sentences with students using this structure.
- Refer students to the explanation about the infinitive of purpose in Workbook Unit 13. They can read the explanation and do the exercises in class or for homework.
- The Workbook also contains an extra grammar point: order of adjectives. This is something many students have difficulties with. Students can read the explanation and do the exercises at home or you can deal with this point in class.

5 LISTEN IN CD1 (Blue) track 19, page 60 SB

Picture / background information

All the people taking part in the radio discussion are British English speakers.

5 A

- Look at the photos with the class. Ask: When is the photo from? Can you describe the car? Who is in the car? What are they doing? How are they feeling?
- Write *Cars:* + on the board. With students, make a list of the good things about cars under the heading. Use the photos to prompt students.
- Leave the list on the board for task **D**.

5 LISTEN IN A **Possible answers**

Convenience: A car is an easy way to transport lots of people and especially good for travelling with children. You can travel door to door and don't have to go to a bus stop / station / airport first. You can travel when you want – you don't have to wait for buses, trains or planes.
Luggage: The car can carry heavy luggage / personal objects / shopping / …
Freedom: It's a good feeling to drive on empty roads, listening to music, especially in an open-top car.

5 B

- Tell students they are going to listen to a radio discussion about cars. Read out the four opinions and check that students understand them.
- Play the CD. Students listen and write the correct speakers for the opinions.
- Students compare their answers with a partner.
- Check the answers.

5 LISTEN IN B **Answers**

1 Deborah **2** Helen **3** Alex **4** Graham

5 C

- Read out the task.
- Play the CD. Students listen again and choose the correct alternatives.
- Students compare their answers with a partner.
- Check the answers.

5 LISTEN IN C **Answers**

1 b **2** b **3** b **4** a

5 D

- Write the word *cars* on the board next to the list of good things about cars. Now make a list of the bad things about cars with the class. Use ideas from the listening and make up others.
- Make sure students make notes on the lists in preparation for task **5D**.

5 LISTEN IN D **Possible answers**

Stress: Traffic jams; aggressive drivers make drivers stressed.
Health: It is healthier to use a bike for short journeys; cars make you lazy.
Space: Roads, car parks, etc. take up lots of space in cities. We could use the space better – for parks, for example.
Environment: Cars pollute the environment (produce carbon dioxide).
Road safety: Millions of people die or are injured in car accidents.

6 YOUR TURN TO SPEAK

A Role play

- Read the task with the class and make sure students understand it.
- Go through the phrases in **LB 21** with the class.
- Prepare the role play by asking students for ideas about why teenagers might need a car (eg lack of public transport; safe travel at night so that parents don't have to take their children everywhere) and why parents might be for or against their teenager having a car (cost of buying and running a car, accidents, risky activity etc).
- Students work in pairs and practise their role play. They can swap roles and do the role play again.
- Ask for volunteers to act out their role play in front of the class.
- With the class, discuss if teenagers really need their own cars.
- To consolidate the language used in this activity, review the phrases in **LB 21** again and do the exercise in **LB 21** orally with the class.

B Conversation

- Read the task with the class and check that students understand it.
- Divide the class into pairs. Students discuss the arguments for and against cars and decide whether they are for a world with or without cars.
- Take a class vote on 'For' or 'Against' by asking for a show of hands. What is the class opinion? Ask students from both sides to explain their reasons.

7 YOUR TOPIC

- Read out the points learners have to prepare to speak about and check that the points are clear.
- This presentation is best done in pairs or groups. Students brainstorm ideas and make notes for each point.
- Students decide who is going to present each point.
- Each pair or group presents its talk to another pair or group. Encourage students to ask and answer questions.
- Ask each pair or group to briefly report back to the class about the other pair or group's presentation.

Optional activity: Safety for cyclists

- Ask students to work in small groups.
- Students brainstorm a list of safety rules for cyclists (for example: wear a helmet; wear bright clothes so that drivers can see you; use lights at night; check bike regularly to make sure it is safe; follow rules of the road – don't cross traffic lights when they are red; don't ride on the wrong side of the road; don't ride on the pavement; use cycle lanes if possible). Help groups with vocabulary as necessary.
- Students make a poster about safety for cyclists. They can add pictures or photos.
- Students display their posters in the classroom.

8 *PHYSICS in English* Page 61 SB

Picture / background information

Land speed record:
www.edition.cnn.com/TECH/9710/15/brits.land.speed/index.html
www.thrustssc.com/thrustssc/contents_frames.html
www.landspeed.com/learn.asp
www.en.wikipedia.org/wiki/Land_speed_record

Sound waves and sonic booms:
www.physicscentral.com/action/action-04-03-print.html
www.physicsclassroom.com/Class/sound/U11L3b.html
www.pbs.org/wgbh/nova/barrier/boom/answer3.html

8 A

- Tell the class this page is about speed. Ask students to give you a definition of speed (how fast a vehicle or object moves). Ask: How do we measure speed? (in kilometres per hour/kph or miles per hour/mph). Ask: What is the top speed of a normal car?
- Look at the photo of the vehicle with the class. Ask: What sort of vehicle is this? What do people use vehicles like this for? (To try and travel as fast as possible; to break speed records).
- Students read the text and find words and phrases in the text which match the definitions in **A**.
- Check the answers.

8 *PHYSICS in English* A — **Answers**

1 supersonic **2** altitude **3** sound wave
4 sonic boom

8 B

- Ask: What was special about the car in the photo, *Thrust SSC*? Read out the task.
- Students complete the notes.
- Check the answers.
- Refer students to the sound waves diagrams and ask: What happens when a vehicle travels faster than the speed of sound? (It hits its own sound waves and pushes them back.); What does this action produce? (Shockwaves.); What happens when the shockwaves hit the ground? (They produce a very loud noise called a sonic boom). Make sure students have understood this process. Ask if they had heard about sonic booms before.

8 *PHYSICS in English* B — **Answers**

1 jet **2** land speed **3** the speed of sound
4 1,221 kph and 1,233 kph

8 C

- Read out the questions in turn and discuss them with the class.

Optional project: Speed records

- Students work in small groups and find out information about one of the following, depending on their interests:
- **air speed** records
- **water speed** records
- further research on **land speed** records: electric/ solar-powered cars, stock car racing etc.
- Students make a small presentation (max. 10 minutes) to the class about their findings. They can include visual material.

Possible sources:
www.bluebird-electric.net/bluebird_site_navigator.htm
www.nasaexplores.com/show2_5_8a.php?id=04-071&gl=58
www.en.wikipedia.org/wiki/Water_speed_record
www.speedace.info

9 PORTFOLIO WRITING

- Read out the task and check that students have understood it.
- Write the title on the board: *A city without cars.*
- Brainstorm with students adjectives or phrases to describe what the city looks like (for example, beautiful, green: more trees, flowers and green spaces; lively, exciting: lots of people on the streets, open-air cafes, market stalls, street entertainers; OR still, deserted: no cars, no movement, no energy) and how the city sounds (for example, peaceful: no traffic, birds singing; happy: children playing, people talking; too quiet, boring; traffic is a part of city life!) how the city smells (for example, clean: no pollution from exhaust pipes).
- Students write their descriptions in class or for homework. Remind them to organise their descriptions into paragraphs and be careful with the order of adjectives.
- Take in the descriptions and check them. Read out the best one(s).

10 *Your answer*

- Ask students to summarise their opinions of ***The BIG Question***: Do cars rule our lives? Focus on the sub-questions asked.
- Refer students to the Workbook Unit 13 activities.

Last word

- After doing the workbook activities, students evaluate their performance in the three areas. Check if any students feel they need extra practice in any area.

WORKBOOK answers — Pages 30–31 WB

1 Language: infinitive of purpose

1 A

1 The government is planning new laws (in order to) stop aggressive driving.
2 I need my bike (in order to) cycle to the station.
3 I'm going to take my driving test (in order to) be more independent.
4 They are building more cycle lanes (in order to) encourage more cyclists.
5 I wear a cycle helmet (in order to) protect me against dangerous drivers.
6 I cycled to the newsagents (in order to) buy a magazine.

1 B

(Example answers)
1 I'd like to have a car to go on trips with my friends.
2 I'm learning English to get a good job.
3 I intend to study hard to get good marks.
4 I phone my friends to talk about everything.
5 I use the internet to get information about lots of different things.

1 C

1 My mum drives a tiny old Fiat.
2 They're planning a big new motorway.
3 I'd like a cool red Ferrari.
4 Inexperienced young drivers often cause accidents.
5 My bike has an uncomfortable black saddle.

1 D

(Individual answers)

2 Vocabulary

2 A

1 c **2** e **3** d **4** g **5** b **6** a **7** f

2 B

1 a **2** f **3** h **4** d **5** e **6** b 7 c **8** g

3 Pronunciation CD1 (Blue) track 20

3 B

1 past	**2** spend	**3** disk	**4** front
5 bank	**6** intend	7 test	**8** sound

4 Use of English

1 I *might* not pass my driving test.
2 I have a *new blue* helmet.
3 They drove at full *speed*.
4 That's the *opinion* of a lot of teenagers.
5 You're a *good driver*.
6 The driver *accelerated*.

5 Portfolio Writing

(Individual answers)

What's new?

Subject:	Special occasions, family
Language:	Asking about and describing past activities and events
Functions:	**LB 22** Asking about and describing past activities
	LB 23 Asking about and describing past events
Pronunciation:	Intonation in statements, CD1 (Blue) track 22

1 *The BIG question:* FAMILIES – HELL OR HAPPINESS?

The theme of this unit is special occasions and families. ***The BIG Question*** is: Families – hell or happiness? How important is your family to you? Do you celebrate special occasions as a family?

- Read out ***The BIG Question***. Write the two words 'Hell' and 'Happiness' on the board with the word 'Family' in the middle. Ask students to suggest words for each one (for example: Hell: rules, lots of people and no space, no time alone, no freedom, too many different opinions, problems and arguments; Happiness: people you know and love, not being alone, help when you have problems, a home, meals.)
- Look at the **FACT** box with the class. Ask for brief reactions.

Picture / background information

The information in the **FACT** box is from the Mental Health Foundation of the UK. For more details, go to their website:
www.mentalhealth.org.uk/page.cfm?pageurl=Stress.cfm
At the start of the millennium a poll asked 'What matters most in life?' 40.1% said 'a happy family life' was most important, second only after good health.
www.gallup-international.com
(Go to the 'Millennium archive' in the 'Survey archive'.)

2 FOCUS ON...

Words

2 A

- Revise words for family members with the class (for example, *parents, grandparents, aunt, uncle, cousin, daughter, son*). You can draw a family tree on the board to illustrate relationships. Ask individual students: Do you have brothers and sisters? How many cousins have you got? etc. Point out that in English we generally say 'brothers and sisters' although sometimes students might encounter the word 'siblings'. Ask how students say the equivalent words for familial relationships in their language.
- Read out the words in the exercise box and ask students to repeat them. Make sure that they put the stress in the correct place: *half-sister* and *stepfather*, but *single parent* and *only child*.
- Students complete the sentences with the correct words. Check the answers.

2 FOCUS ON...Words A — **Answers**

1 only child **2** divorced **3** single parent
4 stepfather **5** half-sister

2 B

- Read out the questions and check that students understand them.
- Students tell each other about their families using the questions to guide them.
- Ask two or three students to report back to the class about their partner's family.

Picture / background information

The greeting cards industry is huge (worth about £1 billion a year in the UK and $7 billion in the USA). Family members send or give each other birthday cards even if they live in the same house, and work colleagues often send each other Christmas cards. People often count the cards they receive and consider them an indication of their popularity. Market research puts the average number of cards received at 55 per person per year in the UK and 45 per person in the USA. The greeting cards industry also promotes other year-round opportunities for people to give each other cards – weddings, births, christenings, Mother's Day, Father's Day, cards for a job promotion, a bereavement (a death

on the family), exams passed, anniversaries and so on.
www.greetingcardassociation.org.uk/info-resource/market-info/facts-and-figures
www.clintoncards.co.uk/main/greetingcardindustry.asp

2 C

- Look at the photos with the class. Explain that in the UK and the USA cards are very important for special occasions; it is expected that people send cards to mark occasions such as weddings, birthdays and particular religious holidays, including Christmas. Try to think of as many events as possible for which a card might be suitable.
- Read out the special occasions in turn. Students match the occasions to the correct cards. Ask students to answer orally.
- Check that students understand what the word 'anniversary' means (the celebration every year of the same event, such as the day two people got married). Ask students if they know what a 25th and a 50th anniversary are called (silver wedding and golden wedding) or if people even use these terms in their country.
- Ask students: When was your last birthday? How old will you be on your next birthday? Are your parents married? Do you know the date of your parents' wedding? Do they celebrate their anniversary?

2 FOCUS ON…Words C **Answers**
1 e **2** c **3** d **4** b **5** a

2 D

- Read out the questions and check that students understand them.
- Students discuss the questions with a partner or in small groups.
- Discuss the questions briefly with the class.

2 E

- Read out the words from the stories.
- Students match the words with the correct definitions. They can use a dictionary to help them.
- Check the answers with the class.
- Ask: Has anyone ever been to a wedding? Where was the reception? Who were the witnesses? Did the bride and her husband go on honeymoon? Has anybody been a bridesmaid? What did you wear? Encourage several students to tell the class about their experiences. Alternatively, you could discuss with the class any famous weddings (royal family, celebrities) which have recently taken place in your country.

2 FOCUS ON…Words E **Answers**
1 d **2** a **3** e **4** c **5** b

2 FOCUS ON…

Ideas

- Read out the questions in turn. Students discuss them with a partner or in small groups. Briefly ask students to report back to the class.

3 READING CD2 (Red) track 15, page 63 SB

Picture / background information

The photo on the left shows a traditional North American wedding in which the bride wears a long white dress and veil and the bridegroom wears a black suit. In the left-hand picture, coloured items falling on the bride and groom are pieces of confetti – little bits of paper thrown in a shower over the couple to wish them good luck. Sometimes the paper is in the shape of a horse shoe – a traditional symbol of good luck. According to tradition the bride should also wear 'something old, something new, something borrowed, something blue'. The bride and groom promise to love each other for the rest of their lives, exchange rings and kiss after the ceremony. Traditionally the bride's parents pay for the wedding but many couples now pay for it themselves with help from both sets of parents.
www.manythings.org/sfi/wedding.html
honeymoons.about.com/cs/eurogen1/a/weddingstats.htm
The photo on the right shows a beach wedding, a type of wedding which is known as a 'destination wedding'. Destination weddings are becoming increasingly popular in the USA and in the UK for many reasons. They help avoid the cost of a huge home wedding, permit the couple to get married in a beautiful location with guaranteed good weather and enable them to celebrate in a more personal and individual way. As families become more fragmented, this may even be a way to avoid

inviting everyone in a large extended family, or to allow family members who live in different countries to get together somewhere accessible to all of them.
www.gonomad.com/traveldesk/0508/destination_weddings.html
honeymoons.about.com/od/weddingsaway/a/destination.htm
www.usatoday.com/travel/destinations/2005-05-02-mexico-weddings_x.htm

3 A

- Look at each photo in turn with the class. Ask: What's happening? Who is in the photos? How are they feeling? What's the weather like?
- Read out the task and the possible headings for the stories.
- Students read the article quickly and choose headings for the stories.
- Check the answers. Ask students to give reasons.

3 READING A	**Answers**
1 c **2** b	

3 B

- Read out the things in sentences 1–8 and check that students understand them.
- Students decide who did the things.
- Students read the article again to complete and check their answers.

3 READING B		**Answers**
1 Rosie and Jack	**2** X	**3** David and Mel
4 R and J	**5** X	**6** R and J
7 R and J	**8** D and M	

3 C

- Read out the questions in turn. Students discuss them with a partner or in small groups.
- Discuss the questions with the class. Talk about what a traditional wedding involves in your country and what special marriage customs there are. Discuss if 'destination weddings' (going to a foreign country to get married) or 'theme weddings' (for example, getting married underwater) are popular in your country.
- If you know your class well and your students wish to discuss this, ask students if they think they will get married and what they think their wedding will be like.

Optional project: Weddings around the world

- Tell students they are going to find out about wedding customs around the world. They should find out about:
  - where people get married
  - if they have witnesses and bridesmaids
  - what people do at the wedding
  - if they have a reception or celebration and what they do and eat
  - if they go on honeymoon
- Students work in small groups and choose one or two countries. They can find information on the internet or ask people they know from the country they have chosen.
- Each group tells the class about the marriage customs of the country or countries they have chosen.

Useful internet links:
www.topics-mag.com/internatl/weddings/wedding-customs.htm
www.weddingguru.com/wedding_traditions.asp
www.ourmarriage.com/planner/html/traditions_around_the_world.html

4 LANGUAGE: The past continuous

4 A

- Look at the first example with the class. Read out the two questions and elicit answers from the class. Draw time diagrams on the board to illustrate the length and completeness of the actions.
- Do the same thing for the remaining two examples.
- Write the examples of the past simple in the examples on the board. Ask students to identify the tense by name and explain when we use it (eg past simple: we use it for completed actions in the past.)
- Write the examples of the past continuous on the board. This time tell students the name of the tense and then ask when we use it (past continuous: we use it for actions which are not completed / in progress and to describe background actions which start before another action and continue while other completed actions take place).

4 LANGUAGE A **Answers**

1 a) *was walking* starts first / *started to cry* is a completed action
b) *everyone was really enjoying themselves* starts first/ *we left* is a completed action
c) *was shining* starts first / *we said* is a completed action

2 No, only one of the activities in each of the sentences is a completed action.

4 B

- Draw students' attention to the structure rule. Complete the rule with the class using the examples on the board.

4 LANGUAGE B **Answers**

Subject + *was* / *were* + verb + *-ing*

- Refer students to the explanation about the past continuous in Workbook Unit 14. They can read the explanation and do the exercises in class or for homework.

5 LISTEN IN CD1 (Blue) track 21, page 64 SB

Picture / background information

A large percentage of women work outside the home in the UK: in 2003, 68% of women with dependent children and 76% without children. Nearly 40% of women with dependent children work part-time.

In the UK on average, women spend over 2 hours 30 minutes a day doing housework, cooking, washing up, cleaning and ironing – 1 hour 30 minutes more than men.

Men in full-time work have more free time on a weekday than women who work full-time. Men spend more time than women watching TV; women spend more time socialising than men.

www.statistics.gov.uk/CCI/nugget.asp?ID=436&Pos=1&ColRank=2&Rank=192

www.statistics.gov.uk/CCI/nugget.asp?ID=440&Pos=2&ColRank=2&Rank=192

5 A

- Look at the photos with the class and read out the task.
- Students describe what they can see in the photos. Prompt them if necessary with questions. Encourage them to speculate what the problem could be.

5 LISTEN IN A **Possible answer**

Dad is sitting in a comfortable chair and watching TV while Mum is making dinner. Perhaps Mum thinks dad is lazy and would like some help in the kitchen.

5 B

- Tell students they are going to listen to a conversation before a family party. Read out the question. Remind students they are only listening for the answer to this question and are not supposed to understand every word.
- Play the CD. Students listen and answer the question.
- Check the answer.

5 LISTEN IN B **Answer**

Mum thinks Dad watches too much TV. She thinks it isn't fair that she does all the work in the house and has a full-time job too.

5 C

- Read out the sentences and check that students understand them.
- Play the CD again. Students listen and answer the questions.
- Check the answers or ask students to check their answers in the listening script.

5 LISTEN IN C **Answers**

1 Their silver wedding anniversary.
2 He was watching TV.
3 He was watching football / the World Cup.
4 Miriam
5 Emma
6 The cooking, the washing up, the shopping and sometimes the ironing.
7 She went clubbing / was out clubbing with her friends.
8 He was thinking about his wedding 25 years ago (and that Miriam doesn't look a day older now.)

5 D

- Read out the sentences. Students discuss them with a partner or in small groups.
- Discuss students' answers with the class.

6 YOUR TURN TO SPEAK

A Role play

- Read the task with the class and make sure they understand it.
- Brainstorm what the person might say and how the boyfriend / girlfriend might react. Write useful language on the board. For example, *You:* I don't think you help enough, I think you're lazy, What about your poor mum?, Can't you …?, Why don't you…?
  Boyfriend / girlfriend: Mum likes cooking / cleaning / …, I don't have time to…, That's why you have parents, OK, I'll…, I'll try and help more.
- Divide the class into pairs. Students decide who is the new boyfriend or girlfriend.
- Students do their role play.
- Ask for volunteers to act out their role play in front of the class.

B Conversation

- Read out the task. Go through the phrases in **LB 22** with the class.
- With the class brainstorm a list of possible activities for the three times given in the questions (for example, *7 o'clock this morning*: be asleep, have breakfast, have a shower, wait for the bus; *8 o'clock in the evening*: have dinner, watch TV, do homework; *Sunday afternoon*: play football, go for a walk, meet friends, visit grandparents).
- Students work in pairs and ask and answer the questions, using **LB 22** and the activities on the board to help them.
- Ask several students to report back to the class.
- To consolidate the language used in this activity, ask students to write the answers to the exercise in **LB 22** and then read out their answers to the class. Alternatively, ask students to review the phrases in **LB 22** at home and do the exercise for homework.

7 YOUR TOPIC

- Read out the task and the points learners have to prepare to speak about. Remind students to make notes about each point.
- Ask students to bring photos if possible to illustrate the event they are talking about.
- Students can talk about their special occasions to the class or smaller groups if you have a large class. Encourage them to ask questions about each other's presentations. If students work in groups, ask them to briefly report back to the class.
- To consolidate the language used in this activity, ask students to write the answers to the exercise in **LB 23** using their imagination. They should then swap their answers with a partner and either read their partner's dialogue silently or read out the dialogue with their partner. Alternatively, ask students to review the phrases in **LB 23** at home and do the exercise for homework.

8 *THE FAMILY in English* Page 65 SB

Picture / background information

The UK, the USA and many other countries have seen traditional, extended families lose their importance over the past few decades. There are fewer and fewer multi-generation households. The proportion of one-person households in the UK almost doubled between 1971 and 2001, from 17% to 31%. People tend to move to other parts of the country, or to other countries because of their jobs, or simply to start a new life. British and particularly Irish families very commonly have relatives living all over the English-speaking world, in America, Canada, Australia and New Zealand in particular. Similarly Greek and Italian families often have connections in America and Australia. In 2004, 24% of all UK children lived with a single parent (in nine out of ten cases with the mother). In 2001, 10% of all UK families were stepfamilies. And 42% of all families did not have any children living with them. Only 1% of households included more than one family.
www.statistics.gov.uk/focuson/families/
In 2000, 9.3 % of all US households were single-parent families (7.2% were single mothers); 31.9% of all households did not have children; 3.7% of all US households were 'multigenerational'.
www.census.gov/prod/2001pubs/c2kbr01-8.pdf
In the UK 'civil partnerships' between same-sex couples, giving them similar legal rights to marriage couples, became law in December 2005. In several European countries same-sex couples can now be married. In the USA same-sex marriage is recognised in the state of Massachusetts and some other states

permit 'civil unions'. However nineteen states forbid the recognition of same-sex marriages.
en.wikipedia.org/wiki/Same-sex_marriage
Many elderly people in the UK and the USA are cared for outside the family in 'care homes' or 'nursing homes' (sometimes informally called 'old people's homes'), or 'retirement homes'.
The number of children in Europe is decreasing: in 2002 it was 1.47 children per woman. Spain (1.25 children), Greece (1.25) and Italy (1.26) have the lowest birth rates in the European Union.
www.staff.city.ac.uk/~ra828/assets/tina/print_page.html
General information on family groups:
www.uk.encarta.msn.com/text_761558266_1/Family_(sociology).html
www.bartelby.com/65/fa/family.html
www.en.wikipedia.org/wiki/Family

8 A

- Look at the photos with the class and read out the captions. Ask: Which is the most common type of family in your / our country? Do families in your / our country have lots of children? Depending on the sensitivity of your class, you may or not may not wish to draw attention to the question of same-sex couples and if it is possible for same-sex couples to marry in your country.
- Students read the text using the photos to support their reading and understanding, and then find the words and phrases for the definitions in **A**. You might like to read the first sentence of the text with the class and find the word for definition **1** together.
- Check the answers.

8 *THE FAMILY in English* A **Answers**

1 society **2** nuclear family **3** extended family
4 childless **5** stepfamily

8 B

- Read out the questions and check that students understand them.
- Students read the text again and decide if the sentences are true or false. Alternatively, ask students to do the exercise and then check their answers in the text.
- Check the answers.
- Talk about the function of the family in your country. Ask: Do family members work together? Does the family educate its children? Does the family look after older family members?

8 *THE FAMILY in English* B **Answers**

1 True
2 False (The number has become smaller.)
3 False (Traditionally families worked and lived together, educated the children and looked after the older people in the family.)

8 C

- Read out the questions and check that students understand them.
- Students discuss the questions with a partner or in small groups and then report back to the class. Alternatively, discuss the questions with the whole class.

Optional project: A class survey about types of family

- Tell students you are going to find out about the types of family in their class.
- Write these headings on the board:
  Nuclear family
  Stepfamily
  Single parents
  Extended family
  Number of children: 1, 2, 3, 4, 5 etc
  (Add up the number of children and divide it by the class size to find the average number of children in each family.)
- Ask for a show of hands for each question. In larger classes, students can work in small groups and conduct the survey within their group with one person making notes. Groups can then write their information on the board or read it out so you can pool the information for the class.
- Look at the results of the survey with the class. Is this typical for the country you are in?

9 PORTFOLIO WRITING

- Read out the task and check that students have understood it. With students, brainstorm reasons why somebody might have an argument with their parents (for example, friends; clothes and appearance; behaviour: drinking, smoking, drugs; rules at home; helping at home; money) and write them on the board.

- Elicit useful words and phrases for talking about arguments, such as:
  have an argument with somebody about something
  to argue with somebody about something
  to shout at
  to cry
  to be fed up with …
- Write a structure for the email on the board, using these questions:
  What did your brother do?
  Why did he leave home?
  How do you and family feel?
  (NB: Keep in mind that some students may be sensitive about the subject if they have had a similar experience at home. Focus on the words for argument rather than on the emotion behind it.)
- Students write their emails in class or for homework. Remind students to be careful with the use of the past simple and the past continuous when they describe what happened.
- Take in the emails and check them. Read out the best one(s). Or ask students to do the optional activity below.

Optional activity: A reply to an email

- Distribute the emails from your students to other students in the class. Each student should write a reply to the email, expressing sympathy and offering help. Elicit or teach language for this (*I was sorry to hear… , I'm sorry that…, It's a shame that… I can understand that…, Do you want to talk about it? Would you like to…?*)
- Students swap emails and read the reply to their own mail.
- Ask individual students if the reply was helpful.

10 *Your answer*

- Discuss the question as a class using the sub-questions.
- Refer students to the Workbook Unit 14 activities.

Last word

- After doing the workbook activities, students evaluate their performance in the three areas. Check if any students feel they need extra practice in any area.

WORKBOOK answers — Pages 32–33 WB

1 Language: past continuous

1 A

1 was thinking **2** was raining **3** was starting
4 were smiling **5** were clapping **6** was crying
7 was clapping **8** were waiting

1 B

1 was getting ready; phoned **2** were you doing
3 made; were watching **4** got; got
5 was shining **6** had

1 C

(Individual answers)

2 Use of English

1 We saved up *to* get married.
2 There are *lots / a lot* of single parent families in Britain.
3 Their son is an *adult* now.
4 She doesn't do *anything* in the house.
5 I fell asleep *while* my dad was giving his speech.

3 Vocabulary

3 A

anniversary birthday wedding graduation

3 B

1 c (got engaged) **2** g **3** a **4** f
5 e **6** b **7** d (got married) **8** h

3 C

1 childless **2** only child **3** half-sister
4 stepchildren **5** single parent **6** extended family

See pages 32–33 WB

4 Pronunciation CD 1 (Blue) track 22

4 A

The speaker's voice falls.

4 B

The speaker's voice rises because he / she is uncertain if the information is correct.

4 C

When the speaker is certain the information is correct, his / her voice *falls*.
When the speaker is uncertain if the information is correct, his / her voice *rises*.

4 D

1 uncertain (rising intonation)
2 certain (falling intonation)
3 certain (falling intonation)
4 uncertain (rising intonation)

5 Portfolio Writing

(Individual answers)

What's new?

Subject: Health
Language: Zero and first conditionals
Functions: LB 24 Talking about facts
LB 25 Requesting and expressing opinions and impressions

1 *The BIG question:* CAN WE STOP DISEASE?

The theme of this unit is health. ***The BIG Question*** is: Can we stop disease? What is the best way to stop disease? What diseases should we worry about?

- Read out ***The BIG Question***. Make sure students understand the word *disease*.
- Look at the **FACT** box with the class. Ask students if they are surprised by the statistics. What reasons can they give for them? (for example, nutrition and diet, vaccinations, disease, medical help).
- Ask students what they think the life expectancy is in their country. Give them the statistics for men and women (see box above or refer to the website list) and compare them with students' predictions.

Picture / background information

The information in the **FACT** box is from *The World Health Report 2003* by the World Health Organization.
www.who.int/en/
On average women live six to eight years longer than men.
www.who.int/mediacentre/factsheets/fs252/en/
Life expectancy in other countries: Brazil: men 65.7, women 72.3; China: men 69.6, women 72.7; France: men 75.9, women 83.5; Greece: men 75.8, women 81.1; Italy men 76.8, women 82.5; Japan: men 78.4, women 85.3; Korea: men 71.8, women 79.4; Russia: men 58.4, women 72.1; UK: men 75.8, women 80.5; USA: men 74.6, women 79.8.
For other countries see:
www.who.int/whr/2003/en/Annex1-en.pdf

2 FOCUS ON...

Words

2 A

- Look at the photos with the class. Ask students: How do you feel when you see photo **5**?
- Read out the words in the box and ask students to repeat them. Make sure that they stress the words correctly: *aspirin* ['æsprɪn], *injection, cough medicine* ['kɒf ˌmedsn], *antibiotics, tissues.*
- Students match the photos with the correct words.
- Check the answers.
- Look at collocations of the words with the class: take an aspirin, have an injection, take / have some cough medicine, take antibiotics, use / buy / carry tissues. Write them on the board as preparation for exercise **B**.

2 FOCUS ON...Words A — **Answers**

1 c **2** e **3** b **4** e **5** d

2 B

- Read out the list of problems with the students. Ask students to repeat key words: *headache, cold, flu, feel sick, virus, allergy, hay fever*. Check the meaning of these words and phrases. Tell students 'flu' is the shortened form of 'influenza'.
- Look at the example with the class. Remind students that they can give advice using *should / shouldn't*.
- In pairs, students take it in turns to read out a problem and give advice using *should / shouldn't* and the words from exercise **A** when possible.
- Read out the problems again and ask for advice. Alternatively, ask pairs of students to act out the mini-dialogues in front of the class. Other students can add their own advice.

2 FOCUS ON...Words B — **Possible answers**

a) You should take an aspirin. You should lie down.
b) You should take an aspirin and buy lots of tissues.
c) You should have an injection against flu. You should eat healthily.
d) You should go to bed. You shouldn't eat anything.
e) You can't do anything. You should wait.
f) You should go to the doctor's and have an injection.

2 C

- Read out the list of words from the text and make sure students can pronounce them properly.
- Students match the words with the correct definitions, using a dictionary to help them.
- Check the answers.

2 FOCUS ON...Words C	**Answers**
1 c **2** e **3** d **4** a **5** b	

2 D

- Read out the words in the shaded boxes.
- Ask students to complete the sentences with the correct words.
- Check the answers. If you have a monolingual class, ask students what these words are in their language.
- Ask: Are these diseases a problem in your country?

2 FOCUS ON...Words D	**Answers**
1 Heart disease **2** AIDS **3** cancer	

2 FOCUS ON...

Ideas

- Read out the sentences and check that students understand them.
- Students discuss the questions with a partner or in small groups.
- Briefly discuss the questions with the class.

3 READING CD 2 (Red) track 16, page 67 SB

Picture / background information

The photo shows a health officer collecting ducks to be killed at a farm in Pathum Thani north of Bangkok, Thailand, after a resurgence of bird flu.
The reading text is based on information from the Communicable Epidemic and Pandemic Alert and Response section of the WHO website:
www.who.int/csr/en/
www.who.int/csr/disease/avian_influenza/en/
At the time of press, cases of bird flu have been discovered in countries all over the world, including parts of Western Europe. Many countries have stockpiled drugs for emergencies.
Influenza pandemics in history (see Chapter 2 in the document below):
www.emro.who.int/syria/PDF/H5N1-9reduit.pdf

3 A

- Look at each photo in turn with the class. Ask: What can you see? What is the person wearing? What is happening? Where is the photo taken, do you think?
- Read out the task. Tell students to read the FAQs quickly for this information.
- Check the answer.

3 READING A	**Answer**
There will be a flu epidemic early in the twenty-first century, so it could be soon. But we don't know exactly when it will be.	

3 B

- Read the paragraph headings above the FAQs with the class. Check that students understand the word *prevent.*
- Students read the text again and match the headings to the correct paragraphs.
- Students compare their answers with a partner.
- Check the answers.

3 READING B	**Answers**
1 Can flu kill?	
2 What is a pandemic?	
3 How many people die in pandemics?	
4 Will there be another pandemic soon?	
5 Can we prevent it?	

3 C

- Read out the sentences. Ask students to mark them true or false.
- Students check their answers in the FAQs.
- Check the answers.

3 READING C	**Answers**
1 F (The are lots of different flu viruses.)	
2 F (Pandemics kill millions of people.)	
3 F (Pandemics have happened regularly in history.)	
4 F (Bird flu is a dangerous virus which can spread to humans.)	
5 T	

3 D

- Read out the task and the figures. Tell students to scan the text for these figures.

- Students look for the figures in the text and find out their meaning.
- Check the answers. Ask: What do you think of these figures? Are you surprised?

3 READING D **Answers**

1 The First World War killed 8.3 million people (over 4 years).
2 There was a flu pandemic in 1918. It was the worst in history.
3 Forty million people died in the 1918 pandemic (in less than a year).
4 People died less than 48 hours after they caught the disease.

3 E

- Read out the sentences in turn and discuss them with the class. If your students feel worried about a flu pandemic or other pandemics, reassure them: the response to a pandemic today will be very different to that of the past. Authorities are continuously monitoring and assessing the situation of current viruses so that far fewer people will die in a possible future pandemic.

3 READING E **Answer**

2 The FAQ text comes from the World Health Organization which is the health organisation for the United Nations. The website provides facts and information about important health topics.

4 LANGUAGE: Zero and first conditionals

4 A

- Read out the task.
- Students read the examples and complete the sentences with *zero* or *first* conditional.
- Check the answers. Make sure students have understood the difference in the way the two conditionals are used. Elicit or give students further examples:
  If you eat too much fat, you can get heart disease = general fact
  If you eat all that ice-cream, you'll feel sick = likely future event after a specific action

4 LANGUAGE A **Answers**

1 We use the *zero* conditional to talk about general facts.
2 We use the *first* conditional for events which will probably happen in the future.

4 B

- Write the examples of the two conditionals on the board and circle the words *if* and *unless*. Tell students that the *if / unless* clause can be the first or second clause in the sentence. Ask when we use a comma (when the *if / unless* clause is the first clause in the sentence).
- Underline the verbs in each clause. Point to each verb and ask: What tense is this? Write the names of the tenses on the board next to the verbs.
- Look at the structure rules with the class. Tell the class to complete them using the examples on the board to help them.
- Check the answers.
- Write further examples on the board for students to complete. For example:
  Unless Jack (wear) his winter jacket, he (get) cold.
  If people (eat) too much, they (get) fat.
  If it (be) nice weather tomorrow, we (go) swimming.
  Unless it (rain), August (usually / be) the best month of the year.

4 LANGUAGE B **Answers**

Zero conditional: *if / unless* + present simple; other clause: present simple or a modal verb
First conditional: *if / unless* + present simple; other clause: *will* future or a modal verb

- Refer students to the explanation about the past continuous in Workbook Unit 15. They can read the explanation and do the exercises in class or for homework.

5 LISTEN IN CD1 (Blue) track 23, page 68

Picture / background information

The photo shows military officers wearing masks and gloves against infection fending off journalists outside a SARS hospital on the outskirts of Beijing,

China. The hospital had just released the last 18 patients out of 680 who had the disease at the height of the SARS epidemic in 2003.
SARS (Severe Acute Respiratory Syndrome) is a type of infectious pneumonia which killed about 800 people in Asia in 2003 and infected over 8,000. SARS evolved from animals to humans, causing serious breathing problems for those infected. After the outbreak, the disease apparently disappeared.
www.guardian.co.uk/print/0,3858,4848583-111420,00.html
en.wikipedia.org/wiki/SARS
www.wednesday-night.com/SARS.asp
www.economist.com/agenda/displaystory.cfm?story_id=2383561

5 A

- Look at the photo with the class and read out the task. First ask students to describe what they can see in the photo and then speculate about where it is and what the problem might be.

5 LISTEN IN A **Possible answer**

The military officers in the photo are wearing masks to prevent infection from disease, in this case SARS, because they are in a job where they have contact with a lot of people.

5 B

- Explain that these words are in the conversation students are going to hear. Read them out in turn and ask students to repeat them. Make sure they pronounce *pneumonia* correctly with a silent 'p' [nju:məʊniɑ] and hypochondriac with the correct stress [ˌhaɪpʊˈkɒndriæk]. Point out that SARS is spoken as a word [sɑ:z] rather than as initials.
- Students check the meaning of the words in their dictionary. Warn them that they may not find SARS in their dictionary.
- Check the answers. Elicit or explain the meaning of SARS.

5 LISTEN IN B **Answers**

to exaggerate: to make something seem better or worse than it really is
pneumonia: an illness which causes problems with breathing
hypochondriac: a person who thinks he / she is always ill, even when he / she is healthy
SARS: (Severe Acute Respiratory Syndrome): a type of infectious pneumonia which killed hundreds of people in Asia in 2003
infection: a disease caused by bacteria

5 C

- Tell students they are going to listen to a conversation between two friends. Read out the question before they listen to the conversation. Remind students they are only listening for the answer to this question and not to understand every word.
- Play the CD. Students listen and answer the question.
- Check the answer.

5 LISTEN IN C **Answer**

Jake has a cold but he thinks he might have pneumonia or bird flu.

5 D

- Read out the sentences and check that students understand them.
- Play the CD again. Students listen and write the correct initial.
- Check the answers or ask students to check their answers in the listening script.

5 LISTEN IN D **Answers**

1 V 2 V 3 J 4 J 5 V 6 J

5 E

- This exercise gives students the chance to characterise the two people from the conversation in the listening. Read out the pairs of opposites and check that students understand their meaning.
- Look at the example with the class. Ask: Do you agree that Jake is pessimistic? Why? Ask students to complete the sentence about Jake.
- Students work in pairs. They describe Jake and Vanessa using the remaining adjectives.
- Check the answers. Ask pairs to say a sentence. Ask other students if they agree.

5 LISTEN IN E **Possible answers**

I think Jake is pessimistic because he thinks there will be a flu epidemic soon.
Jake is selfish because he just thinks about himself. He doesn't think about other people who are really ill.
Jake is realistic because he wants to buy a mask against infection.
I think Vanessa is optimistic because she says the flu epidemic might never happen.
Vanessa is unselfish: she thinks we should spend money on sick people. We shouldn't buy drugs we might not need.
Vanessa is unrealistic because she says we shouldn't worry about things that aren't certain. But it's very hard not to worry about things like that.

6 YOUR TURN TO SPEAK

A Role play

- Read the task with the class and make sure they understand it.
- Go through the phrases in **LB 24** with the class.
- Write these questions on the board: *What is it?, Why are you worried? What can we do about it?* Brainstorm ideas to answer these questions and write them on the board.
- Divide the class into pairs. Students decide which one of them is the person worried about flu.
- Students do their role play.
- Ask for volunteers to act out their role play in front of the class.
- To consolidate the language used in this activity, ask students to review the phrases in **LB 24** at home and do the exercise for homework.

B Conversation

- Read out the task. Go through the questions and phrases in **LB 25** with the class.
- Read out the points listed in the exercise. Make sure students understand them.
- In pairs, students talk about their opinions and impression of the things in the list, using the expressions in **LB 25**.
- Ask some students to report back to the class.
- To consolidate the language used in this activity, ask students to review the phrases in **LB 25** at home and do the exercise for homework.

7 YOUR TOPIC

- Read out the task and the points learners have to prepare to speak about. As this topic is quite demanding, ask students to work in pairs or small groups and give them guidance as necessary.
- Students discuss the points and make notes about them.
- Pairs or groups present their talk about healthcare to the class. Encourage them to ask questions about each other's presentations.

8 *HEALTH AND FITNESS in English* Page 69 SB

Picture / background information

The photographs come from the American Lung Association. Its website at www.lungusa.org contains a great deal of information about lung diseases, such as cancer and tuberculosis. About 17 million people die of heart disease, particularly heart attacks and strokes every year. Many of these deaths are caused by smoking, which increases the risk of dying from heart disease 2-3 times. Lack of exercise and an unhealthy diet also increase the risk.
www.who.int/cardiovascular_diseases/resources/atlas/en/
There is evidence that 70% of all cancers are caused by environmental factors. Cancer can be prevented by stopping smoking, eating healthy food and avoiding exposure to the sun without sunscreen. For more information about smoking and cancer, see these websites:
www.mariecurie.org.uk
www.cancer.org
Smoking-related diseases are the world's leading preventable cause of death but the number of smokers is increasing. Every year four million men and one million women die and it is expected that this number will double in twenty years.
www.who.int/whr/2003/chapter6/en/index2.html
A study by researchers at University College London linked happiness with lower levels of stress hormones in men and women and lower heart rates in men.
www.newscientist.com/article.ns?id=dn7282&print=true

8 A

- Look at the photos of a smoker's lungs. Ask: What is your reaction when you see these photos?

- Ask the class: How interested are you in your health? Is looking after your health an important part of you life?
- Read out the definitions in **A**. Make sure students understand them.
- Students read the text and the **FACT** box about smoking and find words or phrases which match the definitions.
- Check the answers.

8 *HEALTH AND FITNESS in English* A **Answers**

1 infectious **2** genetic **3** a balanced diet **4** exercise **5** passive smoking

8 B

- Read the questions with the class.
- Students read the text and the **FACT** box again and answer the questions.
- Check the answers. For question **1**, ask: Why is Africa the only place where infectious diseases kill more people than non-infectious diseases? (lack of vaccines, drugs, medical care and information, spread of AIDS in particular).

8 *HEALTH AND FITNESS in English* B **Answers**

1 Africa **2** healthy living **3** It helps people stay healthy. **4** about five million every year

8 C

- Read out the task. Look at the healthy living rules with the class and check that students understand them.
- Students work in pairs. First they tick the rules they follow. Then they tell their partner about their lifestyle and discuss whether they have a healthy lifestyle and what they can improve.
- Students report back to the class. Invite volunteers to tell the class if they have a healthy lifestyle. Ask: Do you think you have a healthier lifestyle than your parents? What does the government do to encourage healthier lifestyles in your / our country? What does your school / college / workplace do if anything? What could they do to encourage healthier lifestyles even more?

8 D

- Read out the question and discuss it with the class. Focus on the image of smoking among young people (Is this positive or negative?), why people smoke, how easy or difficult it is to stop smoking and if there are any government rules limiting smoking in public places in your country.

Optional project: A *Healthy You* poster

- Tell students they are going to make a poster that tells people how to stay fit and healthy.
- Suggest to students they make a list of DOs and DON'Ts
- Students work in small groups. They brainstorm DOs and DON'Ts for their poster. They can use the ideas on page 69 and add their own ideas.
- Students agree on the design for their poster. They can research photos or illustrate their own pictures.
- Students make their poster.
- Display the posters on the walls or on desks and allow students time to look at them.
- Students vote for the poster that best represents a *Healthy You*. If possible, make copies of the poster and hang it throughout your school or college.

9 PORTFOLIO WRITING

- Read out the task and check that students have understood it.
- Look at the structure of the essay together:
  For paragraph 1, refer students to their YOUR TOPIC talk.
  For paragraph 2, refer students to the 'healthy living' list on page 69.
  For the conclusion, brainstorm ideas together.
- Students write their essays in class or for homework.
- Ask students to swap essays with a partner and check / comment on them. Then take in the essays and check them.

10 *Your answer*

- Discuss ***The BIG Question*** as a class using the sub-questions.
- Refer students to the Workbook Unit 15 activities.

Last word

- After doing the workbook activities, students evaluate their performance in the three areas. Check if any students feel they need extra practice in any area.

WORKBOOK answers Pages 34–35 WB

1 Language: zero and first conditional

1 A

1 c **2** d **3** e **4** f **5** a **6** b

1 B

1 'll get **2** 'll need **3** 'm not **4** 'll have to get up
5 won't get **6** go **7** don't start **8** won't get
9 won't feel **10** won't miss

1 C

1 Unless he stops drinking, he'll destroy his health.
2 Unless we hurry, the chemist will be closed.
3 Unless it rains, we'll play tennis.
4 Unless the government invests in healthcare, the system will break down.
5 Unless you take your medicine, you won't get better.

2 Vocabulary

2 A

1 c **2** e **3** b **4** a **5** d

2 B

1 disease **2** epidemic **3** virus **4** infectious
5 infection **6** drugs **7** vaccine **8** spread

2 C

1 e **2** c **3** a **4** d **5** b

3 Connections

3 A

1 in **2** to **3** from **4** against **5** with

4 Word Building

4 A

1 death **2** life **3** ache **4** prevention
5 protection

5 Use of English

5 A

1 In my *opinion*, our healthcare system is quite good.
2 The number of people with cancer is *increasing*.
3 I won't go to the doctor's *unless* you come with me.
4 You *should* enjoy life.
5 While I *was playing* football, I suddenly felt sick.

5 Portfolio Writing

(Individual answers)

What's new?

Subject:	Seasonal activities, English-speaking world
Language:	Present continuous for future arrangements
Functions:	**LB 26** Making arrangements
	LB 27 Talking about future arrangements and intentions
Pronunciation:	Intonation in questions, CD1 (Blue) track 25

1 *The BIG question:* WHY ARE YOU LEARNING ENGLISH?

The theme of this unit is seasonal activities, in particular English language summer courses and the English-speaking world. ***The BIG Question*** is: Why are you learning English? Is English important? And are language schools a good way to learn English?

- Begin by talking a little bit about students' language learning experience so far: if English is the students' first foreign language, when they started to learn it, if they think this was early enough, what other foreign languages are offered at school; in multilingual countries, talk about the languages students use at home, when they use which language; in multilingual classes, ask students what their native language is and how easy / difficult it is to learn for foreign students.
- Read out ***The BIG Question*** but don't invite students to respond at this stage. Tell them they will talk about this question shortly.
- Look at the **FACT** box with the class. Make sure students understand what *broadens the mind* and *open doors* means. Ask students *how* language learning can do this. Make a network with students on the board with the phrases 'broadens the mind', 'opens doors'. For example,
  broadens the mind: can talk to people from different countries; learn about different lifestyles, customs and traditions; learn to be tolerant about differences; talk about lots of different subjects in English; improve your general education.
  opens doors: if you can speak another language, you can work in that country; travel there more easily; make friends everywhere; use the language in all sorts of jobs; understand other cultures. If you have your own classroom, you could put a notice on the door: 'Languages open doors'.

Picture / background information

For more information on foreign language learning in Europe, see:
http://ec.europa.eu/education/languages/index_en.htm
For help with learning English:
www.bbc.co.uk/worldservice/learningenglish/index.shtml

2 FOCUS ON...

Words

2 A 1

- Tell students that the phrases in exercise **1** are all things you can do in the summer holidays. Read out the verbs and nouns. Check that students understand *look after* and explain the meaning of *hang out* (spend time in a certain place or with certain people, often doing nothing in particular).
- Read out the example. Students match the other verbs to the correct nouns.
- Check the answers.

2 FOCUS ON...Words A 1	**Answers**
1 d **2** c **3** f **4** a **5** b **6** e	

2 A 2

- Look at the photos with the class. Ask students to describe them. Prompt students with questions if necessary. For example: Who can you see in the picture? Where are they? What are they doing? Are they having fun?
- Students match the photos with the correct phrases in exercise **1**.

2 FOCUS ON...Words A 2	**Answers**
Photo 1: do a language course	
Photo 2: go to an activity camp	
Photo 3: go on a family holiday	

2 A 3

- Students work in pairs. They ask and answer the question using the phrases in exercise **1** if possible. Note: if students have already met the present continuous for future, they might like to use it here. Otherwise encourage students to use the *going to* future.

2 B 1

- Read out the words in the boxes. Ask students to repeat them and check that they have the correct word stress: accent, examinations, intensive course, motivated, self-access.
- Students complete the sentences with the correct words or phrases.
- Check the answers.

2 FOCUS ON...Words B 1		Answers
a) intensive course	**b)** motivated	**c)** accent
d) self-access room	**e)** examinations	

2 B 2

- Read out the questions and check that students understand them.
- Students work in pairs and discuss the questions.
- Students report back to the class. Spend some time on this part of the activity. Ask students how they use English outside the classroom and talk about what other activities they could do to further practise their English: watch English films with subtitles; read teenage English magazines if they have access to them; listen to music in English; use websites in English; write or receive emails in English from teenagers in other countries etc.

2 C

- Tell students they are going to read an article about two students on language courses in the UK. Read out the words from the text. Practise the pronunciation of *accommodation* [əˌkɒmə'deɪʃn] and *excursions* [ɪk'skɜːʃnz].
- Students match the words with the correct definitions.
- Check the answers.
- Ask students: What sort of accommodation do you live in? Do you have a packed lunch on weekdays? What is in it? Do you like going on excursions? Do you prefer going by car or train or bus? Where do you go? What places have you visited?

2 FOCUS ON...Words C					Answers
1 d	**2** e	**3** f	**4** a	**5** c	**6** b

2 FOCUS ON...

Ideas

- Read out the two statements and check that students understand them.
- Discuss the statements with the class. For statement one, ask how you can learn English by yourself (with a book, CD, video) and what the advantages and disadvantages of this are. For example:
  ✓ **(advantages)**: you can go at your own pace, more slowly or quickly than in class; you can hear and repeat things as often as you want; you can spend more time on learning
  ✗ **(disadvantages)**: there is no teacher to correct you and help you; there are no other students to talk to and exchange opinions with; it isn't as much fun.

3 READING CD 2 (Red) track 17, page 71 SB

Picture / background information

The statistic of 600,000 foreign learners is from the British Council magazine *Club UK*:
www.educationuk.org/clubuk/1/index.html
For information on learning English, taking exams and studying in the UK:
www.britishcouncil.org/home
For facts about choosing an English Language School:
www.englishschool.org.uk/
For a critique of the ELT industry, see:
www.english-learning.co.uk/geifr.html

3 A

- Read out the task. Check that students understand the phrase *worth the money* (ie provide good teaching for the money the students pay).
- Students read the article quickly. Remind them to read to answer the question and not worry about things they don't understand.

3 READING A **Answers**

Jiang Li: Yes, she's enjoying the course.
Alessandro: No, he just does exercises and thinks he could do this in Italy for less money.

3 B

- Read through the questions with the class. Check that students understand them.
- Students read the text again and answer the questions. Alternatively, they can answer the questions, then read the text again and correct their answers.
- Check the answers. Compare the two students' experiences by asking further questions: For example,
  Question **1**: Where is Alessandro living?
  Question **2**: What are Alessandro's lessons like?
  Question **5**: Why doesn't Alessandro speak a lot of English outside class?
  Question **6**: What does Jiang Li do in her classes?
  Question **7**: What does Jiang Li say about travel in Preston?
- Ask: Do they like the places (town / city) they are studying in? (Yes, Jiang Li likes Preston because the town is small and the people are friendly; Alessandro likes London because it's an exciting international city.)

3 READING B **Answers**

1 J **2** J **3** A **4** A **5** J **6** A **7** A **8** J

Optional activity: Act out interviews

- Tell students they are going to role play interviews with Jiang Li and Alessandro.
- First, brainstorm questions on the board based on the information in the text: Where did you do your course? What were the lessons like? What was the place like? Where did you stay?
- Students work in pairs. Student A is Jiang Li or Alessandro and reads the appropriate part of the text again. Student B thinks of two or three more questions which are not answered in the text.
- Students role play the interview in pairs. Student B asks his / her questions in random order and Student A responds. Student A should make up information for those questions not based on the text.
- Walk around and listen to the role plays. Invite two strong pairs (one with Jiang Li and one with Alessandro) to role play their interview in front of the class.

3 C

- Read out the first question. If any of your students have done such a course, ask: Where was your course? What was it like? Where did you stay? What did you especially like about the course? What didn't you like? If students have been to the UK, ask them if they can identify with any of the comments in the text (eg about friendly people, the food).
- If students haven't yet done a language course, ask them if they would be interested in doing one and why.
- Read out the second question. (If students are likely to try to find a course on their own, it would be useful to spend some time on this activity in order to give them some practical help.) With students, make a list on the board of the main things mentioned in the text: the course, excursions, place, accommodation. Then ask students what aspects of these things they should consider. Complete the list together.

3 READING C 2 **Suggested answers**

the course: class size, teachers, facilities (computer room/self-access room), type of class excursions (if the course includes excursions, such as theatre trips etc)
the place: small town or large city (might have to travel a lot in a large city, easy to get around in a small town)
the accommodation: student accommodation, host family, own flat or a room in a flat, location

4 LANGUAGE: Present continuous for future arrangements

4 A

- Look at the examples with the class. Read out the first question and elicit the answer. Ask students when we usually use the present continuous (to describe events in progress, often with time references such as *at the moment* or *now*).
- Read out the second question. Give students a short time to look at the examples, then go through each example in turn. Elicit if the sentences refer to the present or the future. Ask students what tells them it is the future (the time references *tomorrow, tonight, after school today*).

- Write the future time references on the board and elicit other future time references from the students (eg *next week, at the weekend, in the summer holidays, next year*).
- Explain the use of the present continuous in the future: for arrangements with other people. Explain that we can also use *going to* to talk about future arrangements but that the present continuous is more natural, especially when we use the word *go* (eg *He's going to the cinema,* rather than *he's going to go to the cinema*). Indicate to students that the latter is not incorrect, just not as natural.
- Refer students to the explanation about the past continuous in Workbook Unit 16. They can read the explanation and do the exercises in class or for homework.

4 LANGUAGE A **Answers**

1 present continuous
2 sentences **1** and **4** refer to the present; sentences **2**, **3** and **5** refer to the future

5 LISTEN IN CD 1 (Blue) track 24, page 72 SB

Picture / background information

For more information on different language learning styles:
www.teachingenglish.org.uk/think/methodology/learning_style.shtml
www.language.com.hk/articles/styles1.html
According to Alistair Smith's book, *Accelerated Learning*, we take in 20% of what we read, 30% of what we hear, 40% of what we see, 50% of what we say, 60% of what we do and 90% of what we read, hear, see, say and do.

5 A

- Look at the photo with the class and read out the task. Elicit suggestions. Tell students to use the word *Perhaps…* to start their predictions.

5 LISTEN IN A **Possible answer**

Perhaps the woman on the right is a teacher, an English teacher.
Perhaps the girl on the left is a student.
Perhaps they are talking about the student's homework or a problem she has.

5 B

- Tell students they are going to listen to a conversation between a student and a teacher. Read out the question.
- Play the CD. Students listen and answer the question.
- Check the answer. Ask: What is the teacher's reply? (She says there's no one way to learn a language.)

5 LISTEN IN B **Answer**

Julia wants to know what the best way to learn English is.

5 C

- Ask students to read through the sentences before they listen.
- Play the CD again. Students listen and complete the sentences.
- Students compare their answers with a partner.
- Check the answers.
- Ask: What do you worry about when learning English? Do you think grammar mistakes are important? Do you think it's necessary to have a perfect accent?

5 LISTEN IN C **Answers**

1 learners	**2** write them down
3 grammar	**4** pronouncing the
5 have to have	**6** thousands

5 D

- Ask: Julia likes writing things down. How do *you* learn best? Discuss students' learning preferences and styles, focussing on whether students prefer to listen (auditory learners), look at things (visual learners) or move (kinetic learners). You might like to suggest tips for different types of learners.
- Ask: Generally speaking, how can people improve their English? Elicit tips for general language learning and write them on the board.
- This is a good chance to get feedback from your students. Ask: What part of class do you enjoy most? What would you like to change?

6 YOUR TURN TO SPEAK

A Role play

- Read the task with the class and make sure they understand it.
- Go through the phrases in **LB 26** with the class.
- Students work in pairs. Students decide on their roles.
- Students do their role play.
- Ask for volunteers to act our their role play in front of the class.
- To consolidate the language used in this activity, ask students to review the phrases in **LB 26** at home and do the exercise for homework.

B Conversation

- Read out the task. Go through the questions and phrases in **LB 27** with the class.
- In pairs, students talk about their arrangements and intentions.
- Ask some students to report back to the class.
- To consolidate the language used in this activity, ask students to review the phrases in **LB 27** at home and do the exercise for homework.

7 YOUR TOPIC

- Read out the task and the points learners have to prepare to speak about. Make sure they understand the word *improve.*
- Students discuss the points and make notes about them.
- Pairs or groups present their talk about learning English to the class or to a smaller group. Encourage students to ask questions about each other's presentations.

8 *ENGLISH-SPEAKING WORLD in English* — Page 73 SB

Picture / background information

The map shows where English is spoken and its relationship to other languages.

For a full list of countries where English is an official language:
www.en.wikipedia.org/wiki/English-speaking_countries

For information on colonisation and the British Empire:
www.bbc.co.uk/history/state/empire/index.shtml
www.en.wikipedia.org/wiki/British_Empire

For more information on the Commonwealth, see:
www.thecommonwealth.org/

The statistics in the text are from the British Council:
www.britishcouncil.org/english/engfaqs.htm
www.britishcouncil.org/learning-elt-future.pdf

Although the number of English speakers will continue to increase, the global percentage of speakers of English as their first language is in decline. A publication by David Graddol for the the British Council in 2006 called *English Next (Why global English may mean the end of English as a foreign language)* states that, 'there are signs that the global predominance of the language may fade in the foreseeable future' and that Asia, especially India and China, probably now holds the key to the long-term future of English as a global language'. According to one estimate there are over 300 million students of English in China.
www.britishcouncil.org/files/documents/learning-research-english-next.pdf

Mandarin Chinese (the language with the most native speakers in the world), Spanish, Urdu/Hindi and Arabic will continue to gain in importance.
news.nationalgeographic.com/news/2004/02/0226_040226_language.html

8 A

- You could start with the optional activity below. This is an area which needs constant revision and practice, particularly as far as pronunciation is concerned.

Optional activity: Countries, nationalities and languages

- Practise the vocabulary and pronunciation of countries, nationalities and languages.
- Elicit a list of about ten countries from students. Write them on the board. Make sure students can pronounce them correctly.
- Elicit the nationality of the people that live there and their language. Again check pronunciation.
- Look at the list. If there is an imbalance of countries from one or more continents (eg Europe), correct it by adding countries yourself and eliciting the nationalities and languages.
- It is impossible to include a comprehensive list here. Don't be afraid to check in a dictionary if you are unsure!

- Ask students (with books closed) what they know about the English-speaking world. Ask: In which countries do people speak English? Write students' ideas on the board. Check that they pronounce the countries correctly.
- Students look at the map on page 73. Briefly compare their ideas on the board to those coloured on the map but don't go into the different status of the English language in those countries yet.
- Read out the definitions in exercise **A** and check that students understand them.
- Students read the facts and figures and find words or phrases for the definitions.
- Check the answers. Make sure that students understand the difference between second language and foreign language. Give examples if necessary (eg English is a second language for native Spanish speakers in the USA, but English is a foreign language for people in Japan).
- Ask: Are there any important community languages in your / our country? Is anybody here bilingual?

8 *ENGLISH-SPEAKING WORLD in English* A **Answers**

1 second language **2** foreign language
3 community language **4** bilingual

8 B

- Look at the map with the students and read out the first question. Elicit answers orally. You might like to refer to the historical background for this. Ask:
  When did the British start building towns in the USA? (in the early seventeenth century: Jamestown, the first settlement, was established in 1607)
  When did the British sail to Australia and New Zealand? (in the late eighteenth century).
  You might also like to give students an overview of the population of these countries. Ask:
  How many people live in the UK? (about 60 million)
  How many people live in the USA? (about 300 million)
  In Australia? (just over 20 million)
  And in New Zealand? (just over 4 million).
- Read out the second question and again, elicit an oral response.
- Read out the third and fourth questions in turn. Allow students time to refer back to the *Fact and figures* and then elicit answers.

8 *ENGLISH-SPEAKING WORLD in English* B **Answers**

1 The UK (Britain and Northern Ireland), the USA and Australia, Guyana in South America. Also (not clear from the map) in Gibraltar and some Caribbean islands such as Jamaica and the Bahamas.
2 French in Canada; Maori in New Zealand
3 The UK has a large immigrant population.
4 An association of former British colonies (countries that were governed by Great Britain before they became independent).

8 C

- Read out the questions and check that students understand them.
- Students discuss the questions in pairs.
- Students report back to the class. (NB: the second question is intended to be provocative and in no way represents the authors' opinion. We are well aware that the spread of English is a sensitive issue in many countries.) You might like to ask students what the most important languages are in the world in term of numbers of native speakers. Ask: What do you think will happen in the future? Will English become more important or less important?

Optional project: An English-speaking country

- Tell students they are going to make a brochure about an English-speaking country.
- Students work in groups and choose a country. They think of ideas for what they might write about.
- Give students time to collect information outside class. They can use the internet, travel brochures, their own or friends' holiday experiences, postcards and any other sources.
- Students pool their information and write a short paragraph each for the brochure.
- Students put their brochure together and add photos or illustrations.

- Groups swap brochures and read them. Do this several times so all the brochures can be read.
- Invite feedback on the brochures.
- Take them in and then give students your own feedback.

9 PORTFOLIO WRITING

- Read out the task and check that students have understood it.
- With the class, brainstorm what the email could contain (for example, the class size and people on the course, the teacher, what the students do in class, an opinion about the teaching, excursions and visits, accommodation, the city itself).
- Elicit words to describe a course and a teacher (fantastic, excellent, terrible, boring,…) and words to describe a city like New York (exciting, amazing, dirty, stressful,…).
- Students write their essays in class or for homework.
- Ask students to swap emails with a partner and comment on them. Then take in the emails and check them.

10 *Your answer*

- Depending on the level of discussion so far, discuss or summarise ***The BIG Question***: *Why are you learning English*? as a class.
- Refer students to the Workbook Unit 16 activities.

Last word

- After doing the workbook activities, students evaluate their performance in the three areas. Check if any students feel they need extra practice in any area.

WORKBOOK answers

Pages 36–37 WB

1 Language: present continuous for future arrangements

1 A

1 'm helping **2** 'm going **3** 're checking
4 Are (you) playing **5** isn't playing **6** is coming
7 's taking **8** 're having

1 B

At 9.30 Victoria is going to the doctor's.
At 11.00 she's meeting Emma in town.
At 13.00 Victoria, Emma and Mel are having lunch.
At 16.00 she's going to the hairdresser's.
At 20.00 Victoria and David are having dinner.

1 C

(Individual answers)

1 D

(Individual answers)

2 Vocabulary

2 A

1 f **2** e **3** d **4** a **5** b **6** c

2 B

1 d **2** a **3** c **4** g **5** b **6** e **7** h **8** f

3 Use of English

1 People speak English all *over* the world.
2 I'd like to *improve* my English.
3 It's *impossible* to have a perfect accent.
4 I'm *doing* a language course in the summer.

4 Pronunciation

CD 1 (Blue) track 25

4 A

In sentences 1–4 the speaker's voice falls.

4 B

In sentences 1–4 the speaker's voice rises.

4 C

In **wh**-questions, the speaker's voice usually *falls*.
In **yes** / **no** questions, the speaker's voice usually *rises*.

5 Portfolio Writing

(Individual answers)

What's new?
Subject: Racism and prejudice
Focus: Reading an extract from a novel

1 *The BIG read:* *FACE*, by Benjamin Zephaniah

This extended reading deals with the themes surrounding racism and prejudice as related by the contemporary writer and poet Benjamin Zephaniah in his novel *Face*.

- Students read the information about the novel in the **FACT** box. Ask: What is the name of the boy in the novel? (Martin); What happens to him? (He has a terrible accident.)
- Students look at the photo of Benjamin Zephaniah and read the information about him. Ask questions about the author:
  How old is he? (He was born in 1958.)
  Where is he from? (Birmingham)
  What else does he do as well as writing novels? (He is a poet, novelist, playwright and performance artist. He has also acted in films and presented TV programmes.)
  Make sure students understand what a performance artist is: he or she performs poems and other pieces of writing using acting, dancing and music. Benjamin Zephaniah was an *oral poet* before he agreed to write his poems down and he says on his website that that is how he would prefer to describe himself.

Picture / background information

Resumé of the book:
Face is about a white teenage boy called Martin Turner. He lives in the racially-mixed East End of London. This area (just east of the City of London) used to be near the port of London, which has since moved to the mouth of the River Thames. The East End was traditionally where new immigrant groups settled first – Huguenots (Protestant Christians) feeling persecution in France in the 17th Century; Jews fleeing pogroms in Eastern Europe in the 19th Century; West Indians and Bangladeshis arriving to find work in England since the 1950s.

Martin is good-looking and has a pretty girlfriend called Natalie. He is in the Gang of Three with his friends Matthew and Mark and they have a reputation for playing tricks at school. Martin doesn't try at school and although he is a good gymnast, he lacks the discipline to take it further.

One night Martin, Matthew and Mark meet Pete Mosley, a member of a tough gang. He is joyriding in a stolen car with an older guy called Apache who seems to be on drugs. He wants the three boys to go with them but they are a bit scared. Matthew leaves but Martin and Mark agree to let Pete and Apache take them home. Apache takes them on a wild ride which turns into a police chase. They finally cross a red light and crash into another car. Mark and Apache get out the car but then the car explodes with Martin inside. He is rescued by police and taken to hospital. Pete Mosely dies and Apache is later sent to prison.

After the accident, Martin has to cope with people staring and making stupid remarks at school ('facial discrimination'). He reacts by becoming more serious and paying more attention to his lessons. His relationship with Mark and Matthew changes and he makes new friends – another badly disfigured boy and a group of black girls. Natalie finds a new good-looking boyfriend. Martin becomes captain of the gymnastics team and trains the team for A competition. The team doesn't win but the experience gives Martin back his confidence and self-respect.

This is what Benjamin Zephaniah says about his idea for *Face*:
One day I was driving through Liverpool when I stopped at a set of traffic lights. I looked to the right of me and in the next car was a man who had a very badly burnt face. I could see that he had received plastic surgery, he was very relaxed and at ease with himself but I could not help staring at him. In fact I was so stunned by the way he looked that I was almost in a state of shock. I didn't realise that he had driven off until the driver behind me started sounding his horn. Afterwards I did not feel happy with myself.

I have been to places where there are no Black people and have been stared at myself, so I should have known better. I wondered what prejudices a person with a disfigured face would come across. Was discrimination by face the same as discrimination by race? Was he ever bullied? What does real beauty mean? Who were his friends and lovers? These were the issues I wanted to explore in 'Face'.
www.benjaminzephaniah.com/teenz.html#face
Reviews of the book:
www.amazon.com/gp/product/1582347743/002-0229443-3904862?v=glance&n=283155
For more about Benjamin Zephaniah:
www.benjaminzephaniah.com/truth.html
www.penguin.co.uk/nf/Author/AuthorPage/0,,0_1000051523,00.html
www.contemporarywriters.com/authors/?p=auth105
For examples of his poems and information on his novels:
www.benjaminzephaniah.com
This extract is from pages 66-73 of *Face* by Benjamin Zephaniah, published by Bloomsbury Publishing, 1999. The extract has been abridged but not changed in any other way.

2 READING — CD2 (Red) track 18, page 75 SB

2 A 1

- Look at the cover of the book on page 75. First ask students to describe the cover (eg It's a boy's head with hair and ears, but no face. There's just white space and no face.) Ask: You now know that Martin, the boy in the novel, had a terrible accident. What do you think happened to him? Elicit ideas and write them on the board.

2 B

- Read out the questions. Tell students to read the extract quickly to find the answers.
- Check the answers. Compare them with students' ideas from exercise **A**.

2 READING B — Answers

Martin is in hospital. (explicit in line 10; *Nurse* should also give students a clue)
He has burns on his face / facial burns (lines 33–39).
He was in car crash / accident (lines 84 and 85).

2 C

- This exercise practises working out the meaning of unknown words from the context. Read out the words from the extract. Tell students to find the words in the text and see which definition best fits the context.
- Students read the text again and choose the correct meaning for the words.
- Check the answers.

2 READING C — Answers

1 b **2** c **3** b **4** c **5** b

2 D

- Read out the sentences and check that students understand them.
- Students read the text again carefully and decide if the statements are true or false.
- Students compare their answers with a partner.
- Check the answers. Ask students to quote evidence from the text. Find the place in the extract and discuss it with the students, focussing on the meaning and any new vocabulary such as *damage* or *nightmare*.

2 READING D — Answers

1 T (He has burns on his face and 'damage' to his legs. lines 38–44)
2 F (He thinks it's too early. He thinks Martin should prepare himself first. lines 28–30)
3 T (He says he thinks he might be locked in a nightmare. line 41)
4 F (He was on his way home. Pete Mosely was taking him home in a car. lines 84–88)
5 F (He cries for his face, for his parents and his friends. Because his face looks terrible, he feels he has hurt his parents and is afraid that he might lose his friends. lines 94–97)

2 E

- Read out the questions and the words to describe feelings in the box. Check that students understand the words, giving examples if necessary.
- Individually or in pairs, have students think about how Martin might feel in the situations given.

- If students have done the task individually, ask them to compare their answers with a partner.
- Students report back to the class. Discuss their answers.

2 READING E	Suggested answers
1 He is curious; he wants to see his face.	
2 He is frightened / scared but he is also determined to see his face.	
3 He is shocked and scared.	
4 He is angry with Pete Mosely and probably regretful that he got in the car.	
5 He is upset and he is worried how his friends will react.	

3 YOUR TURN TO SPEAK

3 A / B

- Read out the questions from **A** and **B** and make sure students understand them.
- Students discuss the questions in pairs or small groups.
- Ask students to report back to the class and discuss their ideas.
- Tell the students what happens to Martin's relationships with his friends after the accident and how he learns to adapt to his changed face (see book resumé in the background information section at the beginning).

3 C

- These questions go beyond what happened in the extract and deal with the main ideas behind the book.
- Read out the questions. Students work in groups and discuss the questions. Alternatively, you might prefer to discuss these questions as a class in order to give students more support. Elicit opinions and reasons from the class and encourage other students to agree or disagree.
- If students worked in groups, ask them to report back to the class. Discuss their ideas. You might like to tell students how Benjamin Zephaniah got the idea for his book (see initial **Background information** again).

3 D

- Read out the question and elicit reactions from the class. Encourage students to give reasons and invite other students to agree or agree.
- Ask students if they would like to read other works by this author. If you have time, you might like to look at one of Benjamin Zephaniah's poems with your class (see his website).

Optional portfolio writing

- Write these optional writing tasks on the board. Ask students to work with a partner or in small groups and choose a task.
  A Write Natalie's diary (about 150 words) for the day she first visits Martin in hospital (before and after her visit).
  B Write out the scene between Pete Mosely and Martin on the night of the crash.
- Students complete the task in class. Give them help with using any new vocabulary and expressing ideas.
- Check students' work. Ask one or two pairs or groups to read out their diary to the class.
- Ask one or two pairs or groups to act out their scene to the class.

WORKBOOK — Progress check 2

The Progress Check 2 after Unit 16 in the Workbook does not correspond directly to the Extended Reading in the Student's Book but revises the vocabulary and structures from the second half of the Student's Book (Units 9–16).

- Give the students the pages to do for homework and when checking the answers with the class, discuss and explain any unclear points.
- Alternatively, if you think your students need more support, revise word fields and structures with the class before students do the exercises either in class in pairs or at home.

WORKBOOK answers — Pages 38–39 WB

Progress check 2 (Units 9–16)

1 Language

1 A

1 are (you) doing **2** getting **3** won't be
4 're going **5** 'll rain **6** might travel **7** 'm doing
8 'll enjoy **9** might not be **10** 'll probably stay

1 B

(Individual answers)

1 C

(Example answers)
1 You have to *eat less.*
2 But you don't have to *stop eating all your favourite foods.*
3 You really need to do *some exercise.*
4 But you don't need to *do more than twenty minutes three times a week.*

1 D

1 I haven't spoken to my sister *for* three weeks.
2 My parents *have been* married since 1985. (Or: My parents were married *in* 1985.)
3 *(correct)*
4 My family *has lived* in the same house since I was born.
5 *(correct)*
6 My grandparents have been dead *for* a long time.

1 E

(Example answers)
1 If everybody has a robot in the future, *people will have more free time.*
2 The printer won't work unless *you switch it on.*
3 You can take fantastic photos if *you have a good camera.*
4 If we buy a flat screen TV, *we won't have to watch films at the cinema.*
5 Unless you get internet access, *you'll have to download music at the internet café.*
6 People get annoyed with machines if *they don't work.*

1 F

1 Everybody needs to learn foreign languages <u>to get</u> a good job.
2 People use English <u>to communicate</u> with people from many countries.
3 Most people do courses <u>to learn</u> foreign languages.
4 A lot of people stay in an English-speaking country <u>to learn</u> English.
5 It's a good idea to listen to CDs <u>to improve</u> your accent.
6 You can use the internet <u>to get to know</u> people from different countries.

1 G

1 was flying **2** had **3** was reading **4** said
5 started **6** had to **7** was screaming
8 were landing **9** stopped **10** landed

2 Vocabulary

2 A

1 medicine, cancer, vaccine, disease, injection
2 engagement, graduation, birth, wedding, anniversary
3 printing press, robot, batteries, dishwasher, wheel

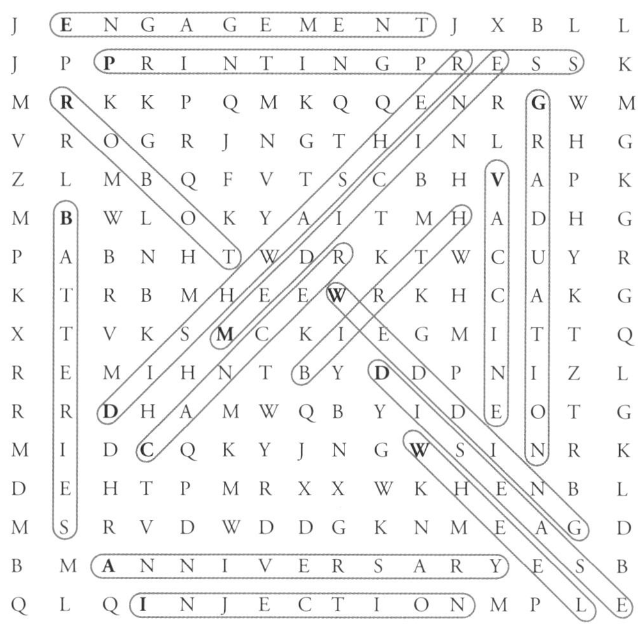

2 B

1 a **2** h **3** g **4** c **5** d **6** f **7** b **8** e

2 C

Bikes: e) handlebars, g) pedal, k) saddle
Cars: a) drive, b) exhaust pipe, f) steering wheel
Planes: c) fare, d) flight, j) passengers
Roads: h) roundabout, i) traffic lights, l) junction

2 D

1 e **2** c **3** d **4** g **5** b **6** a **7** f **8** h

2 E

1 b **2** d **3** a **4** d **5** a **6** b

PET Exam Practice Materials

For each Unit of ***QSE Pre-Intermediate*** there is an **exam practice test** in the style of the Cambridge ESOL Preliminary English Test (PET). These practice tests are found on pages 146 to 161. They are in addition to the many activities in the course which follow the aims and principles of the Cambridge examinations. The PET Exam is set at the Council of Europe's Common European Framework of Reference (CEF) Level B1. This in turn was based on the Threshold Level (1990). Teachers accustomed to the Threshold Level will find that ***QSE Pre-Intermediate*** is designed to cover all of its main elements. At the back of this Teacher's Guide there are two lists of 'Can-do' statements, one for the teacher's reference and the other self-assessment by students. These are derived from the CEF Level B1. Please note that they do not pretend to be comprehensive (a full list is available from the Council of Europe website (http://www.coe.int/t/dg4/linguistic/CADREEN.asp).

The PET Exams covers all four skills. The authors have chosen to practise particularly the Reading and Speaking sections of the examination in these photocopiable pages. The Listening and Writing components are extensively covered in the Student's Book and Workbook. There is an **answer key** to the PET Exams on pages 194-195 of this book.

Paper 1 Reading	Part 1 Part 2 Part 3 Part 4 Part 5	Unit 1 Unit 3, 11 Unit 5, 13 Unit 7 Unit 9, 15	**Paper 3 Speaking**	Part 2 Part 3 Part 4	Unit 4, 8, 12, 16 Unit 2, 6, 10, 14 Unit 2, 6

PET Exam practice can be photocopied for the whole class

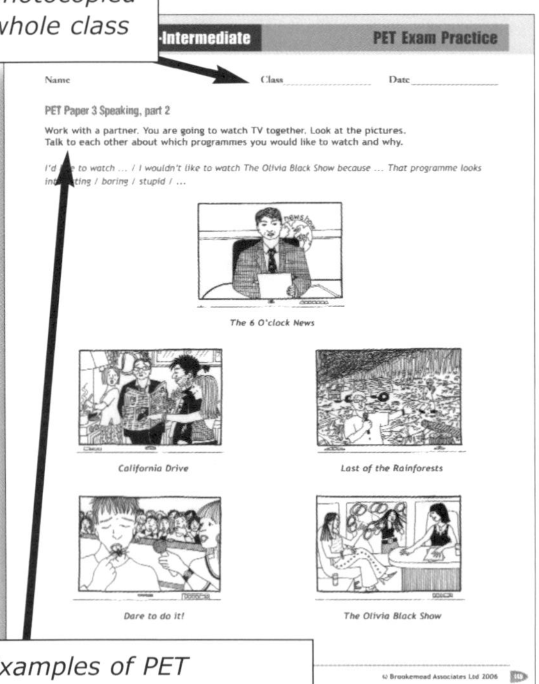
-Intermediate PET Exam Practice

Name Class Date

PET Paper 3 Speaking, part 2

Work with a partner. You are going to watch TV together. Look at the pictures. Talk to each other about which programmes you would like to watch and why.

I'd [illegible] to watch … / I wouldn't like to watch The Olivia Black Show because … That programme looks in[illegible]ting / boring / stupid / …

The 6 O'clock News

California Drive

Last of the Rainforests

Dare to do it!

The Olivia Black Show

© Brookemead Associates Ltd 2006

Examples of PET Speaking Tests for 8 out of 16 Units

Examples of PET Reading Tests for 8 out of 16 Units

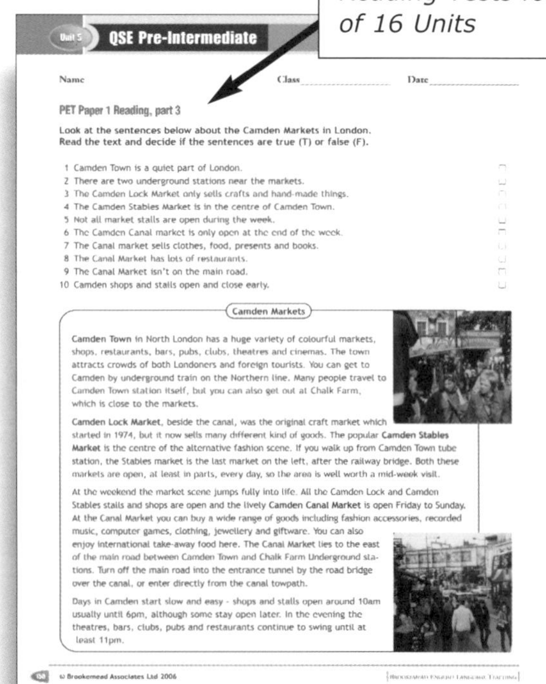
QSE Pre-Intermediate

Name Class Date

PET Paper 1 Reading, part 3

Look at the sentences below about the Camden Markets in London. Read the text and decide if the sentences are true (T) or false (F).

1 Camden Town is a quiet part of London.
2 There are two underground stations near the markets.
3 The Camden Lock Market only sells crafts and hand-made things.
4 The Camden Stables Market is in the centre of Camden Town.
5 Not all market stalls are open during the week.
6 The Camden Canal market is only open at the end of the week.
7 The Canal market sells clothes, food, presents and books.
8 The Canal Market has lots of restaurants.
9 The Canal Market isn't on the main road.
10 Camden shops and stalls open and close early.

Camden Markets

Camden Town in North London has a huge variety of colourful markets, shops, restaurants, bars, pubs, clubs, theatres and cinemas. The town attracts crowds of both Londoners and foreign tourists. You can get to Camden by underground train on the Northern line. Many people travel to Camden Town station itself, but you can also get out at Chalk Farm, which is close to the markets.

Camden Lock Market, beside the canal, was the original craft market which started in 1974, but it now sells many different kind of goods. The popular **Camden Stables Market** is the centre of the alternative fashion scene. If you walk up from Camden Town tube station, the Stables market is the last market on the left, after the railway bridge. Both these markets are open, at least in parts, every day, so the area is well worth a mid-week visit.

At the weekend the market scene jumps fully into life. All the Camden Lock and Camden Stables stalls and shops are open and the lively **Camden Canal Market** is open Friday to Sunday. At the Canal Market you can buy a wide range of goods including fashion accessories, recorded music, computer games, clothing, jewellery and giftware. You can also enjoy international take-away food here. The Canal Market lies to the east of the main road between Camden Town and Chalk Farm Underground stations. Turn off the main road into the entrance tunnel by the road bridge over the canal, or enter directly from the canal towpath.

Days in Camden start slow and easy - shops and stalls open around 10am usually until 6pm, although some stay open later. In the evening the theatres, bars, clubs, pubs and restaurants continue to swing until at least 11pm.

© Brookemead Associates Ltd 2006

Unit-by-Unit Test Materials

For each Unit of ***QSE Pre-Intermediate*** there is a two-page **Quick Smart Test** (see pages 162-193). Each of these Tests marks the students' progress in **Vocabulary, Reading, Language** (grammar) and **Pronunciation**. These photocopiable tests are in addition to the two **Progress checks** in the Workbook (pages 20-21 and 38-39). The **Quick Smart Tests** have been designed to revise the work covered in each Unit, but present it in a slightly different context – still retaining the format of exercises that students will encounter in various examinations.

Each of the **Quick Smart Tests** is marked out of 30 points. This scoring makes it easy for students to check their own progress. The marking scheme for the individual sections (Vocabulary, Language etc) varies, but the overall total for each Test is the same.

There is an **answer key** to the Tests at the back of this Teacher's Guide (see pages 196-197). This key can be used either by the teacher marking the Tests, or by the students themselves. The authors have a slight preference for self-assessment, and encourage students to compete against themselves, rather than against each other for the highest mark in the class. Teachers can suggest that students keep their Tests in a folder, so they can see how they are improving.

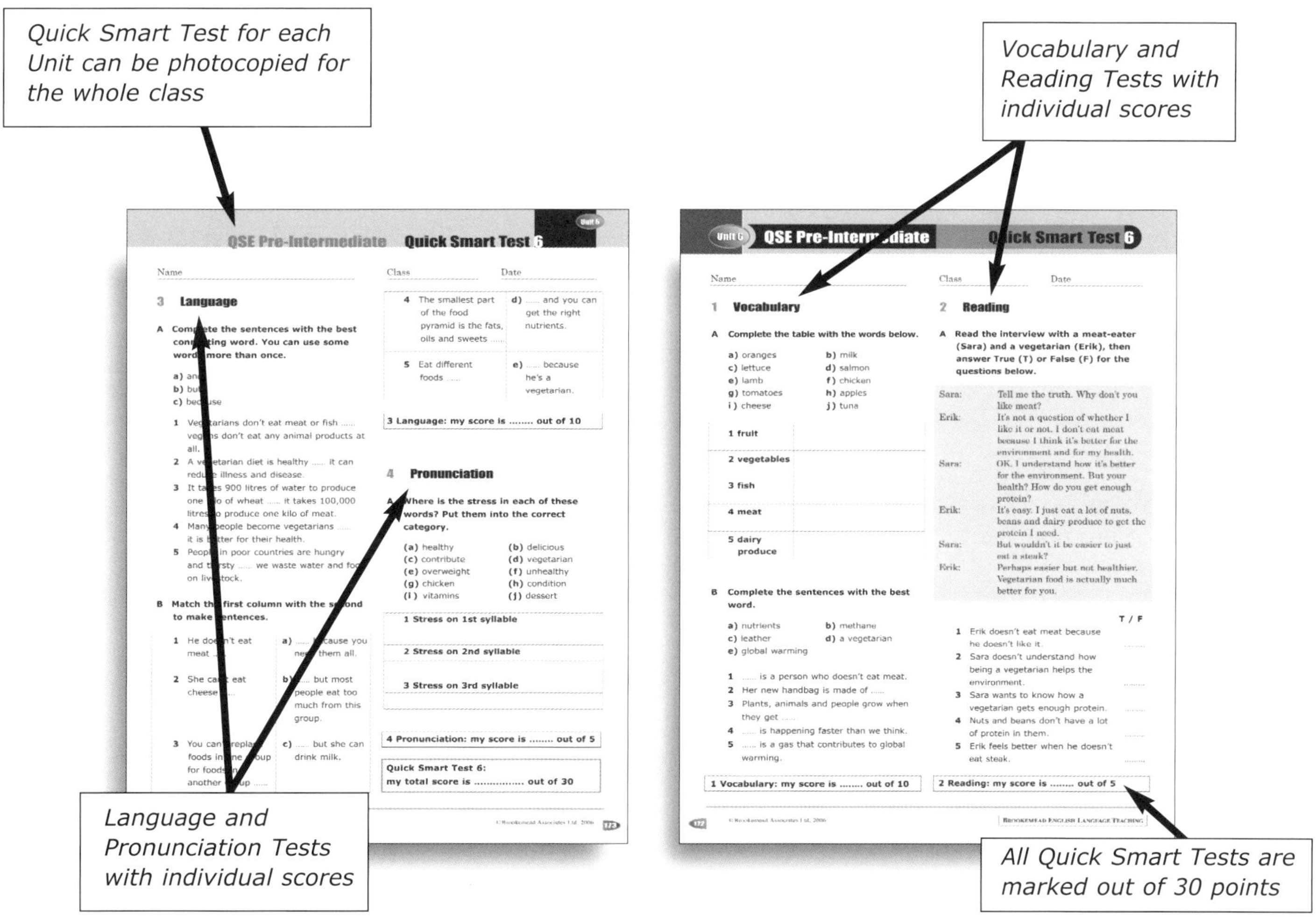

Name ______________________ Class ______________ Date ______________

PET Paper 1 Reading, part 1

Look at the text in each question. What does it say? Choose A, B or C.

1

> **LOST**
>
> I lost my SILVER RING in the changing rooms on Monday. It's not valuable, but it means a lot to me. Did you find it? Please call JASMIN on 7802 74 1094

A Jasmin has lost an expensive ring. ☐
B Jasmin found a ring and wants to give it back. ☐
C Jasmin wants her ring back. ☐

2

> To Fabio
> From Matt
>
> Hi Fabio
> I had a really exciting day yesterday. I went skydiving. I wasn't frightened at all – well, only a bit!
> See you soon
> Matt

Yesterday Matt had...
A ...a bad experience. ☐
B ...a good experience. ☐
C ...a boring day. ☐

3

> The use of this equipment does not guarantee personal safety or freedom from physical injury

This equipment...
A ...is 100% safe. ☐
B ...cannot promise safety. ☐
C ...causes injury. ☐

4

> **To all participants**
> **Please observe the safety regulations at all times.**

A Make sure you always have the right equipment. ☐
B Always follow the rules. ☐
C Always watch the instructors carefully. ☐

5

> Dear Emma
> Wish you were here! The weather is perfect for skiing. Nothing broken so far!
> See you next week
> Olivia

Olivia...
A ...wishes she was at home. ☐
B ...has had a skiing accident. ☐
C ...is enjoying her skiing holiday. ☐

Name________________________ Class______________ Date______________

PET Paper 3 Speaking, part 3

1 SPEAKING TEST

1 

2 

Work with a partner. (*3 minutes*)
Partner A: Describe picture 1 to your partner.
Partner B: Describe picture 2 to your partner.

Think about these questions:

- Where are the people in the picture?
- What time of day is it?
- What kinds of events are shown?
- What are the people doing?
- What are they wearing?
- What is happening?

PET Paper 3 Reading, part 4

2 SPEAKING TEST

(*3 minutes*)
These two photographs show people enjoying themselves at different kinds of events. Talk to your partner about similar events you have been to, or why you would like, or not like to attend events such as those shown in the photographs.

Name____________________ Class__________ Date__________

PET Paper 1 Reading, part 2

The people below are all looking for a job. Look at the eight job adverts (A-H). Decide which job would be the most suitable for each of the people (1-5).

1

Dario is an English student. At the moment his English isn't very good. He would like a job in the evening or at weekends to help him pay for his English course.

2

Alice is a software programmer for a large financial company. She enjoys her job but is looking for something a bit different.

3

Marcelline has just finished a business studies course at college. She would like a challenging, well-paid job with an international company.

4

Ranjit is a geography teacher in a large school. He likes teaching but he's tired of working in a classroom. He would like to spend less time on paperwork.

5

Rose has excellent IT skills. She is looking for a job where she can work with computers as part of a team.

SITUATIONS VACANT – FIND YOUR NEW JOB HERE

A Adult education teacher
Are you an experienced teacher tired of working in a school? Why not teach reading, writing and maths to young adult learners? The job includes preparing and organising courses as well as teaching students individually and in small groups. Most classes are in daytime hours but some evening work can be expected.

B Project accountant
We are a large international company. We are looking for an accountant to work in the company's offices here and abroad. Travel is an important part of the job. You must be able to work independently and under stress. Excellent salary for the right person.

C Ski resort manager
We provide high quality ski holidays. We require a qualified person for a busy ski resort in Switzerland. You will manage a team of people and make sure that guests have a fantastic holiday experience. You must be able to be cool and calm in difficult situations.

D Field studies instructor
Do you want more than just a job? We provide activity holidays and educational courses for children. We are looking for a field studies instructor to help children understand the world around them. The outside world will be your classroom. You need IT skills and an interest in working with children.

E Cleaner
Are you flexible, honest and reliable? We are looking for a cleaner for our large office. The job includes cleaning floors and desks and washing up. Experience preferred but not necessary. 15 hours a week, evenings.

F Weekend sales assistant
We are looking for a person to work in our family-run garden centre. Weekends only. Would suit student. The job includes selling plants and other items and giving advice to customers. Basic knowledge of plants necessary.

G Library / IT assistant
We need an assistant to join our team at the central library. You will sort and organise books and provide help with customer enquiries. You should be friendly, have a positive attitude and be happy to help. Good IT skills necessary but no other experience needed.

H ICT specialist
We are an exciting young company in the sports and leisure industry. We sell fantastic days out to our customers, such as helicopter trips and skydiving. We are looking for a computer specialist to join our enthusiastic team. Normal office hours.

Name____________________ Class______________ Date______________

PET Paper 3 Speaking, part 2

Work with a partner. You are going to watch TV together. Look at the pictures. Talk to each other about which programmes you would like to watch and why.

I'd like to watch ... / I wouldn't like to watch The Olivia Black Show because ... That programme looks interesting / boring / stupid / ...

The 6 O'clock News

California Drive

Last of the Rainforests

Dare to do it!

The Olivia Black Show

Name________________ Class__________ Date__________

PET Paper 1 Reading, part 3

Look at the sentences below about the Camden Markets in London. Read the text and decide if the sentences are true (T) or false (F).

1 Camden Town is a quiet part of London. ☐
2 There are two underground stations near the markets. ☐
3 The Camden Lock Market only sells crafts and hand-made things. ☐
4 The Camden Stables Market is in the centre of Camden Town. ☐
5 Not all market stalls are open during the week. ☐
6 The Camden Canal market is only open at the end of the week. ☐
7 The Canal market sells clothes, food, presents and books. ☐
8 The Canal Market has lots of restaurants. ☐
9 The Canal Market isn't on the main road. ☐
10 Camden shops and stalls open and close early. ☐

Camden Markets

Camden Town in North London has a huge variety of colourful markets, shops, restaurants, bars, pubs, clubs, theatres and cinemas. The town attracts crowds of both Londoners and foreign tourists. You can get to Camden by underground train on the Northern line. Many people travel to Camden Town station itself, but you can also get out at Chalk Farm, which is close to the markets.

Camden Lock Market, beside the canal, was the original craft market which started in 1974, but it now sells many different kind of goods. The popular **Camden Stables Market** is the centre of the alternative fashion scene. If you walk up from Camden Town tube station, the Stables market is the last market on the left, after the railway bridge. Both these markets are open, at least in parts, every day, so the area is well worth a mid-week visit.

At the weekend the market scene jumps fully into life. All the Camden Lock and Camden Stables stalls and shops are open and the lively **Camden Canal Market** is open Friday to Sunday. At the Canal Market you can buy a wide range of goods including fashion accessories, recorded music, computer games, clothing, jewellery and giftware. You can also enjoy international take-away food here. The Canal Market lies to the east of the main road between Camden Town and Chalk Farm Underground stations. Turn off the main road into the entrance tunnel by the road bridge over the canal, or enter directly from the canal towpath.

Days in Camden start slow and easy – shops and stalls open around 10am usually until 6pm, although some stay open later. In the evening the theatres, bars, clubs, pubs and restaurants continue to swing until at least 11pm.

Name_______________ Class_______________ Date_______________

PET Paper 3 Speaking, parts 3 and 4

A

Work with a partner.
Partner A: Describe picture 1 to you partner.
Partner B: Describe picture 2.

Think about these questions:

- Who are the people in the picture?
- Where are they?
- What are the people doing?
- What food can you see?

B

Work with a partner. Talk together about the kind of food you ate as a child and the kind of food you eat now.

Think about:

- your likes and dislikes
- healthy and unhealthy food
- meals at home and meals out
- who prepares the food at home?

1

2

Name______________________ Class______________ Date______________

PET Paper 1 Reading, part 4

Amber Lane, college student and blogger

I started blogging to keep in touch with friends and family when I went away to college. I had a lot of friends who knew about technology, and they were all blogging. A friend who knew about web design helped me and away I went from there. My first entries weren't about anything in particular but I've changed my blog a lot. About a two hundred people read my blog regularly now.

I didn't know the word 'blog' before college, but then I realised that I actually had one with a friend when I was at school. We posted pictures and lots of other stuff on the MySpace website. My blogging has changed a lot since then. Now I focus on certain topics such as the latest technology, internet links that I like and my journalism course. My blog is also where I discuss books I am reading. When I go travelling on holiday, I post pictures of my trip.

My second blog is for my news writing class. All of us have got news blogs. It's a great way for the class to learn and share things with each another. The blogs give us a way to communicate outside the classroom. I actually have blogs for four of my five classes. Three of them are group blogs. I love using new forms of communication; it makes the learning experience much more interesting and valuable.

1 In this text Amber Lane is talking about ...
- A ... what blogs are
- B ... the development of blogging
- C ... how she uses blogs
- D ... the advantages of internet technology

2 How has Amber changed her personal blog?
- A She posts more entries.
- B She focuses on particular themes.
- C She has just got a new blog design.
- D She now shares a blog with a friend.

3 What does Amber say about blogging before college?
- A She didn't know how to post things on the internet before college.
- B She had a blog but didn't call it that.
- C She had a photo website but not a blog.
- D She wasn't interested in blogging then.

4 What does Amber think of class blogs?
- A They're a good way to learn about technology.
- B They improve the learning experience.
- C They make the learning experience more individual.
- D They're good fun.

5 Which of the following is the best description of Amber?
- A A future web designer who likes blogging.
- B A future writer who wants to share ideas about books.
- C A future journalist who uses blogs for professional and personal reasons.
- D A future computer specialist who is interested in the technology of blogs.

Name________________________ Class______________ Date______________

PET Paper 3 Speaking, part 2

Work with a partner. Your friend is going on a backpacking holiday to Peru. Talk together about the clothes and accessories he will need. Agree on the most important things he should take with him. Use the pictures to help you. You can also use your own ideas.

- *I think ...*
- *I prefer / I like ...*
- *What do you think?*
- *I agree / I don't agree.*

Name________________ Class________________ Date________________

PET Paper 1 Reading, part 5

Read the text below and choose the correct word for each space.
For each question, choose the correct letter A, B, C or D.

Example:

0	A	little	B	few	<u>C</u>	lot	D	lots
1	A	what	B	which	C	who	D	how
2	A	make	B	cause	C	develop	D	produce
3	A	by	B	as	C	for	D	to
4	A	good	B	bad	C	well	D	badly
5	A	much	B	many	C	any	D	no
6	A	must	B	doesn't have to	C	shouldn't	D	can
7	A	on	B	for	C	from	D	by
8	A	if	B	when	C	before	D	during
9	A	too	B	as well	C	also	D	in addition
10	A	take	B	speak	C	reply	D	answer

Cultural rules for greetings

A (0) .... of greetings are international: shaking hands, kissing and bowing. But where people shake hands or bow and exactly (1) .... they do it can often (2) .... problems. In the UK, (3) .... example, it is unusual to kiss people you don't know (4) ...., but this is the rule in countries such as Russia or Italy. In the USA and in (5) .... European countries, shaking hands is a quick greeting. In Singapore or in China, a handshake (6) .... last up to ten seconds or longer. Likewise, the number of kisses depends (7) .... the country and sometimes even the regions of a country. In France people usually kiss twice, both (8) .... they meet and when they leave, but it can be three or even four times in Paris. Telephone greetings (9) .... vary. In Germany people (10) .... the phone with their last name, in Denmark with their first name and in the UK with 'Hello' or the telephone number. In the Czech Republic they say 'Please'; in Greece they say 'Can I help you?', and in Italy 'I'm ready'.

Name______________________ Class______________ Date______________

PET Paper 3 Speaking, part 3

Work with a partner.
Partner A: Describe picture 1 to your partner.
Partner B: Describe picture 2 to your partner.

Think about these questions:

- When is the picture from?
- Where is the person in the picture?
- What is the person doing?
- What equipment is he/she using?
- What is he/she wearing?
- How does the person feel?

1

2

Name______________________ Class______________ Date______________

PET Paper 1 Reading, part 2

The people below all want to go on holiday. Look at the eight holiday adverts (A-H). Decide which holiday would be the most suitable for people 1-5.

1

Monty and Daisy are both accountants. They lead busy lives and would like a relaxing holiday in a warm country.

2

Ilona is a college student. She is planning to go on holiday with three friends from college. She would like to see new countries.

3

Christos supports eco-friendly and sustainable tourism. He doesn't like beach holidays. He would like an interesting holiday where he can meet new people.

4

Miki and her parents would like an exciting but very comfortable holiday. Miki's parents are paying for the trip.

5

Luke is an artist. He would like a very cheap holiday where he can paint pictures of the sea.

A Mallorca
Great beaches, lots of bars and some of the best clubs in Europe. Plus restaurants, markets, designer shopping, watersports and sunshine – Mallorca has it all! Are you between 18 and 30? Join us for two weeks of partying in the sun and choose from fifteen fantastic hotels. It'll be a holiday you'll never forget.

B On safari
Safari holiday in Tanzania, East Africa. If you are looking for excitement and serious luxury, this is the holiday for you. This is your chance to see wild animals, including elephants, leopards and lions in their natural habitat. Stay in a luxury camp with wonderful food and service. 100% safety guaranteed.

C Working holiday in Corsica
Want to go somewhere nice in the summer but don't have enough money? What about a working holiday? We need an au pair (male or female) to look after our two small children in the evenings while we work in the family restaurant. We live on the beautiful island of Corsica with fantastic beaches and scenery.

D The Bay Hotel, Whitby
Come to Whitby, the beautiful seaside town on the north-east coast of England. In Whitby, you can explore local fishing and whaling history. You can also visit the beautiful churches and shop for souvenirs in the old town. In the evenings relax in our famous restaurant and enjoy our excellent food and wines.

E Let's surf
Surf Vacations has been the best in the business for over twenty years. We offer top surfing trips and surf camps, with something for everyone – from beginners to professional surfers. Choose Surf Vacations and we guarantee you the best waves, the best facilities and the most exciting experiences.

F Europe by train
On a low budget? Explore Europe by train. Travel through Europe for a month from Norway to Morocco on our special ticket. See new places, meet new people and discover new things about yourself. All you need for an adventure of a lifetime is a sleeping bag, a tent, a guidebook – and our ticket.

G Apartments on Naxos
Naxos is the biggest island of the Greek Cyclades islands with beautiful sandy beaches and a clear blue sea. Visit the island's mountains and pretty villages. Or just relax and enjoy the great weather. All our comfortable apartments have views of the sea, use of the pool and room service.

H Kilimaro climb
A holiday of a lifetime. Climb Africa's highest mountain in eight days. We travel through farmland, forest and ice, with fantastic views. This is a small group adventure holiday – a great way to see a new place and find new friends. The money from this holiday goes to a project that helps local people.

Name______________________ Class______________ Date______________

PET Paper 3 Speaking, part 2

Work with a partner. Your sister has won a lot of money in the lottery. Talk together about how you think she should spend the money. Use the picture to help you. You can also use your own ideas.

- *She should / shouldn't ...*
- *It's a good / bad idea to ...*
- *I agree / I don't agree.*

Name______________________ Class______________ Date______________

PET Paper 1 Reading, part 3

Look at the sentences below about the Cycling Club.
Read the text and decide if the sentences are true or false.
If it is correct, mark it with an A. If it is not correct, mark it with a B.

1 The Cycling Club represents one local area. ☐
2 The club wants better safety for cyclists and fewer cars on the roads. ☐
3 The club wants special roads for cyclists. ☐
4 Cycling makes you happy. ☐
5 Cycling is good for individuals and for our society. ☐
6 The Cycling Club is against public transport. ☐
7 If you join the Cycling Club, you get a free safe cycling course. ☐
8 Members of the club get a new bike. ☐
9 Members can regularly read the club's latest news. ☐
10 The club welcomes ideas from its members. ☐

The Cycling Club

Who are we?

The Cycling Club is a national organisation with over 15,000 members. We promote cycling and are working to improve conditions for cycling. We want:

- more people on bikes
- bike road safety lessons for all school children
- more cycle lanes and safer roads
- traffic lights for bikes
- safe parking for bikes in cities and towns
- regular car-free days
- more participation in National Bike Week
- new rules and regulations for car drivers

Why cycle?

Cycling is good for you and good for the environment. More people on bikes mean fewer traffic jams and other traffic problems and less air and noise pollution. More people on bikes also mean healthier and happier people – if the roads are safe. In addition, cycling is a cheap method of transport. If you can't cycle all the way to work or college, combine a bike ride with public transport: you can take bikes on most trains and trams and on some buses.

Join our club! You get ...

- all the news on our club website.
- regular bike rides and social events
- free cycling maps
- advice on safe cycling
- discounts on safe cycling courses
- discounts on bike repair courses
- discounts on new bikes in bike shops around the country
- cheap cycle insurance

Contact us! Tell us ...

- ... what you think of cycling safety and transport in your area
- ... what you would like to improve in your area
- ... your ideas to get more people on their bikes!

Name________________ Class____________ Date____________

PET Paper 3 Speaking, parts 3 and 4

A

Work with a partner. Partner A: Describe picture 1 to you partner.
Partner B: Describe picture 2.

Think about these questions:

- Who are the people in the picture?
- Where are they?
- What are the people doing?
- How do they feel? Why?

B

Work with a partner. Talk together about the kind of family you have and the kind of family you would prefer.

Think about:

- the size of your family
- the members of your family
- how much you like each other
- what you would like to change about your family (if anything). Use *I think ..., I'd prefer ..., I'd like ...*

Name________________ Class________________ Date________________

PET Paper 1 Reading, part 5

Read the text below and choose the correct word for each space.
For each question, choose the correct letter A, B, C or D.

Example:

0	A	since	B	by	C	in	**D**	for

1	A	become	B	get	C	suffer	D	feel
2	A	virus	B	vaccine	C	epidemic	D	disease
3	A	before	B	while	C	if	D	but
4	A	from	B	of	C	to	D	for
5	A	contain	B	spread	C	include	D	complete
6	A	who	B	which	C	whose	D	where
7	A	lasted	B	was	C	made	D	took
8	A	quick	B	quickly	C	slow	D	slowly
9	A	begin	B	began	C	begun	D	beginning
10	A	discoveries	B	drugs	C	injections	D	answers

What is cancer?

Cancer is not a new illness. It has been around (0) .... thousands and thousands of years. Plants can (1) .... cancer. Dinosaurs probably had it.

People often think of 'cancer' as one (2) .... with one cause, like flu. This is not quite right. Cancer is any illness that results (3) .... the body's cells grow out of control. There are lots of different kinds of cancer. DNA damage is the cause (4) .... most cancers. Things that can damage DNA (5) .... chemicals in cigarette smoke, and ultraviolet (UV) light. People (6) .... have an unhealthy diet are more likely to develop cancer.

It (7) .... a long time for doctors to start treating cancer. But treatment has developed (8) .... in the last fifty years. In 1953 Francis Crick and James Watson worked out the structure of DNA. Since then scientists have (9) .... to study and understand the causes of cancer, and to invent new treatments. At the moment scientists are making new (10) .... about cancer nearly every week.

Find out more at: http://info.cancerresearchuk.org/cancerandresearch/learnaboutcancer/

Name________________________________ Class__________________ Date__________________

PET Paper 3 Speaking, part 2

Work with a partner. Your friend wants to do an English course in the UK.
Talk together about what he or she should think about.
Use the pictures to help you. You can also use your own ideas.

- *He should think about ...*
- *It's a good idea to check if ...*
- *..... is very important.*

Name ______________________ Class ______________ Date ______________

1 Vocabulary

A Match the words with the sentence that best describes the sport.

a) surfing
b) skydiving
c) BMX biking
d) inline skating
e) bungee jumping

1 To do this sport, you have to jump out of an aeroplane. ......
2 To do this sport, you have to like the sea. ......
3 To do this sport, you have to like danger and ride very fast. ......
4 To do this sport, you have to use shoes with wheels. ......
5 To do this sport, you have to like to hang in the air. ......

B Complete the sentences with the best word or phrase.

a) cut or bruise
b) broken leg
c) sprained wrist
d) sprained knee
e) cracked rib

1 When you have a ...... , it hurts when you breathe.
2 When you have a ...... , you can't move your hand easily.
3 When you have a ...... , you can't walk.
4 When you have a ...... , it's difficult to walk.
5 When you have a ...... , you have to wear a bandage.

1 Vocabulary: my score is .... out of 10

2 Reading

A Read the following interview with Erika, a surfer, then answer True (T) or False (F) for the questions below.

I first started surfing seriously when I was 10. Does that seem young? Not where I'm from. Everyone lives near the beach so it was easy to learn how to surf. I loved the ocean and the adrenalin rush I got every time I caught a wave. I surfed every day after school until I was 17. Then I entered a national surfing contest and won! I knew that surfing was more than just fun for me. It was a way of life. I feel more alive when I surf. And what's even better – lots of girls like me are professional surfers now.

T / F

1 Erika was too young when she started to surf. ....
2 Erika surfed every day after school. ....
3 She loved the adrenalin rush of catching a wave. ....
4 Erika didn't surf every day until she was 17. ....
5 Erika won a surfing competition. ....
6 For Erika surfing is just fun. ....
7 Not many girls like to surf. ....

2 Reading: my score is .... out of 7

Name ________________ Class ________ Date ________

3 Language

A Put the following sentences in the correct order 1-5.

a) ...... After that, I went out everyday and practised on my skateboard.
b) ...... I got a skateboard for my birthday two years ago.
c) ...... First I went straight to the shop to buy knee pads and a helmet.
d) ...... That was the beginning of my interest in the best sport in the world.
e) ...... Even today, two years later, my parents can't believe how much I love it.

B Choose the right form of the verb to complete the sentences.

a) thought
b) got
c) learnt
d) planned
e) was

1 The two men ...... to jump out of the plane at exactly 12:05.
2 I ...... so much when I went to ski class last year.
3 Yesterday he ...... very nervous before the race started.
4 As a professional skydiver, he ...... extremely fit.
5 She ...... BMX biking was the best sport in the world.

3 Language: my score is .... out of 10

4 Pronunciation

A Which words contain a sound which is *unlike* the others?

A	B	C
1 player	**1** swimming	**1** wrist
2 baseball	**2** biking	**2** ice
3 started	**3** cycling	**3** fight
4 dangerous	**4** diving	**4** eye

4 Pronunciation: my score is .... out of 3

Quick Smart Test 1:
my total score is .... out of 30

Name ____________ Class ____________ Date ____________

1 Vocabulary

A Complete the sentences with the correct verb.

a) wear
b) celebrate
c) make
d) watch
e) have

1 Some people use controversial floats to ...... a protest.
2 The music and dancing make it fun to ...... the parade.
3 Many people like to ...... amazing costumes at carnivals.
4 The idea behind most festivals is to ...... a good time.
5 Many countries ...... some kind of festival every year.

B Answer True (T) or False (F) to the following questions.

1 A float is part of a carnival parade. ......
2 All floats require sponsorship. ......
3 When something is controversial, people usually have a lot to say about it. ......
4 Slaves are people who aren't free. ......
5 Dancing is not allowed at most festivals. ......

C Put these words into the correct categories.

1 costumes
2 decks
3 floats
4 dancers
5 turntables

a) festivals and carnivals	b) DJ mixing

1 Vocabulary: my score is .... out of 15

2 Reading

A Complete the dialogue with one of the phrases below.

a) tracks
b) mix together
c) musical instrument
d) clubs
e) fastest growing music market

Interviewer:	Is it easy to find jobs as a DJ?
DJ:	No. DJ mixing is the 1) ...... now. You have to be really good at it to get work.
Interviewer:	Do you have to play a 2) ...... to be good at mixing?
DJ:	No, but it helps. You understand the music better.
Interviewer:	How do you know which tracks 3) ...... well?
DJ:	Practice. Sometimes very different 4) ...... sound really good together.
Interviewer:	What's the best part about your job?
DJ:	That I only work at night at my favourite 5) ...... !

2 Reading: my score is .... out of 5

Name ______ Class ______ Date ______

3 Language

A Choose the best word to complete the sentences.

1 Club members work ...... on their floats for the Carnival every year.

a) hard
b) passionate
c) corruptly
d) usually

2 DJ mixing is growing ...... in the music market today.

a) slow
b) often
c) fast
d) sometimes

3 To be a performer at a carnival, you have to dance ......

a) perfectly
b) hardly
c) always
d) unlikely

4 People support their schools ...... at Carnival.

a) usually
b) likely
c) slowly
d) passionately

5 Music, costumes and dancing are almost ...... a part of all festivals.

a) always
b) never
c) not usually
d) really

3 Language: my score is .... out of 5

4 Pronunciation

A Where is the stress in each of these words? Put them into the correct category.

(a) mixer	**(b)** support
(c) celebration	**(d)** politicians
(e) corrupt	**(f)** traditions
(g) music	**(h)** carnival
(i) decorations	**(j)** costume

1 Stress on 1st syllable
2 Stress on 2nd syllable
3 Stress on 3rd syllable

4 Pronunciation: my score is .... out of 5

Quick Smart Test 2:
my total score is .... out of 30

Name ____________ Class ____________ Date ____________

1 Vocabulary

A Match the words with the sentence that best describes the job.

a) accountants
b) gardeners / garden specialists
c) managers
d) ski instructors
e) computer programmers

1 ...... love the outdoors and cold weather.
2 ...... look at a screen and write software.
3 ...... know a lot about plants.
4 ...... attend a lot of meetings.
5 ...... work with numbers.

B Complete the sentences with the correct phrase.

a) ...... you're a techie ......
b) ...... work with people ......
c) ...... have a good salary ......
d) ...... see other countries ......
e) ...... work with numbers ......

1 If you want to ....., then a job as a freelance reporter is good for you.
2 If you like to ..... more than people, then a job as a financial analyst is right for you.
3 If you want to ..... but little free time, consider a job as a managing director.
4 If you think ....., then a job as a computer programmer is best for you.
5 If you love to ...., consider a job as a sales manager.

1 Vocabulary: my score is .... out of 10

2 Reading

A Read the following text, then answer True (T) or False (F) for the questions below.

My name is Ron and I am a sales manager at a large toy company. I have to attend a lot of meetings. Sometimes I have to organise them myself. This takes some planning. First I tell everyone where the meeting is and also the time. It's very important to make this clear. Then I prepare an agenda. It's easier to stay on topic if you've got an agenda. Sometimes I use flip charts and somebody always takes the minutes so we all remember what we discussed. The time together is important. It makes us feel more like a team.

		T / F
1	Ron has to attend a lot of meetings.	....
2	Ron never has to organise the meetings himself.	....
3	It's important to state the time and place of the meeting.	....
4	An agenda makes it easier to stay on topic.	....
5	One person should take the minutes.	....
6	Time together as a team is not important.	....

2 Reading: my score is .... out of 6

Name ______ Class ______ Date ______

3 Language

A Choose the best comparative to complete the sentences.

a) happier
b) more important
c) less stressful
d) more secure
e) healthier
f) riskier
g) more creative

1 Some people feel that it is ...... to have free time than a lot of money.
2 If you are working too hard, you need to get a ...... job.
3 A ...... lifestyle includes exercise, good food and more time outside.
4 Many people are ...... if they spend less time in their car.
5 Sometimes a ...... job is a less exciting one.
6 People with lots of ideas do better in ...... jobs.
7 A ...... job sometimes means more money but is often less secure.

B Now choose the best superlative(s) to complete the sentences.

a) largest
b) most beautiful
c) most fun
d) most expensive
e) best
f) hardest
g) most

1 The ...... places in the world are often the ...... to live in.
2 The ...... job I ever had also had the ...... pay.
3 Some people have the ...... in jobs that don't pay very much.
4 The ...... companies don't always have the ...... exciting jobs.

3 Language: my score is .... out of 11

4 Pronunciation

A Which words have the *sh* sound? Mark them.

...... **a)** spe<u>ci</u>alist
...... **b)** expres<u>si</u>on
...... **c)** te<u>ch</u>ie
...... **d)** job satisfac<u>ti</u>on
...... **e)** bu<u>si</u>ness

4 Pronunciation: my score is .... out of 3

Quick Smart Test 3:
my total score is .... out of 30

Name ________________ Class ________ Date ________

1 Vocabulary

A Complete the sentences with the best word.

a) game shows
b) the news
c) documentaries
d) soap operas
e) talk shows

1 ...... are so boring. Who wants to see the same people on the same show all the time?
2 I don't like to watch ...... The world is so depressing these days.
3 There are some interesting ...... in the afternoons. I like the presenter who invites all of the celebrities.
4 ...... are so fun to watch. I can always answer all of the questions.
5 Sometimes I like to watch ...... , especially if they are about strange animals in different parts of the world.

B Match the words with their definitions.

a) viewers
b) a producer
c) a series
d) contestants
e) a critic

1 ...... answer questions on game shows.
2 ...... watch the shows on TV.
3 ...... writes comments about a programme or film.
4 ...... makes a programme or film.
5 ...... is a group of programmes on TV.

1 Vocabulary: my score is .... out of 10

2 Reading

A Read the following interview, then answer True (T) or False (F) for the questions below.

Interviewer:	What made you decide to have plastic surgery?
Sherry:	I wasn't happy with my looks. I really wanted to look like Madonna.
Interviewer:	Was it painful to have the surgery?
Sherry:	Yes, it was. But I wanted to look like her so badly.
Interviewer:	And do you think you look like Madonna now?
Sherry:	My face does but my body still needs some work.
Interviewer:	Are you going to get that done then too?
Sherry:	I have to save up some more money first!

		T / F
1	Sherry wasn't happy with her looks.	....
2	Plastic surgery wasn't painful for her.	....
3	Sherry only wanted her face to look like Madonna's.	....
4	It's expensive to have plastic surgery.	....
5	Sherry wants to have surgery on her body too.	....

2 Reading: my score is .... out of 5

Name ______________ Class ______________ Date ______________

3 Language

A Complete the sentences with the best word or phrase.

a) do you
b) are you going
c) are
d) going to
e) are you

1 What ...... your plans this evening?
2 ...... to see a film?
3 What ..... going to do tomorrow morning?
4 ...... have plans for this weekend?
5 I'm not .... do anything special.

B Complete the sentences with the gerund or the infinitive.

1 ...... sports all day is not my idea of fun.
a) To watch
b) Watching
2 I'm interested in....film.
a) to study
b) studying
3 What are you going....on TV this week?
a) to watch
b) watching
4 I'm good at....the questions on game shows.
a) to answer
b) answering
5 She's going.....a film on Saturday night.
a) to see
b) seeing

3 Language: my score is .... out of 10

4 Pronunciation

A How many syllables does each word have? Put them in the appropriate box.

a) celebrity
b) fantasy
c) fictional
d) visual
e) news
f) critic
g) documentary
h) programme
i) prize
j) series

1 One syllable
2 Two syllables
3 Three syllables
4 More than three syllables

4 Pronunciation: my score is .... out of 5

Quick Smart Test 4:
my total score is .... out of 30

Name ______________________ Class ______________ Date ______________

1 Vocabulary

A Complete the table with the words below.

a) handbag (US: purse)
b) store card
c) backpacks
d) magazines
e) clothes
f) cash
g) cameras
h) credit card
i) cheque
j) wallet (US: billfold)

1 What you can use to buy things
2 What you can use to hold your money
3 What things you can buy with money

B Complete the sentences with the best word.

a) sales assistant **b)** refund
c) receipt **d)** sale **e)** customer

1 If you buy something you don't like, go back to the shop and get a ......
2 I don't like to pay for anything full price. I always look for a ......
3 Ask the ...... if you need some help.
4 I'm a regular ...... at that shop.
5 You can't get a refund without a ......

1 Vocabulary: my score is .... out of 10

2 Reading

A Read the following text about Adrienne, a shopaholic, then answer True (T) or False (F) for the questions below.

I spent too much money again today. The new clothes at my favourite shop were so beautiful. And since I have their store card, there was no reason not to buy. The sales assistant showed me so many lovely new things. I went in to buy just one thing but left with two bags of clothes! I can't use my credit card anymore because I've spent too much already. I need help because I just don't know how to stop. Shopping makes me so happy but I can't pay my bills.

Adrienne,
Shopaholic

		T / F
1	Adrienne hasn't spent too much money on clothes.	....
2	A store card makes it easier to spend money.	....
3	The sales assistant showed Adrienne some beautiful clothes.	....
4	Adrienne wanted to buy a lot of clothes that day.	....
5	Adrienne can't spend any more money on her credit card.	....
6	Adrienne goes shopping because it makes her happy.	....

2 Reading: my score is .... out of 6

Name ______ Class ______ Date ______

3 Language

A Complete the sentences with the best adverbial of quantity.

a) at all
b) a lot
c) very much
d) not much
e) a little

1 He doesn't have good taste .... Look at that suit!
2 Talk to the sales assistant. They know ...... about fashion.
3 I don't like that shop .... It has almost no selection.
4 I know you're nervous about it but even my mum uses online shopping ...... and likes it.
5 That shop is ...... open ...... , only at the weekends.

B Match the first column with the second to make sentences.

1 I'm afraid this item	a) to speak to the manager.
2 I'd like	b) about that.
3 Here's my	c) doesn't work.
4 I'm not happy	d) for your help.
5 Thank you	e) receipt.

3 Language: my score is .... out of 10

4 Pronunciation

A Do these words have a *hard* 'c' or a *soft* 'c'? Put the words in the correct box.

a) customer
b) service
c) credit card
d) account
e) cancel
f) cell phone (US)
g) receipt
h) complaint

1 *hard* 'c'	2 *soft* 'c'

4 Pronunciation: my score is .... out of 4

Quick Smart Test 5: my total score is .... out of 30

Name ______ Class ______ Date ______

1 Vocabulary

A Complete the table with the words below.

a) oranges **b)** milk
c) lettuce **d)** salmon
e) lamb **f)** chicken
g) tomatoes **h)** apples
i) cheese **j)** tuna

1 fruit	
2 vegetables	
3 fish	
4 meat	
5 dairy produce	

B Complete the sentences with the best word.

a) nutrients **b)** methane
c) leather **d)** a vegetarian
e) global warming

1 ...... is a person who doesn't eat meat.
2 Her new handbag is made of ......
3 Plants, animals and people grow when they get ......
4 ...... is happening faster than we think.
5 ...... is a gas that contributes to global warming.

1 Vocabulary: my score is .... out of 10

2 Reading

A Read the interview with a meat-eater (Sara) and a vegetarian (Erik), then answer True (T) or False (F) for the questions below.

Sara: Tell me the truth. Why don't you like meat?
Erik: It's not a question of whether I like it or not. I don't eat meat because I think it's better for the environment and for my health.
Sara: OK. I understand how it's better for the environment. But your health? How do you get enough protein?
Erik: It's easy. I just eat a lot of nuts, beans and dairy produce to get the protein I need.
Sara: But wouldn't it be easier to just eat a steak?
Erik: Perhaps easier but not healthier. Vegetarian food is actually much better for you.

		T / F
1	Erik doesn't eat meat because he doesn't like it.	....
2	Sara doesn't understand how being a vegetarian helps the environment.	....
3	Sara wants to know how a vegetarian gets enough protein.	....
4	Nuts and beans don't have a lot of protein in them.	....
5	Erik feels better when he doesn't eat steak.	....

2 Reading: my score is .... out of 5

Name ______________________ Class ______________ Date ______________

3 Language

A Complete the sentences with the best connecting word. You can use some words more than once.

a) and
b) but
c) because

1. Vegetarians don't eat meat or fish ...... vegans don't eat any animal products at all.
2. A vegetarian diet is healthy ...... it can reduce illness and disease.
3. It takes 900 litres of water to produce one kilo of wheat ...... it takes 100,000 litres to produce one kilo of meat.
4. Many people become vegetarians ...... it is better for their health.
5. People in poor countries are hungry and thirsty ...... we waste water and food on livestock.

B Match the first column with the second to make sentences.

1 He doesn't eat meat	**a)** ...... because you need them all.
2 She can't eat cheese	**b)** ...... but most people eat too much from this group.
3 You can't replace foods in one group for foods in another group	**c)** ...... but she can drink milk.
4 The smallest part of the food pyramid is the fats, oils and sweets	**d)** ...... and you can get the right nutrients.
5 Eat different foods	**e)** ...... because he's a vegetarian.

3 Language: my score is .... out of 10

4 Pronunciation

A Where is the stress in each of these words? Put them into the correct category.

(a) healthy	**(b)** delicious
(c) contribute	**(d)** vegetarian
(e) overweight	**(f)** unhealthy
(g) chicken	**(h)** condition
(i) vitamins	**(j)** dessert

1 Stress on 1st syllable
2 Stress on 2nd syllable
3 Stress on 3rd syllable

4 Pronunciation: my score is .... out of 5

Quick Smart Test 6:
my total score is .... out of 30

Name ______ Class ______ Date ______

1 Vocabulary

A Match the first column with the second to make sentences.

1 I feel scared ……	**a)** …… when I finish all of my work.
2 I feel relieved ……	**b)** …… when my friends aren't around.
3 I feel relaxed ……	**c)** …… when I enter a dark house.
4 I feel angry ……	**d)** …… when someone is mean to me.
5 I feel lonely ……	**e)** …… when I'm on holiday.
6 I feel proud ……	**f)** …… when I do well on an exam.

B Match the words with their definitions.

a) posting
b) an editor
c) a blogger
d) access

1 This person can help you with your mistakes.
2 People with computers have this.
3 Putting your details on a website.
4 This person writes about his / her life online.

1 Vocabulary: my score is …….. out of 10

2 Reading

A Read about Fiona's experience with a web diary, then answer True (T) or False (F) for the questions below.

I started writing my own web diary eight months ago when my boyfriend and I had our last fight. I thought it was a good way to talk about my feelings. I wanted to see what other people thought about my experience. At first, I didn't hear from many people and often from just the same people. But then I started going out and dating again a couple of months ago and more people got interested. Suddenly I got comments from all kinds of people. In the last month, I've received hundreds of comments about my new experiences. Someone's even suggested that I get my own TV programme. What a good idea! I never thought of my dating life as that interesting but everyone says it is.

	T / F
1 Fiona started her web diary after she and her boyfriend had their last fight.	………
2 Only the same people wanted to talk to her about her feelings.	………
3 She heard from a lot of people in the beginning.	………
4 When she started dating, she got more comments.	………
5 She has received thousands of comments.	………
6 She has never thought about having her own TV programme.	………

Name ____________________ Class ____________ Date ____________

7 Fiona didn't realise that her dating life was so interesting. ....

8 Everyone says Fiona's dating life is interesting. ....

2 Reading: my score is .... out of 8

3 Language

A Complete the sentences with the past or present perfect tense.

1 He ...... a web diary from September until December.
a) wrote
b) has written

2 I ...... online but many people I know have done this.
a) never dated
b) have never dated

3 Over the last two years, some people ...... very personal things on their blogs.
a) wrote
b) have written

4 I ...... a trip to Japan and had a marvellous time.
a) finished
b) have just finished

5 I ...... about becoming a writer last year.
a) thought
b) have thought

B Match the first column with the second to make questions and sentences.

1 Have you ever	**a)** just finished your web diary?
2 Have you	**b)** thought about online dating.
3 Haven't	**c)** you visited a chat room before?
4 I've never	**d)** shouted in public?

3 Language: my score is .... out of 9

4 Pronunciation

A Which words contain a sound which is *unlike* the others?

A	**B**	**C**
1 chat	**1** lonely	**1** relieved
2 sad	**2** blog	**2** private
3 happy	**3** self-exposure	**3** excited
4 scared	**4** proposed	**4** outline

4 Pronunciation: my score is .... out of 3

Quick Smart Test 7:
my total score is .... out of 30

Name ______________________ Class ____________ Date ____________

1 Vocabulary

A Match the words with their definitions.

1 watch	**a)** piece of jewellery you wear on your ears
2 sunglasses	**b)** something you use to talk to people
3 mobile phone	**c)** something you use to listen to music
4 music player	**d)** something you wear to protect your eyes from the sun
5 necklace	**e)** piece of jewellery you wear on your wrist
6 earrings	**f)** something you wear that tells time
7 hat	**g)** piece of jewellery you wear around your neck
8 bracelet	**h)** something you use to carry things
9 scarf	**i)** something you wear around your neck to keep warm
10 bag	**j)** something you wear on your head

1 Vocabulary: my score is .... out of 10

2 Reading

A Read the interview with Mr Brand and Ms Individual, then match the phrases to make true sentences below.

Interviewer: Here we have two very different dressers: Mr Brand and Ms Individual. Let me ask you first, Mr Brand. Where do you buy your clothes?
Mr Brand: The best shops, of course.
Interviewer: And you, Ms Individual?
Ms Individual: I always buy second-hand. Why pay full price?
Interviewer: Right. Do you always pay full price, Mr Brand?
Mr Brand: You have to pay full price if you want the real thing. And I want the logos. Doesn't everyone?
Ms Individual: Not me. I make my own street fashion. I don't need logos.
Mr Brand: That's cool but I'm not giving up my brands.

1 Mr Brand and Ms Individual don't	**a)** ...... from clothes at second-hand shops.
2 Mr Brand buys his clothes	**b)** ...... doesn't need logos.
3 Ms Individual makes her own fashion	**c)** ...... only at the best and most expensive shops.

Name ______ Class ______ Date ______

4 Mr Brand accepts that Ms Individual	**d)** ...... because he wants the real brands.
5 Mr Brand pays full price	**e)** ...... dress the same.

2 Reading: my score is .... out of 5

3 Language

A Choose the appropriate article to complete the phrases.

a) a / an **b)** the **c)** --

1 Fashion is not only for ...... rich.
2 He always wears ...... black trousers.
3 ...... designer sunglasses complete the outfit.
4 She has ...... expensive haircut.
5 Fashion and style are not ...... same thing.
6 Have you got ...... style you prefer?
7 ...... street fashion is very popular in some places.
8 My friends and I like ...... same style.
9 ...... fashion comes from all over the world.
10 My mother always wears ...... scarf.
11 I feel more confident when I wear ...... logos.
12 ...... new look is not for me.

3 Language: my score is .... out of 12

4 Pronunciation

A What sound does the *–ed* make in these words?

a) spott<u>ed</u>
b) strip<u>ed</u>
c) pattern<u>ed</u>
d) check<u>ed</u>
e) dy<u>ed</u>
f) well-dress<u>ed</u>

1 *(t)*	2 *(ed)*	3 *(d)*

4 Pronunciation: my score is .... out of 3

Quick Smart Test 8:
my total score is .... out of 30

Name ______________________ Class ____________ Date ____________

1 Vocabulary

A Match the words with their definitions.

a) graffiti
b) shoplifting
c) murder
d) fraud

1 killing someone deliberately
2 illegal art on walls
3 taking money from people by tricking them
4 stealing from a shop

B Match the words from the first column with the second to make phrases.

1 commit	**a)** litter
2 arrest	**b)** prison
3 go to	**c)** a crime
4 drink	**d)** photos
5 drop	**e)** a criminal
6 take	**f)** alcohol

1 Vocabulary: my score is .... out of 10

2 Reading

A Read the interview with a prisoner, then answer True (T) or False (F) for the questions below.

Interviewer: I understand you're in prison for fraud? Is that correct?
Prisoner: That's what they say. But I don't think that fraud is the right word for what I did.
Interviewer: And why do you say that?
Prisoner: I don't have to answer that, do I?
Interviewer: No, but it's my job to find out as much information as I can. Maybe I can even help you.
Prisoner: I don't need your help. I just need to get out of prison.
Interviewer: Didn't you lie to your boss about money you got from a client?
Prisoner: No, it wasn't a lie. I just didn't tell him about it.
Interviewer: I see.

	T / F
1 The interviewer wants to find out more information.	....
2 The prisoner doesn't like the interviewer's question.	....
3 The prisoner has to answer all of the questions.	....
4 The interviewer thinks he can help the prisoner.	....
5 The prisoner lied to his boss about money from a client.	....

Name ______ Class ______ Date ______

6 The prisoner told his boss about the money. ....
7 The interviewer thinks the prisoner is there for fraud. ....

2 Reading: my score is .... out of 7

3 Language

A Complete the sentences with *have to* or *don't have to*.

a) have to
b) don't have to

1 I ...... eat something. I am so hungry suddenly.
2 You ...... be quiet. The neighbours will hear you and get angry.
3 You ...... help us. We've already finished.
4 We ...... pay to get in. Somebody gave us free tickets.
5 If you work at night, you ...... sleep during the day.
6 If you own a dog, you ...... talk it for walks.
7 You ...... find the best people for the team if you want to win.
8 If you have enough money in the bank, you ...... work.
9 I ...... answer any of your questions if I don't want to.

3 Language: my score is .... out of 9

4 Pronunciation

A How many syllables does each word have? Put them in the appropriate box.

a) Parliament
b) union
c) European
d) individual
e) criminal
f) commune
g) law
h) freedom

1 One syllable
2 Two syllables
3 Three syllables
4 More than three syllables

4 Pronunciation: my score is .... out of 4

Quick Smart Test 9:
my total score is .... out of 30

Name Class Date

1 Vocabulary

A Match the words to make phrases.

1 plug in	a) the TV
2 switch on / off	b) the button
3 press	c) the cable

B Complete the sentences with the best word.

a) test
b) experiment
c) solve
d) laboratory
e) robot

1 The scientists worked long into the night in their ......
2 A ...... is not like a person because it doesn't have feelings.
3 The ...... failed because there weren't enough people on the project.
4 It was not easy to....the problem.
5 He didn't have time to study but he had to take the ...... anyway.

1 Vocabulary: my score is .... out of 8

2 Reading

A Read about what Laura thinks life will be like fifty years from now, then answer the questions.

Life is going to be very different fifty years from now. Technology is moving so fast already. I think that in fifty years, people won't need cars anymore. We will just have special machines that run on rubbish. And there won't be any phones because we will be able to talk to anyone from a mini-computer on our clothes. Computers as we know them today will be a thing of the past. Robots will be everywhere we go. They will be so similar to humans we won't always know the difference!

1 What does Laura think life is going to be like fifty years from now?
a) completely different
b) similar but with some differences
c) almost the same
d) a little different

2 What does she think will happen to cars and phones?
a) We will still need them in emergencies.
b) They will still be everywhere.
c) We won't need them because there will be something better.
d) Everyone will still own one.

3 According to Laura, robots will...
a) not be at all like humans.
b) will be so similar that we won't know the difference.
c) will run on rubbish.
d) will be like mini-computers.

2 Reading: my score is .... out of 6

Name Class Date

3 Language

A Complete the sentences with the *will* future.

a) won't
b) will happen
c) will
d) will you learn
e) will be like

1 What do you think ...... in the future?
2 I ...... go to the party on Saturday night if it's too late.
3 What do you think your life ...... in five years?
4 ...... it be hard to find a job after university?
5 What ...... in that class?

B Put the instructions in the correct order (1-9). The first one is done for you.

...... This one?
...... Where? I can't see.
..1.. First plug that cable in there.
...... But the button doesn't work.
...... Oh, dear. It can't work without the button.
...... I see now. What do I do next?
...... Choose the programme.
...... That's fine. But remember to push the button.
...... Right here.

3 Language: my score is .... out of 13

4 Pronunciation

A Where is the stress in each of these words? Put them into the correct category.

a) robot
b) population
c) information
d) hardware
e) connect
f) laboratory
g) data
h) prediction
i) technological

1 Stress on 1st syllable
2 Stress on 2nd syllable
3 Stress on 3rd syllable

4 Pronunciation: my score is .... out of 3

Quick Smart Test 10:
my total score is .... out of 30

Name ______________________ Class ____________ Date ____________

1 Vocabulary

A Complete the sentences with the best word.

a) traffic
b) flight
c) fares
d) climate change
e) fuel
f) passengers
g) airlines

1 ...... costs have gone up a lot in the last two years.
2 Air travel is causing ......
3 The ...... are fighting to offer the lowest ......
4 I was late because there was too much ......
5 There were 200 ...... on that ......

B Complete the phrases with the best preposition.

a) by
b) into
c) on / off

1 to travel ...... boat
2 to get ...... the plane
3 to climb ...... the back seat of the car
4 to go ...... bus
5 to get ...... at Euston Station

2 Reading

A Read these notes from a cheap airline, then answer T (True) / F (False) for the questions below.

Our airline started about two years ago. We only had five planes to keep costs low. At first we only had short flights between London, Paris and Frankfurt. But since then, we've added other flights to cities in Eastern Europe. Our idea was to make travel by air quick and convenient. We know how people hate to queue and wait for delayed planes. So we made the process easier with e-tickets and self-check-in. So far we've had no problems in our two short years of business.

		T / F
1	This airline has been in business for a long time.	....
2	They saved money with only five planes.	....
3	They only travel within Western Europe.	....
4	The airline didn't want people to wait in long queues.	....
5	E-tickets and self-check-in have not made it easier.	....
6	The airline has been successful so far.	....

1 Vocabulary: my score is .... out of 12

2 Reading: my score is .... out of 6

Name ______________________ Class ______________ Date ______________

3 Language

A Complete the sentences with a) *for* or b) *since*.

1. We went on holiday last year ...... two weeks.
2. It has been five years ...... I travelled abroad.
3. I have been in this English class ...... September.
4. She has studied English ...... two years.
5. I've been in London ...... a long time.

B Complete the sentences with the past or present perfect tense.

1. We ...... a very long time for the government to do something about climate change.
   a) 've waited
   b) has waited
   c) waited

2. People ...... millions of trees over the past year to fight global warming.
   a) planted
   b) have planted
   c) has planted

3. Since cheap travel ...... several years ago, more people are flying than ever before.
   a) has started
   b) started
   c) 've started

3 Language: my score is .... out of 8

4 Pronunciation

A How many syllables does each word have? Put them in the appropriate box.

a) energy
b) environmentalist
c) conference
d) overcrowded
e) fuel
f) cell
g) luxury
h) climate
i) pollute
j) speed

1 One syllable
2 Two syllables
3 Three syllables
4 More than three syllables

4 Pronunciation: my score is .... out of 4

Quick Smart Test 11:
my total score is .... out of 30

Name ____________ Class ____________ Date ____________

1 Vocabulary

A Complete the sentences with the best word.

a) pin number
b) earn
c) cashpoint (ATM)
d) bank accounts
e) coins
f) note
g) bank balance

1 I need to check my ……. It was low yesterday.
2 I don't have enough cash. I will have to stop at the …….
3 We have two …… at that bank.
4 I forgot my …… so I'll have to speak to someone at the bank.
5 That machine only takes …… so you have to have change.
6 I don't have anything more than a 5 pound …….
7 I hope to …… a good salary in my first job.

B Choose the *opposite* of each verb.

1 to save	**a** to lose
2 to win	**b** to steal
3 to borrow	**c** to spend

1 Vocabulary: my score is …….. out of 10

2 Reading

A Read the conversation between Catherine and a bank assistant, then answer T (True) / F (False) for the questions below.

Catherine: Hello. My name is Catherine Nisbet. I'd like to check my bank balance, please.
Agent: Certainly. Can I have your account number, please?
Catherine: Yes. It's 0077-645600.
Agent: Thank you. And for security, can you tell me your mother's maiden name?
Catherine: Yes, it's Logie.
Agent: Thank you. And your address, please?
Catherine: 45 Kensington Church Street. London W8 4LS.
Agent: Thank you. Your balance is 165 pounds.
Catherine: OK. Great! That's more than I thought it was.

T / F

1 The bank tells Catherine her balance before she tells them her account number. ………
2 They bank asks Catherine for her mother's maiden name for security. ………
3 Catherine gives her mother's address. ………

Name Class Date

4 Catherine's bank balance is less than she thought it was. ....

5 Catherine is pleased about her bank balance. ....

2 Reading: my score is .... out of 5

3 Language

A Complete the student's responses with *might be* or *will be*.

a) might be **b)** will be

1 Interviewer: In 50 years do you think the world will be a better place?
Student: I don't know. It ......

2 Interviewer: In 50 years do you think travelling will be even easier?
Student: I think it definitely ......

3 Interviewer: In 50 years do you think you will still be working?
Student: I'm not sure. I ......

4 Interviewer: In 50 years do you think you will be rich?
Student: I ...... It's possible.

B Complete the sentences with *too* or *enough*.

a) too **b)** enough

1 She is never going to make ...... money.
2 He talks ...... much for most people.
3 He doesn't talk to his friends ......
4 She isn't ...... good at languages.

C Put the sentences in the correct order (1-5). The first one is done for you.

...... Do you think there's a chance it will happen again?
..1.. Did you hear about the cash machine that gave out free money?
...... It might but the banks will be more careful now.
...... Yes. That was amazing.
...... True. But I really hope it happens again!

3 Language: my score is .... out of 12

4 Pronunciation

A Which word sounds most *like* the first word?

1 euro	**a)** queue	**b)** your	**c)** put
2 yen	**a)** your	**b)** yes	**c)** you
3 pound	**a)** fond	**b)** down	**c)** choose

4 Pronunciation: my score is .... out of 3

Quick Smart Test 12:
my total score is .... out of 30

Name ______________________ Class ______________ Date ______________

1 Vocabulary

A Match the words with their definitions.

1 overtake	**a)** to stop
2 crash	**b)** to hit another car
3 park	**c)** to pass
4 accelerate	**d)** to speed up
5 brake	**e)** to put your car somewhere

B Complete the sentences with the best word.

a) accident
b) traffic lights
c) vehicle
d) speed
e) traffic jams

1 It's not right to use your ...... as a weapon.
2 Watch your ...... as you pass through the town.
3 She had a very bad ...... last December and still can't walk.
4 My parents have to leave work early to avoid the ......
5 Turn right at the ...... on High Street.

1 Vocabulary: my score is .... out of 10

2 Reading

A Read the text about Tom, a cyclist, then answer T (True) / F (False) for the questions below.

I live in the city so I really don't need a car. I started riding my bike about two years ago and now I can't live without it. I used to take public transport everywhere but now I ride my bike instead. It's easy for me to cycle to college since it's not far from my house. There is even a secure place for me to park my bike when I get there. I cycle every morning and often with friends. I feel better when I cycle and I am also doing something good for the environment. I want to save money too and this is a good way to do it!

		T / F
1	Tom doesn't need a car because he lives in the city.	....
2	He can't live without his bike.	....
3	He doesn't have to take public transport anymore.	....
4	Tom only cycles to college alone.	....
5	Tom feels he is doing something good for the environment.	....
6	Cycling doesn't help him save money.	....

2 Reading: my score is .... out of 6

Name ______________________ Class ______________ Date ______________

3 Language

A Match the first column with the second to make sentences.

1 I want to cycle	**a)** ...... to get to school.
2 She is going to England this summer	**b)** ...... to be more independent.
3 He takes the bus every morning	**c)** ...... to chat with my friends.
4 I use the internet	**d)** ...... to get fit.
5 He needs his helmet	**e)** ...... to protect his head.
6 I learned to drive	**f)** ...... to study English.

B Complete the sentences with the correct order of adjectives.

1 He wants to replace his ...... bicycle.
a) slow old
b) old slow

2 There's a ...... motorway outside the city.
a) big new
b) new big

3 She has a ...... car.
a) new gorgeous red
b) gorgeous new red

4 It's easy to get a ticket if you're a ...... driver.
a) fast young
b) young fast

5 I still love my ...... bike.
a) lovely old blue
b) old blue lovely

3 Language: my score is .... out of 11

4 Pronunciation

A Which words contain a sound which is *unlike* the others?

A	B	C
1 traffic	**1** read	**1** bike
2 accident	**2** speed	**2** pipe
3 crash	**3** steering	**3** line
4 hate	**4** bleed	**4** circle

4 Pronunciation: my score is .... out of 3

Quick Smart Test 13:
my total score is .... out of 30

Name ______________________ Class ____________ Date ____________

1 Vocabulary

A Match the words with their definitions.

1 stepmother	**a)** when two parents are not together anymore
2 half-brother	**b)** the mother of children who are not hers
3 single parent	**c)** a child in the family who has just one of the same parents
4 divorced	**d)** a person who doesn't have any brothers or sisters
5 only child	**e)** a mother or father who is alone

B Match the special occasions with the words in the right column.

1 birth	**a)** presents and cake
2 wedding	**b)** jewellery
3 birthday	**c)** honeymoon
4 graduation	**d)** baby
5 anniversary	**e)** degree certificate

1 Vocabulary: my score is .... out of 10

2 Reading

A Read the conversation between Maureen, a recent bride, and her wedding planner, then answer T (True) / F (False) for the questions below.

Maureen:	Hello. I'm calling about my wedding in September.
Wedding planner:	Yes. Your name, please?
Maureen:	Maureen White.
Wedding planner:	Yes. I have your information here. You got married in Spain, is that correct?
Maureen:	Yes, just south of Barcelona.
Wedding planner:	And you were planning to have the reception outside but it rained.
Maureen:	That's right. So we'd like to have some of our money back.
Wedding planner:	I'm afraid we can't be responsible for the weather. While you were planning your wedding with us, we offered you insurance but you didn't take it.
Maureen:	We wanted to but we couldn't spend any more money.
Wedding planner:	I'm sorry. We can't give you any money back.

T / F

1 Maureen was happy with her wedding. ....

2 Part of the wedding was going to be outside. ....

Name Class Date

3 Maureen wanted all of her money back. ....

4 The wedding planner offered insurance to Maureen. ....

5 Maureen didn't buy the insurance because she thought it wasn't going to rain. ....

2 Reading: my score is .... out of 5

3 Language

A Complete the sentences with the correct combination of verb tenses.

While I ...... for my wedding, my grandmother ...... to visit.

1 a) prepared **b)** was preparing
2 a) came **b)** was coming

When we ...... the reception, everyone ......

3 a) left **b)** were leaving
4 a) danced **b)** was dancing

Our friends ...... from the balcony when we ...... rings at our wedding.

5 a) watched **b)** were watching
6 a) exchanged **b)** were exchanging

When my sister ......, my stepmother and I ...... the invitations.

7 a) phoned **b)** was phoning
8 a) wrote **b)** were writing

My father ...... while I ...... abroad.

9 a) remarried **b)** was remarrying
10 b) studied **b)** was studying

3 Language: my score is .... out of 10

4 Pronunciation

A Where is the stress in each of these words? Put them into the correct category.

(a) honeymoon **(b)** celebration
(c) occasion **(d)** birthday
(e) stepfather **(f)** divorced
(g) reception **(h)** witness
(i) anniversary **(j)** husband

1 Stress on 1st syllable
2 Stress on 2nd syllable
3 Stress on 3rd syllable

4 Pronunciation: my score is .... out of 5

Quick Smart Test 14:
my total score is .... out of 30

Name ____________ Class ____________ Date ____________

1 Vocabulary

A Complete the sentences with the best word.

a) epidemic
b) harmless
c) spread
d) vaccines
e) disease

1 ...... are important for small children.
2 Many people fear an ...... of bird flu.
3 An illness can ...... very quickly.
4 You cannot always prevent ......
5 Some viruses are ...... but others can kill.

B Complete the sentences with the best phrase.

1 When you have a bad infection	**a)** take an aspirin tablet.
2 When you have a cough	**b)** take antibiotics.
3 When you have a headache	**c)** use lots of tissues.
4 When you need a vaccine	**d)** take cough medicine.
5 When you have a cold	**e)** get an injection.

1 Vocabulary: my score is .... out of 10

2 Reading

A Read Steve's comments about his health, then answer T (True) / F (False) for the questions below.

I worry a lot about my health. Everyone in my family is overweight so I have to be very careful about my diet. But I don't exercise very much. My doctor says that unless I start exercising soon, I will continue to gain weight. I told her that I can't find the time to exercise, but she said that I have to make the time. I study very hard and spend a lot of time on my computer. I'm not very good at sports so it's going to be hard for me to find something I like. Perhaps I'll try swimming or running so I can still eat sweets.

		T / F
1	Steve's family is all overweight.	....
2	Steve isn't careful about his diet.	....
3	He exercises a lot.	....
4	His doctor says that he needs to make more time for exercise.	....
5	Steve spends a lot of time studying.	....
6	He is good at sports.	....
7	He wants to find a sport he likes so he can still eat sweets.	....

2 Reading: my score is .... out of 7

Name ______________________ Class ______________ Date ______________

3 Language

A Mark the sentences that can take *will*.

1 Most people worry if they ...... get flu. ......

2 Fewer people ...... get ill if we give them special vaccines. ......

3 You ...... feel better after you eat a good breakfast. ......

4 If you eat less, you ...... lose weight. ......

5 Unless you ...... get the injection, you can't go to Africa. ......

6 If you ...... want to get better, take antibiotics. ......

7 If you're a smoker, you ...... have a greater risk of heart disease. ......

8 If you don't watch your diet, you ...... gain weight. ......

3 Language: my score is .... out of 8

4 Pronunciation

A Match the words that rhyme.

1 cough	**a)** rug
2 flu	**b)** make
3 ache	**c)** new
4 drug	**d)** off
5 spread	**e)** said

4 Pronunciation: my score is .... out of 5

Quick Smart Test 15:
my total score is .... out of 30

Name ______________________ Class ____________ Date ____________

1 Vocabulary

A Complete the sentences with the best word or phrase.

a) the tube
b) a packed lunch
c) host family
d) accommodation
e) excursions
f) included in

1 The ...... I'm staying with lives outside the city.
2 Meals are not ...... the price of the course.
3 The ...... is going to be very expensive for two months.
4 When I live in London this summer, I intend to take ...... to my language school.
5 There are going to be ...... every Saturday.
6 I am going to bring ...... since I don't like the food at the cafeteria.

B Match the words with their definitions.

1	self-access room	**a)**	class taught in a short period of time but with a lot of information
2	examinations	**b)**	space with books and materials for students
3	intensive course	**c)**	the way someone speaks a language
4	accent	**d)**	tests often given at the end of a course

1 Vocabulary: my score is .... out of 10

2 Reading

A Read about where Phil is going this summer, then answer T (True) / F (False) for the questions below.

I'm doing an intensive English course in Edinburgh, Scotland this summer. The course is only six weeks long but we are going to have lessons for eight hours a day. Fortunately, we won't be in the classroom all the time. We have excursions planned on Wednesdays and Saturdays. The instructors are going to take us to see the sights in the city. And we're even travelling all the way to the Isle of Skye for one of the weekends. I don't intend to get a lot of rest while I'm on the course. There are too many people to get to know and too many things to do.

		T / F
1	Phil is going to do a course in England this summer.	....
2	The course is short but the days are long.	....

Name ____________________ Class ____________ Date ____________

3 Not all of his time is going to be in the classroom. ....

4 The excursions are only for one day. ....

5 Phil plans to get a lot of rest on the course. ....

2 Reading: my score is .... out of 5

3 Language

A Complete the sentences with the correct verb to talk about Christina's plans for the day.

a) is seeing art
b) is going
c) is having dinner
d) is having breakfast
e) is going to be
f) is having lunch
g) is travelling
h) is watching

1 At 7 o'clock in the morning, Christina ...... with her host family.
2 At 8 o'clock, she ...... to school by tube.
3 At 9 o'clock, she ...... in her English class.
4 At 12:30, she ...... with a friend.
5 At 3 o'clock in the afternoon, she ...... at a museum.
6 At 7 o'clock in the evening, she ...... with her host family.
7 At 9 o'clock at night, she ...... her favourite TV programme.
8 At half past 10 at night, she ...... to bed.

B Choose the best verb to complete the sentences about the future.

a) 're meeting
b) plans to stay
c) intend to go
d) am going to take

1 This summer I ...... an intensive course in London.
2 She ...... with a host family for two months.
3 We ...... for lunch at 1 o'clock.
4 I ...... to bed early tonight.

3 Language: my score is .... out of 12

4 Pronunciation

A Which words contain a sound which is *unlike* the others?

A	B	C
1 tube	**1** host	**1** good
2 food	**2** most	**2** rule
3 lunch	**3** course	**3** school
4 noon	**4** toast	**4** tool

4 Pronunciation: my score is .... out of 3

Quick Smart Test 16:
my total score is .... out of 30

Unit 1:
PET Paper 1 Reading, part 1

1 C 2 B 3 B 4 B 5 C

Unit 2:
PET Paper 3 Speaking, part 3

1 (*Example answers*)
Picture 1: These women appear to be in the old centre of a city. (It is Venice in Italy). It is day and they are wearing beautiful costumes or traditional dress as there is a Carnival. I think the women in costumes are part of a carnival parade. I think they are on their way to the celebration.
Picture 2: These people are at a music concert. The music is jazz, or rap, or rock. It appears to be night. They are watching a band on stage. They are dancing and having a good time. Most of the people are wearing T-shirts. The band is playing for the crowd.

PET Paper 3 Speaking, part 4

2 *(Individual answers)*

Unit 3:
PET Paper 1 Reading, part 2

1 E 2 H 3 B 4 D 5 G

Unit 4:
PET Paper 3 Speaking, part 2

(*Individual answers*)

Unit 5:
PET Paper 1 Reading, part 3

1 F (It is a lively part of London.)
2 T
3 F (It used to sell only crafts but now it has many different kinds of goods.)
4 F (It's the last market on the left, after the railway bridge.)
5 T
6 T
7 F (Books aren't in the list.)
8 F (The Canal Market only has take-away food.)
9 T
10 F (They open late at 10am and often stay open after 6pm.)

Unit 6:
PET Paper 3 Speaking, parts 3 and 4

(Example answers)
A
Picture 1: A large family, including parents, grandparents and children, are sitting round a dinner table having a meal together. They are all talking, and they are enjoying having a meal together. They are eating vegetables, including lettuce, carrots and tomatoes, meat, including chicken or possibly lamb, possibly fish, such as salmon, pasta and bread. They appear to be drinking water.
Picture 2: Two friends, possibly a couple, are eating take-away Chinese or possibly Japanese food and pizza. They aren't sitting at a dinner table, they are sitting in front of the TV with the food on their knees. They aren't taking to each other, they're watching TV.

B
(Individual answers)

Unit 7:
PET Paper 1 Reading, part 4

1 C 2 B 3 B 4 B 5 C

Unit 8:
PET Paper 3 Speaking, part 2

(Example answer)
I think...he will need a good pair of shoes and some sandals. He will also need a watch and lots of casual, comfortable clothes, for example, some trousers, a warm sweater for cold nights and a pair of jeans. He can also take a backpack, a guidebook and an international mobile phone.

Unit 9:
PET Paper 1 Reading, part 5

1 D
2 B
3 C
4 C
5 B
6 D
7 A
8 B
9 C
10 D

Unit 10:
PET Paper 3 Speaking, part 3

(Example answers)
Picture 1: This picture is from a long time ago before there were washing machines. The woman is washing the dirty clothes by hand. She is wearing a black dress with an apron. She looks very tired.
Picture 2: This picture shows a young man in a laundrette. He is watching his clothes in a washing machine. He is wearing shorts and a shirt and he isn't wearing any shoes. He looks a little bored.

Unit 11:
PET Paper 1 Reading, part 2

1 G
2 F
3 H
4 B
5 C

Unit 12:
PET Paper 3 Speaking, part 2

(Example answers)
buy expensive jewellery / buy presents for her friends / go on a beach holiday / save the money / buy a large house / go shopping and buy lots of clothes

Unit 13:
PET Paper 1 Reading, part 3

1 B (It's a national organisation.)
2 A
3 B (The club wants more cycle lanes and safer roads.)
4 A
5 A
6 B (The club wants members to combine cycling with public transport.)
7 B (You only get a discount on a safe cycling course.)
8 B (Members get discounts on new bikes.)
9 A
10 A

Unit 14:
PET Paper 3 Speaking, parts 3 and 4

(Example answers)
A
Picture 1: A family of five is having a holiday at the beach. There is a mum, a dad, a daughter and two sons. The eldest son and his dad are playing ball while the mum and the youngest son are making sandcastles. The daughter is sunbathing. The children look happy with their parents. Everyone is having a good time on their holiday.

Picture 2: A grandfather is sitting on the sofa next to his grandson. The grandson has just got some bad news and is crying. His grandfather has his hand on his grandson's arm and he's trying to make him feel better. The grandfather has made them a cup of tea.

B
(Individual answers)

Unit 15:
PET Paper 1 Reading, part 5

1 B
2 D
3 C
4 B
5 C
6 A
7 D
8 B
9 C
10 A

Unit 16:
PET Paper 3 Speaking, part 2

(Example answers)
He should think about... going to an exciting place / doing an intensive course.
It's a good idea to check if... accommodation is included in the price of the course / the course provides access to computers and the internet / there are weekly excursions and day trips.
A good host family / Small class size / A good teacher / A self-access room...*is very important.*

Quick Smart Test 1:

1 Vocabulary

1 A
1 b 2 a 3 c 4 d 5 e
1 B
1 e 2 c 3 b 4 d 5 a

2 Reading

2 A
1 F 2 T 3 T 4 F 5 T
6 F 7 F

3 Language

3 A
1 b 2 c 3 a 4 d 5 e
3 B
1 d 2 c 3 b 4 e 5 a

4 Pronunciation

4 A
A 3 B 1 C 1

Quick Smart Test 2:

1 Vocabulary

1 A
1 c 2 d 3 a 4 e 5 b
1 B
1 T 2 F 3 T 4 T 5 F
1 C
a 1, 3, 4
b 2, 5

2 Reading

2 A
1 e 2 c 3 b 4 a 5 d

3 Language

3 A
1 a 2 c 3 a 4 d 5 a

4 Pronunciation

4 A
1 a, g, h, j
2 b, e, f
3 c, d, i

Quick Smart Test 3:

1 Vocabulary

1 A
1 d 2 e 3 b 4 c 5 a
1 B
1 d 2 e 3 c 4 a 5 b

2 Reading

2 A
1 T 2 F 3 T 4 T 5 T
6 F

3 Language

3 A
1 b 2 c 3 e 4 a 5 d
6 g 7 f
3 B
1 b, d 2 f, e 3 c 4 a, g

4 Pronunciation

4 A
a, b, d

Quick Smart Test 4:

1 Vocabulary

1 A
1 d 2 b 3 e 4 a 5 c
1 B
1 d 2 a 3 e 4 b 5 c

2 Reading

2 A
1 T 2 F 3 F 4 T 5 T

3 Language

3 A
1 c 2 b 3 e 4 a 5 d
3 B
1 b 2 b 3 a 4 b 5 a

4 Pronunciation

4 A
1 e, i
2 f, h, j
3 b, c, d
4 a, g

Quick Smart Test 5:

1 Vocabulary

1 A
1 b, f, h, i
2 a, c, j
3 d, e, g
1 B
1 b 2 d 3 a 4 e 5 c

2 Reading

2 A
1 F 2 T 3 T 4 F 5 T
6 T

3 Language

3 A
1 a 2 b 3 c 4 e 5 d
3 B
1 c 2 a 3 e 4 b 5 d

4 Pronunciation

4 A
1 a, c, d, h
2 b, e, f, g

Quick Smart Test 6:

1 Vocabulary

1 A
1 a, h 2 c, g 3 d, j 4 e, f 5 b, i
1 B
1 d 2 c 3 a 4 e 5 b

2 Reading

2 A
1 F 2 F 3 T 4 F 5 T

3 Language

3 A
1 b 2 c 3 a 4 c 5 b
3 B
1 e 2 c 3 a 4 b 5 d

4 Pronunciation

4 A
1 a, g, i
2 b, c, f, h, j
3 d, e

Quick Smart Test 7:

1 Vocabulary

1 A
1 c 2 a 3 e 4 d 5 b
6 f
1 B
1 b 2 d 3 a 4 c

2 Reading

2 A
1 T 2 T 3 F 4 T 5 F
6 F 7 T 8 T

3 Language

3 A
1 a 2 b 3 b 4 b 5 a
3 B
1 d 2 a 3 c 4 b

4 Pronunciation

4 A
A 4 B 2 C 1

Quick Smart Test 8:

1 Vocabulary

1 A
1 f 2 d 3 b 4 c 5 g
6 a 7 j 8 e 9 i 10 h

2 Reading

2 A
1 e 2 c 3 a 4 b 5 d

3 Language

3 A
1 b 2 c 3 c 4 a 5 b
6 a 7 c 8 b 9 c 10 a
11 c 12 b

4 Pronunciation

4 A
1 b d, f
2 a
3 c, e

Quick Smart Test 9:

1 Vocabulary

1 A
1 c 2 a 3 d 4 b
1 B
1 c 2 e 3 b 4 f 5 a
6 d

2 Reading
2 A
1 T 2 T 3 F 4 T 5 F
6 F 7 T

3 Language
3 A
1 a 2 a 3 b 4 b 5 a
6 a 7 a 8 b 9 b

4 Pronunciation
4 A
1 g
2 b, f, h
3 a, e
4 c, d

Quick Smart Test 10:
1 Vocabulary

1 A
1 c 2 a 3 b
1 B
1 d 2 e 3 b 4 c 5 a

2 Reading
2 A
1 a 2 c 3 b

3 Language
3 A
1 b 2 a 3 e 4 c 5 d
3 B
6, 2, 1, 8, 9, 4, 5, 7, 3

4 Pronunciation
4 A
1 a, d, g
2 e, f, h
3 b, c, i

Quick Smart Test 11:
1 Vocabulary

1 A
1 e 2 d 3 g, c 4 a 5 f, b
1 B
1 a 2 c 3 b 4 a 5 c

2 Reading
2 A
1 F 2 T 3 F 4 T 5 F
6 T

3 Language
3 A
1 a 2 b 3 b 4 a 5 a
3 B
1 a 2 b 3 b

4 Pronunciation
4 A
1 e, f, j
2 h, i
3 a, c, g
4 b, d

Quick Smart Test 12:
1 Vocabulary

1 A
1 g 2 c 3 d 4 a 5 e
6 f 7 b
1 B
1 c 2 a 3 b

2 Reading
2 A
1 F 2 T 3 F 4 F 5 T

3 Language
3 A
1 a 2 b 3 a 4 a
3 B
1 b 2 a 3 b 4 a
3 C
3, 1, 4, 2, 5

4 Pronunciation
4 A
1 b 2 b 3 b

Quick Smart Test 13:
1 Vocabulary

1 A
1 c 2 b 3 e 4 d 5 a
1 B
1 c 2 d 3 a 4 e 5 b

2 Reading
2 A
1 T 2 T 3 T 4 F 5 T
6 F

3 Language
3 A
1 d 2 f 3 a 4 c 5 e
6 b
3 B
1 a 2 a 3 b 4 a 5 a

4 Pronunciation
4 A
A 4 B 3 C 4

Quick Smart Test 14:
1 Vocabulary

1 A
1 b 2 c 3 e 4 a 5 d
1 B
1 d 2 c 3 a 4 e 5 b

2 Reading
2 A
1 F 2 T 3 F 4 T 5 F

3 Language
3 A
1 b 2 a 3 a 4 b 5 b
6 a 7 a 8 b 9 a 10 b

4 Pronunciation
4 A
1 a, d, e, h, j
2 c, f, g
3 b, i

Quick Smart Test 15:
1 Vocabulary

1 A
1 d 2 a 3 c 4 e 5 b
1 B
1 b 2 d 3 a 4 e 5 c

2 Reading
2 A
1 T 2 F 3 F 4 T 5 T
6 F 7 T

3 Language
3 A
2, 3, 4, 8

4 Pronunciation
4 A
1 d 2 c 3 b 4 a 5 e

Quick Smart Test 16:
1 Vocabulary

1 A
1 c 2 f 3 d 4 a 5 e
6 b
1 B
1 b 2 d 3 a 4 c

2 Reading
2 A
1 F 2 T 3 T 4 F 5 F

3 Language
3 A
1 d 2 g 3 e 4 f 5 a
6 c 7 h 8 b
3 B
1 d 2 b 3 a 4 c

4 Pronunciation
4 A
A 3 B 3 C 1

Common European Framework (CEF) of Reference
These are extracts from the CEF 'Can-do' statements with indications to help the teacher identify where in the ***QSE*** materials each of the 'Can-dos' can be found. As the syllabus of ***QSE*** was built round the requirements of the CEF, many feature throughout the course, so only examples are given.

LISTENING: ***OVERALL LISTENING COMPREHENSION***	***Where to find it in QSE***
Can understand straightforward factual information about common everyday or job-related topics, identifying both general messages and specific details, provided speech is clearly articulated in a generally familiar accent.	*Units: 2, 9, 11, 13:* **Listen in**
Can understand the main points of clear standard speech on familiar matters regularly encountered in work, school, leisure etc, including short narratives.	*Units: 1, 3, 4, 5, 6, 7, 8, 10, 12, 15, 16:* **Listen in**
UNDERSTANDING CONVERSATION BETWEEN NATIVE SPEAKERS	
Can generally follow the main points of extended discussion around him / her, provided speech is clearly articulated in standard dialect.	*Unit: 1, 3, 4, 6, 7, 8, 11:* **Listen in**
LISTENING TO AUDIO MEDIA AND RECORDINGS	
Can understand the main points of radio news bulletins and simpler recorded material about familiar subjects delivered relatively slowly and clearly.	*Unit: 2, 9, 13:* **Listen in**
UNDERSTANDING A NATIVE SPEAKER INTERLOCUTOR	
Can follow clearly articulated speech directed at him / her in everyday conversation, though will sometimes have to ask for repetition of particular words and phrases.	*Unit: 1, 3, 6, 7, 10, 12, 14, 16:* **Listen in**
READING: ***OVERALL READING COMPREHENSION***	
Can understand short, simple texts on familiar matters of a concrete type which consist of high frequency everyday or job-related language.	*Units: 1, 3, 5, 7, 8, 12, 14, 16:* **Reading**
READING CORRESPONDENCE	
Can understand the description of events, feelings and wishes in personal letters well enough to correspond regularly with a penfriend.	*Unit 5:* **Reading**
READING FOR ORIENTATION	
Can find and understand relevant information in everyday material, such as letters, brochures and short official documents.	*Units: 1, 5, 9:* **CLIL**
Can find specific, predictable information in simple everyday material such as advertisements, prospectuses, menus, reference lists and timetables.	*Units: 6, 12, 15:* **CLIL**
READING FOR INFORMATION AND ARGUMENT	
Can identify the main conclusions in clearly signalled argumentative texts.	*Units: 2, 6, 11, 13, 15:* **Reading**
Can recognise significant points in straightforward newspaper articles on familiar subjects	*Units: 1, 3, 9, 12, 14, 16:* **Reading**
READING INSTRUCTIONS	
Can understand clearly written, straightforward instructions for a piece of equipment.	*Unit 2:* **CLIL**
SPEAKING: ***OVERALL ORAL PRODUCTION***	
Can reasonably fluently sustain a straightforward description of one of a variety of subjects within his / her field of interest, presenting it as a linear sequence of points.	*All Units:* **Your topic, Your turn to speak**
SUSTAINED MONOLOGUE: Describing experience	
Can relate details of unpredictable occurrences, (eg an accident).	*Unit 1:* **Conversation**
Can relate the plot of a book or film and describe his / her reactions.	*Unit 4:* **Your topic**
Can describe dreams, hopes and ambitions.	*Unit 3:* **Conversation**
Can describe events, real or imagined.	*Unit 7:* **Your topic**

Can narrate a story.	*Unit 1:* **Conversation** *Unit 7:* **Your topic**
Can describe plans and arrangements, habits and routines, past activities and personal experiences.	*Unit 2:* **Conversation, Your topic** *Unit: 4* **Conversation** *Unit: 16* **Conversation**
SUSTAINED MONOLOGUE: Putting a case (eg in a debate)	
Can briefly give reasons and explanations for opinions, plans and actions.	*All units: 5, 6, 13, 15* **Ideas, Conversation** **Your topic** *Unit 9* **Role play**
PUBLIC ANNOUNCEMENTS	
Can give a short, rehearsed presentation on a topic pertinent to his / her everyday life, briefly give reasons and explanations for opinions, plans and actions.	*All Units:* **Your topic**
Can cope with a limited number of straightforward follow-up questions.	*All Units:* **Your topic**
CONVERSATION	
Can maintain a conversation or discussion but may sometimes be difficult to follow when trying to say exactly what he / she would like to.	*All Units:* **Your turn to speak**
Can express and respond to feelings such as surprise, happiness, sadness, interest and indifference.	*All Units:* **Your turn to speak**
TRANSACTIONS TO OBTAIN GOODS AND SERVICES	
Can cope with less routine situations in shops, post offices, banks, (eg returning an unsatisfactory purchase). Can make a complaint.	*Unit 5:* **Your turn to speak** *Unit 12:* **Focus on words**
Can deal with common aspects of everyday living such as travel, lodgings, eating and shopping.	*Unit 6:* **Your turn to speak**
WRITING: ***OVERALL WRITTEN PRODUCTION***	
Can write straightforward connected texts on a range of familiar subjects within his / her field of interest, by linking a series of shorter discrete elements into a linear sequence.	*All Units:* **Portfolio writing**
CREATIVE WRITING	
Can write accounts of experiences, describing feelings and reactions in simple connected text.	*All Units:* **Portfolio writing**
Can write a description of an event, a recent trip – real or imagined.	*Unit 2:* **Portfolio writing**
Can narrate a story.	*Unit 7:* **Portfolio writing**
Can write about everyday aspects of his / her environment, (eg people, places, a job or study experience) in linked sentences.	*Units 8, 9:* **Portfolio writing**
REPORTS AND ESSAYS	
Can write short, simple essays on topics of interest.	*Units 6, 11, 12, 15:* **Portfolio writing**
CORRESPONDENCE	
Can write personal letters describing experiences, feelings and events in some detail.	*Units 1, 9, 14, 16:* **Portfolio writing**

Name ______ Class ______ Date ______

LISTENING

I can:	Very well	OK	Not very well
... understand the main points of what people say in clear English about familiar topics			
... understand simple factual or technical information			
... guess the meaning of some unknown words			
... follow a lecture or talk on a familiar topic			
... understand broadcasts or recordings on familiar subjects			
... follow and understand action films in which the language is simple			
... follow detailed directions			
... listen and understand in other ways, such as...			

I find that it is useful to practise my listening skills by:

- ☐ listening to music with English words
- ☐ listening to English-language radio
- ☐ watching music television
- ☐ watching other English-language TV
- ☐ watching films in English in the original version
- ☐ watching films in English with subtitles
- ☐ talking to native speakers of English
- ☐ talking to people from other countries using English as a common language
- ☐ having extra English lessons
- ☐ in other ways, for example...

READING

I can:	Very well	OK	Not very well
... understand the main points of short newspaper articles on familiar topics			
... understand easy text on subjects I'm interested in			
... find and understand general information in letters and brochures			
... understand clear technical instructions			
... understand descriptions of events and feelings well enough to be able to correspond with a penfriend			
... search a longer text, or several shorter ones, to find specific information			
... read in English in other ways, such as...			

I find that it is useful to practise my reading skills by:

- ☐ reading magazines in English
- ☐ reading books in English
- ☐ reading English-language websites online
- ☐ reading letters, emails and texts in English from friends
- ☐ reading signs, notices and advertising in English
- ☐ reading for homework
- ☐ having extra English lessons
- ☐ in other ways, for example...

Name ______________________ Class ______________ Date ______________

SPEAKING

I can:	Very well	OK	Not very well
... start, keep up and finish simple conversations on familiar topics			
... tell a story			
... express feelings like surprise, happiness, sadness and interest			
... describe things			
... give detailed instructions			
... express my opinion and (dis)agree politely			
... summarise the plot and say what I thought of a film, book or concert			
... speak English in other ways, for example...			

I find that it is useful to practise my speaking skills by:

- ☐ talking to my teachers and fellow students
- ☐ talking to native speakers of English
- ☐ talking to people from other countries using English as a common language
- ☐ talking to friends on the phone
- ☐ having extra English lessons
- ☐ in other ways, for example...

WRITING

I can:	Very well	OK	Not very well
... write simply about things that have happened to me in personal letters or emails to friends			
... describe my feelings			
... tell a simple story			
... give reasons for my opinions, plans or actions			
... write a review of a film, book or concert			
... write simple instructions or directions			
... write short, simple essays on topics of interest			
... write English in other ways, for example...			

I find that it is useful to practise my writing skills by:

- ☐ writing emails in English
- ☐ writing texts in English on my mobile phone
- ☐ writing letters in English to a penfriend
- ☐ writing my blog or diary in English
- ☐ writing stories in English
- ☐ having extra English lessons
- ☐ in other ways, for example...

In future, English will ...

..be useful to me:	Very useful	Fairly useful	Not useful at all
... for work and my career			
... for going on holiday in English-speaking countries			
... for travelling to any part of the world where my own language is not widely spoken			
... for making new friends in the 'global village'			
... for understanding other cultures			
... for reading literature in English			
... for technical and scientific purposes			
... for other reasons such as....			

Language Bank exercises **Example answers** **See pages 40-48 WB**

Language Bank 1

(Example answers)
1 *I always eat breakfast in the morning.*
2 *I usually watch TV in the evening.*
3 *Surfing makes me happy.*

Language Bank 2

[1] ...... My friend went inline skating.
[4] *Then* I put my coat around him.
[7] ...... I asked for an ambulance.
[6] *After that*, I rang Emergency Services.
[9] *Finally* the ambulance came and took him to hospital.
[8] ...... I told them we were in the park.
[3] *First* I helped him to sit down.
[5] *Next* I got him to support his injured foot.
[2] ...... He fell and broke his ankle.

Language Bank 3

1 You *should* have singing lessons.
2 *Make sure* you learn to dance.
3 You *should* get a new look.
4 *Why don't* you apply for one of those pop academy TV shows?
5 You *shouldn't* expect to become a star too quickly.
6 You *should* get a manager.
7 *(Example answer) You should choose a new name.*
8 *(Example answer) Make sure you don't forget your friends.*

Language Bank 4

Lola	How often do you practise the drums?
Tom	1 *Hardly ever*. I don't have time.
Lola	2 *How well* can you play?
Tom	Very badly!
Sam	How well can you sing?
Lisa	3 *Quite well*. I sing in a band.
Sam	4 *How often* do you perform?
Lisa	About twice a month.

Language Bank 5

Sales manager	This meeting is about ideas. I want only your very (1) *brightest* ideas.
Chairperson	Let's sit in a circle at the round table. That's (2) *more democratic* and (3) *more creative*.
Accountant	We made some big decisions at our last meeting, but this time we have to make even (4) *more important* ones.
Chairperson	OK. Then it's (5) *easiest* to sit at the long table, so I can be in the (6) *best* place to hear everyone's opinion.

Language Bank 6

(Example answers)
1 I love *watching game shows.*
2 I hate *going to the cinema.*
3 I don't mind *documentaries* but *I hate the news.*
4 I'm not keen on *soap operas.*
5 My favourite *show is...*

Language Bank 7

1 On Monday *Lenny is going to take the DVD back to the shop.*
2 *On Tuesday he hasn't got any plans.*
3 *On Wednesday he's going to go jogging.*
4 *On Thursday he's going to watch* Survivor *on TV.*
5 *On Friday he hasn't got any plans.*
6 *On Saturday he's going to go swimming with Matt.*
7 *On Sunday he's going to write emails.*

Language Bank 8

Assistant	Can I help you?
Customer	Yes, (1) *I'm afraid* this jacket is (2) *dirty*. Look here!
Assistant	Yes, you're right.
Customer	I'd like (3) *to exchange it*, please. Here's my (4) *receipt*.

Assistant I'm sorry, we don't have another one in that size.
Customer Then I'd like a (5) *refund*.
Assistant I'm sorry. I can't give you your money back.
Customer Right, I (6) *'d like* to speak to the manager, please.

Language Bank 9

(Example answers)

1 Do you read much? *Yes, a lot.*
2 Do you like staying at home? *No, not much.*
3 Do you go to museums much? *A little.*
4 Do you enjoy cycling? *No, not at all.*

Language Bank 10

(Example answers)

1 I eat chocolate *because of the taste.*
2 I don't enjoy sport *because I don't like to run.*
3 A good body is important *for a long life.*
4 I don't eat out *because I like to cook at home.*

Language Bank 11

Waiter Can I help you?
Customer (1) *May I have* the menu, please?
Waiter (2) *Certainly*, I'll just get it. (3) *Here you are*, sir.
Customer Thank you.
Waiter Are you ready to order?
Customer Yes, (4) *I'd like* an orange juice, please. And to eat, (5) *I'll have* the vegetable lasagne and a salad.
Waiter (6) *Would you like some* bread?
Customer Yes, please.

Language Bank 12

(Example answers)

1 I've *seen that film* lots of times.
2 I've *gone skiing* two or three times.
3 I've never *played volleyball.*
4 I've just *read that book.*

Language Bank 13

A Lilly Can you tell her I've got the tickets for the concert? ...5...
B Dad I'm afraid she's out, Lilly. ...2...
C Lilly Thanks, bye. ...7...
D Dad Sure. ...4...
E Lilly Oh, ... er can you give her a message, please? ...3...
F Dad Yes, I'll tell her, Lilly. Thanks for calling. ...6...
G Lilly Hi, it's Lilly. Can I speak to Charlotte, please? ...1...

Language Bank 14

1 **Matt** *Which do you prefer, the black jacket or the blue jacket?*
Chloe I prefer the black jacket. The blue jacket is horrible.
2 **Ryan** *Do you prefer shopping in small clothes shops or department stores?*
Oliver I prefer shopping in small clothes shops. I don't like going to department stores.
3 **Rosie** *Which designer do you like best?*
Lucy I like Stella McCartney best. I think she's a really interesting designer.

Language Bank 15

Laura (1) *Do* you *have to* do anything special at home this weekend?
Christina I (2) *have to* help my mum with Dad's birthday meal on Sunday. It's (3) *my job* to make the dessert.
Laura (4) *Do* you *have to* stay at home all day Sunday?
Christina Yeah, I think so.
Laura That's too bad. I (5) *don't need to* do anything at home this weekend because my parents are away. But I (6) *need to* go to town tomorrow to buy Suzie a present.
Christina You (7) *don't have* to buy her a present. You can just burn a CD or something.

Laura I know, but it's (8) *my turn* to get her something. You got her a present last time.

Language Bank 16

A David Er, Holly. Remember to put the DVD in the player. ...8...
B Holly Oh. I've done that! What do I do next? ...5...
C Holly But nothing is happening. ...7...
D David It means plug the cable in and switch it on at the socket. ...4...
E David Then just switch it on and press 'play'. That's not difficult. ...6...
F Holly Oh no, the new DVD player doesn't work! ...1...
G Holly What? I don't understand that. ...3...
H David Let me see the instructions. It says here 'First connect to the mains'. ...2...

Language Bank 17

Dave What do you think your life (1) *will be like* in ten years?
Jane I think I (2) *'ll have* children. I want to have children soon. What about you?
Dave No, I don't (3) *think I'll have children.* I don't like children.
Jane Do you think you'll still be in England?
Dave (4) *I think so.* I can't really imagine moving.
Jane Really? I definitely (5) *won't be* here in ten years. I want to live abroad.

Language Bank 18

(Example answers)
1 *I've known my best friends for ages.*
2 *I've had my mobile phone since 2007.*
3 *I've been interested in surfing since last year.*
4 *I've liked chocolate for as long as I can remember.*

Language Bank 19

Anna Hello, I'd like to (1) *check* my bank balance, please.
Assistant Certainly, What's your (2) *name?*
Anna Oh sorry, Anna Worthington.
Assistant Worthington? Can you (3) *spell* that please?
Anna W-O-R-T-H-I-N-G-T-O-N.
Assistant Right. I need your (4) *account number*, please.
Anna BQZ07.
Assistant Thank you. Can you (5) *confirm* your address?
Anna 67 Newton Road, Doncaster, DN4 6GP.
Assistant Thank you. Your (6) *balance* is two hundred and ten pounds and twenty pence.

Language Bank 20

(Example answers)
1 *I think so.*
2 *People might get richer.*
3 *I don't know. We'll see.*
4 *Possibly.*

Language Bank 21

(Example answers)
1 *I'm going to visit a friend.*
2 *The purpose is to practise these questions and answers.*
3 *The point in studying is to learn.*
4 *I intend to go to the beach with my friends.*

Language Bank 22

(Example answers)
1 *I was watching a film on TV.*
2 *I was dancing at a club with my friends.*

Language Bank 23

(Example answers)
Friend What was your brother's wedding like?
You The weather was (1) *fantastic*. It (2) *was sunny and warm.*
I was wearing (3) *a blue summer dress.*
The best part was when (4) *the band started to play.*
The worst part was when (5) *my brother dropped the cake.*

Friend Did you enjoy it?
You (6) *Yes! But I don't think my brother did.*

Language Bank 24

(Example answers)

1 The fact is *smoking is very dangerous.*
2 The problem is *it's hard for people to stop smoking.*
3 If people smoke, *they can get lung cancer.*
4 As far as passive smoking is concerned, *you can still get cancer.*

Language Bank 25

(Example answers)

1 I think medical progress is too slow.
2 I reckon she's a good doctor.
3 My impression is that they can't give the best care because the costs are too high.
4 It seems to me that it's incredibly important to give money to poor countries to fight disease.

Language Bank 26

Carrie Hi Anna, it's Carrie. Listen, (1) *would you like to* play tennis on Saturday?
Anna Oh, I'm (2) *afraid* I'm going on an excursion with my parents.
Carrie OK. What (3) *about* on Sunday?
Anna Sorry, I already have plans for Sunday. But (4) *why don't* we play tennis on Friday?
Carrie That's a good idea. What time (5) *would suit* you?
Anna Can we say 4 o'clock at the sports centre?
Carrie That's fine. (6) *See you* then.

Language Bank 27

(Example answers)

1 *Tomorrow I've arranged to meet my friend Judy in the centre.*
2 *Tomorrow evening I'm having dinner with my parents.*